P9-CEG-704

HOT
TODDY

HOT TODDY

THE TRUE STORY OF HOLLYWOOD'S
MOST SENSATIONAL MURDER

Andy Edmonds

WILLIAM MORROW AND COMPANY, INC.
New York

Library of Congress Cataloging-in-Publication Data

Edmonds, Andy.
Hot Toddy : the true story of Hollywood's most sensational murder
/ Andy Edmonds.
p.   cm.
ISBN 0-688-08061-8
1. Todd, Thelma, d. 1935. 2. Murder—California—Los Angeles—
Case studies. 3. Hollywood (Los Angeles, Calif.) I. Title.
HV6534.L7T634 1989
364.1'523'0979494—dc19

88-38657
CIP

Printed in the United States of America

First Edition

1   2   3   4   5   6   7   8   9   10

BOOK DESIGN BY NICOLA MAZZELLA

DEDICATED TO:

Ann D. McMahon Wilson, "Mac," because Thelma would have wanted it that way

Ginny Mullaney, who bridged the past with the present through her generosity

"Trust me."

 *Preface*

No murder can really be considered solved until every question is answered, every shred of evidence taken into account, every alternate theory unraveled, and every loophole closed. A murder must be considered in its entirety, weighed against the events of the time and in relation to the people in proximity to the victim. All aspects must be fully explored, all the pieces of the puzzle must be measured, and they must all fit. A murder should be considered the final sequence in a chain of events; the events leading up to the murder are often as important as the actual killing—if not more important in some cases.

The brutal murder of comedienne Thelma Todd has captured the imagination and fascination of film fans and murder-mystery buffs for more than fifty years. Since the 1935 killing, many theories have surfaced; some died a natural death, others remain because they were based on fragments of evidence. Numerous magazine writers and book authors have claimed the murder "solved," only to dredge up further questions, leave more loopholes, without ever reaching an unshakable conclusion. In any event, no murder has garnered more bizarre solutions and as much false information through the years.

When the beautiful blond actress was found battered and bloodied in her Lincoln Phaeton convertible on a cold December night, authorities immediately declared it a suicide, and desperately tried to close the case. But they achieved just the opposite. By insisting it was suicide, they opened the floodgates of fantastic speculation, a succession of confessions by strangers and friends, and lurid details of Thelma Todd's private life—a life that skirted death in the fringes of the underworld.

Those who were suspected had plenty of reason to kill the woman known as "Hot Toddy."

Roland West, her sometime lover/business associate in the Sidewalk Cafe, wanted out of the business because of continued pressure to lease the third floor as a gambling casino. That pressure came from gangster Charles "Lucky" Luciano, a companion of Todd's. Thelma refused to buy West out, and then refused to lease the floor to Luciano, bringing further pressure on West. West was also jealous of an affair Thelma was having with a San Francisco businessman, and in many ways he blamed his fall from grace in the movie industry on Thelma and their ill-fated film project *Corsair*. West remained a prime suspect for fifty years.

Charles Smith, cafe treasurer, was suspected by both Todd and West of juggling the cafe's books, draining the account, and either pocketing the money or turning over a cut to the underworld, which had been infiltrating the cafe and other restaurants. Todd was going to have a professional accountant examine the books after the first of the year. Her death stopped the audit, and there was no solid evidence against Smith.

Lucky Luciano had been intimate with Thelma for the last two years of her life. He put her on the road to drug addiction, hoping to force her into leasing the cafe for his gambling operation. She also started getting close to the heart of Luciano's West Coast business—gambling, drugs, and prostitution—and she suspected Luciano and others in the "Million Dollar Movie Shakedown," which established gang rule in the movie industry. He had plenty of reason to see Toddy dead.

Her former husband, Pasquale "Pat" DiCicco had a violent temper and had beaten Todd during their whirlwind courtship and brief, stormy marriage. He introduced her to

Luciano, who, he felt, stole her away. DiCicco felt betrayed by Todd because of her interest in Luciano. He reportedly returned after their cold and abrupt divorce to claim a new part of the cafe, a steakhouse Toddy was just about to open. He was seen with Toddy hours before she was found dead, and he was identified by several witnesses as the last man to see her alive.

Thelma had also been receiving a series of death threats and extortion notes from strangers who used such names as "The Ace" or "A Friend." She bought a bull terrier for protection and carried a gun in her purse.

I first became interested in the murder of Thelma Todd a number of years ago, in 1980, while researching a book on comedian Charley Chase, a popular but forgotten funnyman who died in 1940. Todd made eleven comedies with Chase and he returned the favor by directing what is considered to be her best comedy, *The Bargain of the Century*. While talking to Chase's co-stars at the Hal Roach Studios, I started learning about this beautiful, bright, bubbly blonde they lovingly called Toddy.

Those stories sent me digging through old newspaper and magazine clippings, court, police, and coroner's records, as well as interviewing men who live on the other side of the law, who had inside knowledge of the killing or of the workings of Luciano, Al Capone, and Frank Nitti. My research took me from Los Angeles to Florida, Chicago to Lawrence, Massachusetts. It was through seven years of exhaustive research, based upon the stories and accounts given to me by these people and gleaned through transcripts and records, that the final, shocking solution to the murder came to light.

The incidents related in the book were obtained through interviews and from personal letters and memorabilia of Thelma Todd's. The dialogue also is based upon these stories or gleaned from letters saved or conversations remembered by friends of the actress.

What follows is, I believe, the true story of the murder of Thelma Todd—a woman who had a compulsive attraction to gangsters learned at her father's knee, an attraction that eventually cost her life. Thelma was destined to die young; the most tragic part of the story is that she realized it.

Acknowledgments

Sincere thanks to Robert Gottlieb of the William Morris Agency and Lisa Drew of William Morrow Publishers, without whom *Hot Toddy* would still be a dream.

I would also like to thank the many people who shared their time and memories with me through the years and helped add invaluable pieces of information for this book. "Tall oaks from little acorns grow." Among the many—Mr. Hal Roach, June Chase Hargis, Anita Garvin Stanley, Venice Lloyd, Roy Seawright, T. Marvin Hatley, Lassie Lou Ahern, Muriel Evans, Lois Laurel Hawes, Dorothy Granger, Mike Hawks, historian/author Randy Skretvedt, Dick Bann, my dearest Joe Rock, the folks at the Academy of Motion Picture Arts and Sciences Herrick Library, Douglas Hart of Backlot Books, Malcolm Willet of Collectors Book Store, Chicago P.D. Detective "Bald Eagle," Betty Brown (Mrs. Thad Brown of the LAPD), Andy Reynolds and Tom McDonald of the Los Angeles District Attorney's office, the men in "Docky's kitchen," and several others who must remain anonymous, who loved Thelma and her movies, and shared files and information that provided the glue.

The following books have also provided a wealth of information:

The Legacy of Al Capone by George Murray
Laurel and Hardy (The Magic and the Movies) by Randy Skretvedt
The Warner Bros. Story by Clive Herschhorn
The Paramount Story by John Douglas Eames
The Great Movie Shorts by Leonard Maltin (which helped cut several large corners when compiling the filmography)

Most of all, I'd like to thank my mom and dad, Leona and Norman, for their help and encouragement, and for putting up with a seven-year obsession.

"There's going to be a change in my life, and it's going to happen before the first of the year."

—THELMA TODD (to dressmaker Helen Ainsworth)

"Now be a good girlie, or I'll lock you up in the garage."

—GROUCHO MARX (in their movie *Monkey Business*)

"My daughter has been murdered!"

—ALICE TODD (to newspaper reporters)

"There are so many mysterious and unusual circumstances in this case that I recommend a grand jury investigation."

—FRANK NANCE (Los Angeles County coroner)

"I have obtained independent information that could indicate foul play in Miss Todd's death."

—GEORGE ROCHESTER (grand-jury foreman)

"We have a middle-aged woman here who claims she knows the identity of the man who killed Thelma Todd . . . that man is staying in a hotel here in Ogden, Utah."

—RIAL MOORE (Ogden police chief in an unanswered telegram to the Los Angeles police)

"I can't speak out of fear I'll be kidnapped and killed."

—ALEX HOUNIE (Trocadero head waiter)

"Witnesses before the grand jury are not being as helpful as they might be. Why? Are they afraid?"

—BURON FITTS (Los Angeles County district attorney)

"You'll open a gambling casino in my restaurant over my dead body!"

—THELMA TODD (during an argument with mobster Lucky Luciano)

"That can be arranged."

—CHARLES "LUCKY" LUCIANO (in response to Todd's threat)

Chapter One

It was just after midnight in the quiet Southern California beachside community. A typical winter night: cold, damp, the temperatures struggling to climb above the nighttime low of 37 degrees. It was a winter chill that cut right to the bone of Southern Californians, who were better prepared for the hot, smoggy afternoons than the frosty December nights. The waves settled down from their earlier high tide, cresting three to four feet, crashing down hard against the sandy shoreline. It was a crash that should have been heard echoing a mile away, but was oddly muffled by the thick, choking fog that was still rolling in offshore. It was the type of fog that cut a scream down to a whisper; so thick it was impossible to see five feet ahead. It was an eerie fog that sent wealthy Palisades residents locking doors and windows out of fear someone might be lurking in the shadows or standing right outside, concealed under the shroud of darkness. Only a week before, on a night like this, three beachside homes had been robbed, one woman beaten. The robber was still out there, somewhere.

Expensive, Spanish-style houses dotted the coastline, tucked away between the rolling hills that edged the shoreline and the rambling, winding coastal road, Roosevelt Highway (now called Pacific Coast Highway). At the edge of the high-way, nestled on the Palisades/Malibu border, was a popular restaurant, usually crowded with movie stars, politicians, and, as 1935 wound to a close, gangsters.

Posetano Road snaked up three levels above the restau-rant, each level dead-ending, dotted with expensive homes breaking up the seemingly endless brush and weeds that blanketed the hillside. A two-car garage was set into the hill-side at the point where Posetano Road met Stretto Way. It had two wooden doors, separated in the middle by a cement post; a small apartment was just above the garage; to the far right of the double doors—a single doorway; behind the doorway—a stairway that led to an opulent, massive house in the hills above. The garage and apartment shared an address—17531 Posetano Road. Both the garage and the main house in the hills above were owned by Roland West and his fading beauty-queen wife, Jewel Carmen. The front entrance to the main house was one road above Posetano Road at 17320 Robelo Drive. Everything appeared quiet on this cold De-cember morning. Yet in the garage, behind the closed wooden doors, a macabre and horrifying death scene was unfolding.

A young blond woman was slumped forward across the steering wheel of her 1934 Lincoln Phaeton convertible. The engine was sputtering, choking, misfiring, burning up what little oxygen was left in the dank garage. The room was rapidly filling with deadly carbon monoxide, enough to choke the car's engine, enough poison gas to kill an adult in min-utes. The young woman coughed, fighting to bring herself back to a state of semiconsciousness. As she struggled to lift her head off the steering wheel of her chocolate-brown car, she coughed again, this time coughing up blood that slowly trickled out of the corner of her mouth. It was a warm sensa-tion against her cold skin, which was growing numb from the ravages of a savage beating and suffocation from carbon mon-oxide.

Still drowsy, still teetering on the brink of death, she clumsily reached for the keys, dangling in the ignition near the steering column. She could not muster the strength to turn off the engine. Taking one last breath, she reached to her left for the thick, leather-lined car door, which had been left ajar. The door was just beyond her feeble touch and she was too weak to slide toward it. She collapsed, wedged between the steering wheel and the seat, her fists clenched in frustration. Her life had slipped away; her once beautiful body, now brutally disfigured from a beating, her once creamy-white skin a contorted crimson-red, her blond curls scattered across the face that had catapulted a naïve little girl from Lawrence, Massachusetts, to movie-star status.

As her body lay limp, the last bit of life flowed from her mouth, across her cheek, and dripped onto the lining of her elegant fur coat. The young woman died alone in the garage, above the restaurant that bore her name: "Thelma Todd's Sidewalk Cafe."

Mae Whitehead arrived on schedule that fatal Monday, shortly before ten o'clock as she did every morning. Her first duties as Thelma Todd's maid were to take the Phaeton convertible out of the main house and drive it two streets below, to the apartments at Castellemmare Drive, at the rear of the Sidewalk Cafe. The right garage door was now mysteriously open about six inches, enough to have allowed the carbon monoxide to dissipate during the night. When Whitehead discovered Todd's bloodied and battered corpse, she thought her mistress was merely asleep behind the wheel, passed out from yet another night of heavy drinking and partying. Whitehead, a usually calm and cautious woman, walked to the Phaeton, gently shaking the body, whispering, "Get up, honey. C'mon now, wake up, baby." The body was still limp but cold. When Whitehead saw Thelma's crimson-colored face, she knew she was staring at the face of death. She ran from the garage, hysterical, screaming, "She's dead! She's dead! Miss Todd's dead!"

Delirious and frightened, Mae Whitehead raced down the 270 cement steps that led from the death garage to the rear of the Sidewalk Cafe. Out of breath, nearly fainting from panic and dizzy from exhaustion, Whitehead pounded on the rear door, a door used as an entryway to the apartments of Todd and her part-time lover, former movie director Roland West. She pounded frantically, raving wildly about blood, death, and murder.

The pounding and maniacal ranting roused West from a fitful night's sleep. He stared groggily at Whitehead as she rambled on about the gruesome scene in the garage above.

She grabbed West by the arm and dragged him to the site. He was still bleary and confused until they peered into the garage together. But when West saw Todd's lifeless body and bright-crimson face, he was jolted to his senses. A horrible nightmare had actually come true.

Suddenly taking control, West ordered Whitehead to close the door, leave everything as she had found it, and get Rudy Schaefer, the cafe business manager, who was staying upstairs in the Carmen home. He phoned Todd's doctor, J. P. Sampson, who then called the police. West headed back to his apartment. The time was 10:45 A.M. Usually quick to arrive on the scene of a crime, especially when a celebrity was involved, this time the police were surprisingly slow. The first investigators did not show up until forty-five minutes after Sampson's phone call.

The first official at the scene was Los Angeles Police Captain Bert Wallis, head of the LAPD's homicide squad. When he arrived at the cafe, he ordered the now-calm Mae Whitehead, Schaefer (who had just emerged from the Carmen house ahead of cafe treasurer Charles Smith, who was also living there), and the increasingly nervous Roland West to accompany him and his officers to the garage. When they opened the heavy door, they saw a shocking sight—Thelma's body had moved.

When Whitehead and West left the body nearly an hour earlier, it was wedged between the seat and the wheel. When Wallis brought them back to the scene, the corpse had fallen to the left, slumped across the leather seat, clear of the steering wheel. How could the body have moved so drastically? Had someone returned to the garage to alter the evidence, to erase fingerprints from keys and car, and in doing so, inadvertently moved the body? Whitehead screamed and fainted. West turned white and shook violently. As Wallis peered at Todd's body, Los Angeles County Medical Examiner A. F. Wagner drove up to the garage. Wallis conferred with Wagner, filling him in on what little information he was able to obtain from Whitehead, who had been taken into Carmen's house, and West, who babbled on with vague and rambling stories. Wallis ordered his crew to halt their investigation immediately and get out of the garage, to conduct their probe elsewhere on the premises. Wagner was then free of intruders and began his preliminary examination before police had dusted the car, the keys, and the garage for fingerprints and remnants. Valuable evidence was now being permanently altered and destroyed.

In his notebook, Wagner detailed Todd's bright-crimson skin color, immediately determining the cause of death to be carbon-monoxide poisoning. He noted bruises around her neck, and attributed them to "postmortem lividity" caused by an involuntary jerking motion of her neck triggered by a violent reaction to the poisoning moments before death. Her nose was broken, obviously, Wallis asserted, from a jolting forward of her head, which slammed into the hard, rigid steering wheel. He accounted for two cracked ribs on the right side of Thelma's rib cage as resulting from the same incident. Bruises and swelling, Wagner claimed, were caused by the deadly gas—a common reaction, he pointed out in his notebook. He took a blood sample, and later found it contained 70 percent carbon-monoxide saturation (the identical saturation level as blood samples taken off the running board). Her blood-alcohol content was .13, with .10 being considered enough to intoxicate. Wagner believed his findings pointed to one conclusion.

As Wagner wrapped up his examination inside the garage, police carried out their investigation of the surrounding area, primarily questioning West, Whitehead, Smith, and Schaefer. West told authorities that he waited for Todd to return from a Saturday night of partying at the Trocadero. When she stayed out past two in the morning against his orders, he went to bed, locking the doors, assuming she had the proper keys to get into the building.

The building had an elaborate key system because the cafe had had several close calls with prowlers. Questions about which keys fit what locks, and which of the keys Thelma had or had not been carrying the night of her death caused tremendous confusion throughout the inquest.

The front entrance to the building was just off the highway. The door to the cafe was to the left, a drugstore off to the right. In the center were two wooden doors: This was considered the "main entrance." It had one lock and Todd and West each had a key. It is believed Thelma was not carrying this key when she was killed.

Behind the wooden doors, inside the building, was a stairway; at the top of the stairway was another set of doors that opened to an isolated courtyard off Castellammare. These doors on the second floor were considered the "outside door" and most vulnerable to breakins because of their secluded location. These doors required two, separate keys as an extra security measure. Todd and West each owned both keys in the two-key set. The doors were double-locked from the inside by West on the fateful Saturday night. Todd and West used these doors during the day to avoid cafe customers entering near the main door, but Thelma rarely used these doors at night out of fear because of their seclusion. It was at this door that Whitehead usually parked Thelma's car.

Just to the right of those doors was a small apartment, with its own door and lock, used primarily as a guest room because of its privacy and easy access to the nearby footbridge that led to the beach. Todd and West rarely carried this key and almost never used this entrance.

The actual apartment shared by Todd and West was on the right of the building, above the drugstore, overlooking the ocean, with Thelma occupying the area nearest the center of the building, West living in the area nearest the footbridge to the extreme right. This had a front entrance just off the landing above the staircase, and a common entrance through a sliding door, erected to give the appearance of "friendship" rather than romance. How often that door remained locked is unclear.

When Thelma returned and found herself locked out of the main entrance, West surmised, she walked around the block, up the 270 cement steps from the restaurant to the garage, thinking she would sleep in her car. (If this was the case, it would be logical to assume Thelma would go through the garage to the West/Carmen home, or wake up the Smiths in the apartment above the garage.) West guessed that to stay warm, Thelma turned on the ignition, passed out, and died. To help make his tale stick, he offered "inside information," the little-known fact that Thelma suffered from a heart condition, one so bad she was refused life insurance. That, coupled with the climb and her drinking, he claimed, did her in.

A policewoman made the climb herself to verify West's story. Though she was in adequate physical condition, she was out of breath by the time she completed the hike. It seemed likely West was telling the truth. Thelma could have passed out from drink and exhaustion. Then the policewoman noticed something unusual, something that seemed to contradict evidence uncovered before Wallis ordered everyone out of the garage. The officer's shoes were scuffed from the climb on the rough, concrete steps. An initial exam of Todd's shoes showed few scuff marks. Had she changed her shoes inside the car, or had she not made the climb as West insisted? Was it even possible that Todd had been placed in the car? The first of many puzzling fragments surfaced.

Wagner was now heading back down the hill, with Wallis close behind. They had already ruled out robbery as a motive. Twenty thousand dollars' worth of jewelry was left on the corpse, along with an expensive fur coat, still wrapped around Todd's body. Wagner felt certain his conclusions would stick, and stated the cause of death as suicide, though he had no real evidence to support his claim. But such a ruling would allow a quick investigation and a closed file. He pinpointed the time of death at 2:00 A.M. Sunday, ignoring the basic fact that rigor mortis sets in after twelve hours. If his time was accurate, Thelma would have been dead for more than thirty-five hours, but her body was just beginning to grow rigid when police arrived. The discrepancy seemed to cause no initial concern. Case closed. Wagner and Wallis were pleased with themselves.

As the two detectives headed back down to Roosevelt Highway, they were mobbed by reporters, who had by now heard something unusual was going on at the Sidewalk Cafe. Word spread quickly that it was Thelma Todd who had been found dead in her car. Reporters swarmed over the restaurant and garage, bulbs flashed, questions were fired off in rapid succession and just as quickly brushed away by police. When backed into a corner, Wagner finally passed his determination to the press. "I believe the cause of Thelma Todd's death to be from carbon-monoxide poisoning. The time of death, approximately two A.M. Sunday. I also believe her death to be a suicide." An onslaught of questions echoed through the hills. Why would a beautiful, popular, successful comedienne take her own life? The trunk of her car was filled with Christmas presents, and she had told friends she would be delivering them the following week. She had had signs printed up, already posted on the front door, announcing a gala New Year's Eve bash—the grand opening of the new third-floor restaurant. She was madly in love with a "mystery man," a businessman from San Francisco. Certainly these were not the actions of someone despondent, planning suicide. Something was wrong; dead wrong! Obviously there was a sensational story here, and the group demanded details and pictures. Wallis stepped in and agreed to appease the press. He led the procession back up the hill, opened the garage, and paraded over to Thelma's corpse. In a grotesque display, he leaned over the body and posed. The picture would sell papers.

Moments later, a lone car headed slowly up the hill, past police barricades that had just been erected to fence off the growing number of spectators. A heavyset, middle-aged woman carefully emerged and slowly walked toward the garage. She was recognized by a reporter from the *Los Angeles Examiner* who had seen a number of bizarre publicity photos showing Thelma and this woman together, an odd gesture because studios usually promote stars, not their mothers.

"Mrs. Todd! Mrs. Todd. A few questions!" Suddenly a crush of reporters appeared. "The medical examiner says your daughter killed herself. What can you tell us?"

Alice Todd took a deep breath, her eyes narrowed. She glared at the reporters through her thin, wire-rimmed glasses, and spoke somberly. "My daughter was murdered. Thelma Todd would never kill herself. She died at the hands of someone else, and I promise you this. I won't rest until the man who killed her is brought to justice."

Her statement sent shock waves through the crowd. She had used the term "man." Did she know who had killed her daughter, or at least have someone in mind? Was it Roland West, a lover scorned? Alice Todd seemed definite enough, but refused to elaborate. She shoved past the reporters and police and headed straight toward Wagner. She had touched off a powder keg that was about to blow up in Wagner's face. He knew a full investigation was imminent, and he knew his findings would not hold up under scrutiny. He would have to alter his report. Wagner brushed past Alice, refusing to talk. Captain Wallis ushered her back into her car, telling her this was neither the time nor place for discussion. She should meet him in his office tomorrow. Little did Alice Todd know that she was the catalyst for a succession of horrifying and frightening events that would send investigators, reporters, and curiosity-seekers on a fifty-year wild-goose chase; a chase that would weave through implications of police cover-ups, death threats, and murder.

The area surrounding the Sidewalk Cafe and the death garage was now a circus, with police shagging spectators off the premises, reporters insisting they be allowed to take pictures, and investigators doing a quick once-over, too obviously overlooking evidence.

Across the highway, a thin, dark man stood alone, silently watching the chaos spiraling out of control in the hills. He stared, expressionless, watching every move made by the police. Though he was too far away to hear what was being said, he seemed confident that nothing conclusive would come of this initial probe. He walked to his black Ford parked three feet away from the steps that led to the Sidewalk Cafe highway overpass, the same overpass that Thelma Todd, Roland West, and hundreds of others had used to walk from the beach to the cafe over the Roosevelt Highway. He climbed into his car and drove off. As far as he was concerned, his mission was complete. He would board a plane for Utah, the last place detectives would think of tracking him down.

The last thing Buron Fitts needed was another Hollywood scandal. His reputation as Los Angeles district attorney was already tainted from a series of inept criminal investigations over his fifteen years in the department. By 1928 he had worked his way up from deputy D.A. to district attorney. He had been involved in a number of questionable deaths of movie figures, beginning with the "unsolved" murders of directors William Desmond Taylor and Thomas Ince. (The Taylor killing was inherited from Thomas Woolwine and his successor, Asa Keyes, who bungled the case from square one; Fitts continued that tradition, making sure the case remained a mystery.) Later came the alleged suicide death of movie mogul Paul Bern shortly after his marriage to Jean Harlow, the closed-file drug overdoses of actress Barbara La Marr and Alma Rubens (Fitts refused to hunt down their drug suppliers though most everyone knew where they bought their junk), and the homosexual scandal involving the death of Fox director F. W. Murnau's sidekick Garcia Stevenson. Every story was sensationalized, snapped up by newspapers around the country and blown up into what Fitts perceived as gross exaggerations of the truth. Most of his cases involved film stars, and Los Angeles had its share of problems with that segment of the population—a community that often considered itself above the law with ready cash to "fix" any problem that threatened to taint a star's pristine image. The studios spent millions to create their celluloid gods and goddesses; a few thousand in the right pockets was petty cash.

Every time a sensational murder was committed and the killer never found, scandalous insinuations followed close behind. And most were aimed right at Buron Fitts. The D.A.'s office was developing a suspect reputation, more sinister than those of the thieves and killers it was assigned to convict. Some reporters staked out Fitts's office as part their regular beat, sniffing out murder investigations, hoping to snag another "D.A. debacle" in the making. Whether Fitts himself was guilty of playing a direct hand in haywire investigations will probably never be proved. But by December of 1935, Fitts's reputation was on the line, and the scuttlebutt around town was that someone in the office was on the take.

Alice Todd was a pushy, confident, aggressive woman who rarely failed to carry out her intentions. She was determined to get to the bottom of her daughter's murder. Believing that she would get nowhere with Captain Wallis, Alice stormed into Fitts's downtown Los Angeles office and demanded immediate action. She assumed that the District Attorney's office would get to the heart of the murder and had more clout to convict a killer than the LAPD.

Fitts full well expected Mrs. Todd to come to him. Her reputation preceded her, and he knew he was in for a rough ride. He sat back in his big leather chair and listened to Alice vent her anger. Fitts got nowhere trying to quiet her down, pacify her, or pass her along to the LAPD homicide squad. She handed him her daughter's murder and insisted he solve the case. After an endless session of accusations, name-calling and posturing, Alice Todd left Fitts with one final piece of advice, thinly disguised in the form of a threat.

"You know my daughter was murdered. I know my daughter was murdered. You also know that I know a lot of people in town. Big people. Important people, and you know who I'm talking about. There's going to be an investigation. Either you solve this, or I'll do a little investigating of my own. Good-bye, Mr. Fitts."

Alice slammed the door. Fitts was not quite sure whom Mrs. Todd knew, or how far her alleged connections would carry, but he did know she was not afraid to speak up. Here was a woman who knew how to rattle cages; she knew the power of the press and she had her daughter's reputation as a movie star to open doors. Reporters always had an eager ear for gossip, especially this type of gossip.

Fitts deemed the best way to rid himself of the problem was to pass it off to his assistants. He assigned Deputy D.A.s George Johnson and Vince Blalock to the case. Johnson and Blalock in turn enlisted investigators Jess Winn and Lloyd Yarrow. The group was eager to get its hands on a case as juicy as this to make a name for itself. The Johnson/Blalock team combed through the evidence taken at the crime scene. They studied Wagner's medical report. They reviewed statements made by witnesses at the scene. And they came to one realization: An autopsy was needed to find out what had actually killed the actress. Johnson filed an offical request with Wagner for an immediate autopsy to be performed on the body of Thelma Todd. He knew he had to scramble to wrap up the case under the D.A.'s banner. His request went unanswered. The LAPD was already deep into its initial investigation, and the race was on.

Though the District Attorney's office had always considered itself the more elite of the two agencies, the LAPD often beat the D.A. to the initial punch. The police department usually had more contacts and informants, and did more of the initial "dirty work" before the "boys in the gray suits" stepped in. It looked upon the D.A.'s gang as a lofty group that usually chose the more notorious cases for publicity's sake. The two agencies had long been fierce competitors when it came to sensational cases. Sometimes the competition worked to solve a crime, each spurring the other into quick action and risk-taking. But there were also times when each was reluctant to pool evidence, not wanting its rival to gain the upper hand. This was one of those cases where the rivalry further hampered the probe. Evidence was lost in the scramble, and as time has shown, this eventually allowed the real villans in this case to slip away. But shockingly, though both sides seemed bent on a race to solve the case, the "team leaders," Wallis and Fitts, appeared to be working against their own underlings; independent actions by both men indicated each wanted the murder swept under the rug. The reason, at this stage of the probe, had still not surfaced.

Bert Wallis turned the police portion of the Thelma Todd investigation over to Captain Steen and Detective Lieutenant Thad Brown, who, along with several homicide investigators, returned to the Palisades that afternoon, Tuesday, December 17, to attempt to reassemble the evidence, reinterrogate the witnesses, and mop up the mess Wallis and Wagner had made of the initial probe. The task force was broken into units; each looked into specific aspects of the case: Thelma's friends and associates, her business dealings with the restaurant, her film career, and rumors about her wild private life. If it was a murder, they believed something would turn up somewhere.

Unfortunately, all that remained were fragmented pieces of evidence. A dusting of the garage, car, and car keys proved futile—they were marred with smudged fingerprints—and hair fragments were inconclusive. The team had one last option; Steen and Brown returned to Wagner to repeat Johnson's request for an autopsy, something Wagner had reportedly wanted to avoid. Caving in to pressure from the LAPD, and knowing a tough new team from the D.A's office was also on the track, Wagner capitulated. The Los Angeles County Coroner's office now received the requests from both the LAPD and the D.A. The autopsy would begin as soon as he received the go-ahead from Alice Todd.

Though Wagner held the official title of Los Angeles County medical examiner and county autopsy surgeon, the order to perform the autopsy was given to R. J. Abernathy, under the supervision of County Coroner Frank Nance. Wagner's at-the-scene exam was questionable, and he knew the autopsy would show Todd was killed much later than his estimate. He already planned to attribute the time discrepancy to the cold temperatures, which "preserved" the body. But he had no idea the operation would explode the case wide open.

No one, not even the detectives and investigators on the case, were prepared for the next series of revelations.

As expected, Abernathy and Nance corroborated the blood-alcohol content of .13; they also verified the lacerations and contusions around Thelma's neck and the cracked ribs, the broken nose, and the chipped front tooth. As Wagner expected, they found that according to the deterioration of tissue, Thelma Todd could not have been killed at 2:00 A.M. Sunday. What Wagner had not expected was the significant variation in estimates. Nance and Abernathy pushed the time closer to Sunday night, more than fifteen hours after Wagner's estimate. Wagner was known as a competent and professional doctor and the two could not understand why he was so off on his estimated time of death. Then another fact emerged that clearly indicated something was amiss. When the team examined the contents of Todd's stomach, they found evidence that was unexplainable; they found partially digested food—peas and carrots. This discovery appeared insignificant at first. In fact, Nance made little of it until the autopsy report was released and newspaper accounts of the findings were published, reports that ignited a fury of protest from Thelma Todd's friends. Only then, the full impact of that gruesome discovery was realized.

The newspapers, still hungry for new information on the now-famous puzzle, constructed their own versions of the last day of Thelma Todd's life. They all arrived at the same basic story: Todd enjoyed a hearty dinner and an evening of drinking at a Saturday night party at the Trocadero nightclub on Sunset Boulevard. The party was hosted by English comedian Stanley Lupino as a "thank you" for Thelma's appearing in an English picture with him three years before. It broke up shortly after 2:00 Sunday morning. When Thelma returned home to her apartment at the Sidewalk Cafe, Roland West locked her out in a fit of anger over her late-hour arrival. She climbed up to the garage above the restaurant, started the car to keep warm, inhaled carbon monoxide and died, accidentally. It was a nice, neat little story. No one had ever bought the conclusion of suicide; the death seemed accidental to even the most casual observer.

Friends who partied with Thelma on that fateful night refuted the newspaper stories, very definitely insisting Thelma did not eat a "hearty dinner," certainly not peas and carrots as uncovered in the autopsy, and each insisted Thelma only sipped two glasses of champagne. All claimed they were telling the truth and would swear so under oath, in court if necessary. The list of witnesses read like a 1930s Hollywood Who's Who; theater mogul Sid Grauman, Mrs. Wallace Ford (whose husband was a star at Universal Studios and featured in the "Mummy" series of films), film choreographer Arthur Prince, the Lupinos, and Todd's former husband, millionaire playboy/agent Pat DiCicco. If the coroner's report was accurate, and her friends were telling the truth, then the medical examiner was absolutely wrong: Thelma Todd could not have died shortly after she left the Trocadero; she must have made another stop, where she ate, drank, and possibly died.

The ball next went back to Buron Fitts, and the investigators in this bizarre probe turned to him, as the county's leading attorney, for a decision. Fitts had several options. He could publicly denounce Wagner and his report, which would take the pressure off Fitts and possibly throw the heat back on Wallis, who was in Wagner's corner. But Wagner had knowledge of other, questionable, murder investigations conducted through Fitts's office, and he in turn could expose Fitts and allude to corruption. Wagner was too volatile. Fitts considered making light of the case, hoping his casual attitude would lessen the importance of what was unfolding. But with a pushy Alice Todd firing off accusations to the newspapers, he knew he could wind up with an even stickier problem on his hands. He did not want some nosy reporter pinning his future as an investigative journalist on an exposé of Fitts's career. There was only one viable option, and Fitts took what he thought would be the more prudent course of action. He ordered a grand-jury investigation to get under way immediately. Unknowingly, Fitts had just made one of the biggest blunders of his career.

Chapter Two

Word that the grand jury would be looking into Thelma Todd's death spread through the Hollywood community. Newspapers devoured this latest twist that kept the death on the front page, giving readers scandalous gossip from Hollywood, something to take their minds off the ongoing Great Depression. The event itself had skyrocketed from a mysterious, but probably accidental, death to speculation of murder, political cover-ups, inept police work, and even mob involvement.

Suddenly, from out of nowhere, friends, associates, and strangers harassed police and hounded newspapers, offering inside information about what they had seen or heard that could wrap up the investigation. Palisades neighbors offered tips on Sidewalk Cafe customers they thought looked "shady," conversations between Thelma and West that they had heard echoing through the hills, casting doubts on West's innocence in the affair; rumors spread about the wild nights and drunken parties hosted by the dead movie star. Literally overnight, the police and District Attorney's office had hundreds of witnesses demanding to be called before the grand jury.

As investigators started weeding out the cranks from the

legitimate witnesses, they stumbled upon a series of statements that sent the case skidding off course. A succession of
friends and strangers insisted they had seen Thelma alive
more than nineteen hours after Wagner's recorded time of
death; they told stories about Thelma driving around town
with a mysterious-looking man, tales about Todd making
phone calls at different locations. The accounts grew more exciting and intriguing as people made claims of personal death
threats and harassment by "tough-looking men," and said
they could offer details of Todd's involvement with some of
the most infamous and notorious figures in the underworld.
Each witness insisted he had not collaborated with anyone
else. Each offered testimony independent of the others, and
each story seemed to pick up where another left off, with the
times of these sightings flowing in a logical progression. Was
it possible?

The case veered off in a frightening and eerie direction.
Too many people had seen the "ghost" of Thelma Todd. Too
many people remembered too many things that threatened to
shake the preliminary investigation. Too many witnesses held
firm to their stories and had other witnesses to back their
claims. These people were rational, sane, and respected; some
were even famous. But most disturbing was that their testimony promised to hold up under scrutiny. The statements
were handed over to Fitts, who turned ashen. He knew he
could no longer ignore Todd's friends who refuted early
newspaper accounts that she was killed within an hour after
leaving the Trocadero. The floodgates had burst open. Fitts
felt queasy and sick; he knew he had a full-blown mess on his
hands.

Fitts had a very real concern that the inquest would drag
on, witnesses would not be discredited, and questions about
his part in the probe would eventually seep to the surface. He
knew he had to go ahead with the grand jury. Right now his
only hope was that the hearing would end quickly and in confusion, that he could wrap it up by convincing not only the
jury but the press and Alice Todd that the blond actress had
died an accidental death. Fitts pinned his hopes on Roland
West, whose testimony was already suspect, who appeared
nervous and contradicted himself, and seemed to be hiding
the truth. If Fitts could throw suspicion on West's testimony,

he would remove a tremendous burden. Fitts homed in on his pigeon.

Nineteen men were called to serve on the Los Angeles County grand-jury panel. The jury convened on the fifth floor of the Hall of Justice in downtown L.A. on Thursday, December 19, 1935, just three days after the gruesome find in the Pacific Palisades garage. The opening session was a field day for the scores of reporters who now flocked to Los Angeles from all over the country. Tall metal lightpoles with bright bulbs snarled foot traffic in the tiled corridor, flashing and temporarily blinding unsuspecting strangers who wandered into the chaos. Men in uniform barked commands to clear the hall and usher witnesses and spectators into the proper rooms. Reporters grabbed anyone who looked as if he had a story to tell, stopping everyone from courthouse clerks to potential witnesses. A stream of movie stars, studio workers, and now-famous faces shoved their way through the mass of flesh pressing outside the giant varnished-wood courtroom doors. But for this press party, there were neither smiles nor witty remarks. The mood was somber, and each witness appeared tense and guarded, as if he were being stalked and his words reported to someone unknown.

In all, more than forty witnesses were paraded before the grand-jury panel. The first group called for the opening proceedings included Margaret Lindsay, a raven-haired actress who had been dining at the Trocadero with Todd's former husband, Pat DiCicco—Lindsay would offer testimony about the confrontation between herself, DiCicco, and Todd on that fateful night; Jewel Carmen, in whose garage Thelma had died—she would clear up some confusion about the Sidewalk Cafe, which she financed for her husband, and offer what she knew about the relationship between her husband and the dead movie star; Charles Smith, the thin, elderly cafe treasurer who should have heard Todd's Lincoln Phaeton convertible start up on that cold night—his room was directly above the garage, and the engine was reportedly loud enough to rouse the dead; Ernest Peters, Thelma's chauffeur, who drove Todd from the Troc to her apartment—Thelma was unusually distraught and kept ordering Peters to drive faster, as if the devil himself was chasing her; Rudy Schaefer, who knew about the cafe's shaky finances and could offer information as to why nefarious "outside interests" had purportedly been trying to buy into the business; Mae Whitehead, who discovered the body; Alice Todd, who insisted she had a lot to tell; and finally, the man who promised to be the key witness in the grisly affair, Roland West.

West sat next to Schaefer outside the courtroom on an old narrow bench as the jury was given its instructions. He appeared exhausted, drawn, and irritable, and shouted at reporters to stay away, to mind their own business. He snapped at Schaefer, who was doing his best to reassure his boss that everything would resolve itself. West held his hat in his hands and stared at the floor. At 10:15 A.M., an officer opened the courtroom doors and called West's name. Pale and shaking, he slowly walked to the witness stand.

West's voice cracked as he took the oath, barely audible as he swore to tell the truth. He slowly looked at the jurors, all dressed in dark suits, and felt cheap and obvious, as if they were already convinced he had committed the crime and were looking for any reason to pin the murder on him. Deputy District Attorney Johnson began the interrogation, assisted by Detective Lieutenants W. J. Clark and E. J. Romero.

"State your full name."

West took a deep breath before he spoke. "Roland Van West."

"Where do you live?"

"I stay at 17320 Robelo Drive and at the Sidewalk Cafe."

"What is your business?"

"Well, at the present I am a landlord."

"Are you also in the cafe business?"

"No, I am not in the cafe business. But I will be."

Muffled whispers rolled through the courtroom. Everyone knew, or at least thought, he was the owner of the Sidewalk Cafe. Sure, it was his wife's money that financed the restaurant, but the title was established under Roland West's name. Though the marriage was shaky, West was still Jewel Carmen's husband. Thelma had supposedly supplied only her name for her stake in the venture. Was West going to buy out his wife and divorce her? Or had he already calculated to get his now-dead partner out of the way? Photographers took shots, reporters scribbled in their notebooks. Another shock wave rippled through the room when Johnson surprisingly let

West's answer drop and detoured onto another line of questioning. The judge pounded his gavel for silence.

"You were acquainted with Thelma Todd?"

"Yes. She was one of my best friends, if not my best friend."

"You have been acquainted with her for how long?"

"I have known her for four years. I have been associated with her in business for about two years."

Johnson steered back on track. "Are you interested with her in this cafe business?"

"Only that I am the financial backer of the cafe."

"You say that you live at the cafe?"

"Yes." West suddenly seemed distant and began looking around the courtroom. He was remembering how they had first met, on a boat trip to Catalina four long years ago. It was one of those days you always associate with the beginning of spring, warm, breezy, the air fresh and crisp; just the right setting to fall in love. He remembered how beautiful Thelma was and how immediately he was smitten with the vivacious blonde. He had felt all alone then, trying to recover from yet another nasty, violent quarrel with his estranged wife. Thelma was fresh, vibrant, and more than a bit of a flirt. She was breathtaking, without a doubt the most beautiful girl in Hollywood; curly blond hair glistening in the sun, sparkling white teeth, dimples, sky-blue eyes, and a sweet, innocent face that seemed so open, so tender, as if yearning for someone to reach out and hold her. Her honesty offered a sharp contrast to Jewel's dark looks and strong but somber personality. She was what he needed at the time. He remembered the trip as one filled with laughter, hand-holding and promises to conquer Hollywood together. He would make her a dramatic actress, take her away from pratfalls and pies in the face. She would revive his near-dead career as a movie director. Her name, his connections and know-how, an unbeatable combination. They became instant friends, and West had hoped the friendship would turn into a romance. But Thelma always kept him at bay, just out of reach, and he never could break through to win her heart. He was married, Thelma recently divorced, both reluctant to encumber what promised to be a free and platonic flirtation. He thought he had tried to make it more.

West smiled, then seemed to snap back to the present. He looked at Johnson, repeating his answer to the question of whether he lived at the cafe. "Yes, yes I do."

"Were you there last Saturday evening or in that apartment?"

"I was there and I escorted Miss Todd and her mother to the car." West's mind began wandering again. He had already told police it was the last time he saw her alive. Thelma and her mother had planned their outing several days earlier. Alice was heading out on a Saturday evening shopping spree, Thelma to a private party at the Trocadero, dressed to kill; a party to which West was flatly not invited. He remembered Thelma's driver, Ernie Peters, pulling his car behind the cafe, on Castellammare Drive, the first street above the highway. Peters never said much to West. They were cordial but he was Thelma's employee and Peters considered himself such.

Thelma was in an unusually foul mood, bickering with West all evening right up to the moment she climbed into Peters's car. They had argued about everything: the cafe finances, her responsibilities, her drinking and carousing. Thelma lectured him on how it was her name that had made the cafe and public appearances were necessary to draw customers. West scolded her, accusing her of finding any excuse to go out drinking and picking up men behind his back. It was an emotionally violent battle, a scene they had played many times before.

"Did you have any conversation with her before that about what she was intending to do that evening?"

West returned to the questioning at hand. "I knew what she was intending to do and had been invited by her to go along." He lied. He wasn't invited to the party, but did not want to be made a fool of in front of everyone. He tried to stay with the answers rehearsed and practiced the day before with his attorney. He knew Johnson was getting close to the critical area of questioning, so he spoke slowly and deliberately.

"Will you please relate in your own way what that conversation was and what happened?"

"Well, she said, 'Can you go tonight?' and I said, 'No, not tonight, not on a Saturday. You know we're very busy.'" West thought to himself that it was typical of Thelma, running off to a party, leaving him alone to take care of the business on a hectic night, especially right before Christmas. He spoke again. "She had been very busy buying Christmas presents and was rather tired, and I said in a joking manner in front of her mother and everyone else up there and the chauffeur, 'Be home by two o'clock,' and she said, 'I will be here at two-five,' and every time I said that, she would open the door and laugh and I said two o'clock and she kept saying two-five."

"It was all in fun or good spirits?"

"As far as I was concerned. It was joking, as everyone would notice." Alice Todd hadn't noticed. Ernie Peters hadn't noticed. Both remembered the discussion as a near brawl.

Johnson seemed suspicious of West's story. "Did you say, 'If you are not home at two, I will lock you out'?"

"No, I said, 'After two the outside door is locked.'"

"What did you mean by that?"

"We have heard people around there and I had bars put up at the window." West knew Johnson and his crew had already heard about the rash of burglaries in the area. It was all over the newspapers.

"Prowlers?" Johnson was steering his questions toward the mystery surrounding the keys to the apartments. West had claimed he didn't know Thelma was locked out, justifying his theory that she had locked herself in the garage to keep warm overnight. Two keys were needed to enter the outside doors, as a safety precaution. Thelma had also been receiving a constant stream of death threats and was in fear of her life.

"Prowlers. The manager told me that, and I had bars put on the windows, especially after she got those messages. She would never go out that door on Saturday night, and she had three keys, one for the main door, one for the main entrance door and the back apartment. The outside door was a separate key and she never used that door on Saturday night except once and it was locked and she wanted to get in and couldn't."

"She didn't have any other keys? Let's see what they look like." Johnson showed the keys confiscated from the cafe to Coroner Nance, who was in the courtroom to testify at a later date. "Which key is which?" Nance handed the keys back to West.

"There is a pass key that Miss Todd had to the outside. I

thought she had these keys with her that night. She had more keys, like to the ladies' boudoir, that I haven't got, and if I had known she didn't have that one key, I would have stayed up and waited for her."

"Where did you go?"

"I didn't go anywhere. I was at the cafe until closing time, which I imagine was about two o'clock, when I received a call from [theater mogul] Sid Grauman."

"Where were you when you received the message?"

"I was in the cocktail lounge."

"At the cafe?"

"Yes. I went to the main dining room and talked to Grauman." West recollected he was worried that Thelma had not yet arrived, but the phone call from Grauman eased his mind. Grauman told West Thelma was wrapping up a conversation with the Skouras brothers, who were Fox movie-theater executives, and was about to head home. The conversation between Grauman was friendly, with Grauman inviting West to the party which was still going strong. They talked about Thelma staying out late, and Grauman assured West that Peters had already been called and was on his way to pick her up. It would take approximately half an hour for Thelma to reach the Palisades if she left immediately. She had stayed out past two, as she had threatened. She had won again.

West continued his testimony. "After I got the message I went upstairs and got the dog [White King, a white pit bull Thelma had bought for protection], took him for his walk, and then brought him back and locked that side door and bolted it. The other door was not bolted, the main door, the entrance we always use. Then I went to my room, closed the apartment, locked it, and took the dog in with me and covered him up." West paused, then went on.

"I fell asleep, I imagine it was about two-thirty. I was awakened about three-thirty by the dog whining. He has a habit of whining when he gets uncovered, and I looked over to see, to cover him up, and he was all covered, and I looked at the clock and it was exactly three-thirty. Whether or not that clock was right, I don't know. I called out to see if Miss Todd was home and received no answer, but I heard the water running in the building and figured somebody was up. I figured she had come in from the outside the regular way and gone to bed. The dog was quiet again and I went to sleep."

Johnson glossed over the reference to 3:30 and continued with his prepared questions. It was possible he had no idea the dog's whining at that time would have proved critical in uncovering the fact that Thelma Todd was alive at that hour and just outside the apartment. A valuable clue had just been ignored.

"On that particular occasion, or any time recently, had you noticed she was at all moody or unhappy about anything?"

"Miss Todd was never unhappy; she had everything to be happy about. . . . She was finishing a Roach contract and Mr. Schenck [Nick Schenck, who headed Loew's and MGM, which was distributing the Hal Roach/Thelma Todd comedies] told her that as soon as she was finished with Roach he was ready to sign her up. She has her mother whom she was taking care of, and she has her cafe."

Then the interrogation edged toward another gray area, the question of Thelma Todd's health. West maintained that Todd had a bad heart, that she had already been denied life insurance because of it, and that the climb from the cafe to the garage possibly triggered a heart attack. Though he held firm in his claim, he was unable to get Todd's doctor to back him. Again, Johnson moved quickly, skipping to the car, the noise, and the deadly fumes.

"How long do you suppose it would take to fill that garage with smoke or fumes from that exhaust pipe?"

West took a deep breath and braced himself for what he was about to say. The sentences rambled a bit, but his meaning was clear. "Well, I don't know. I tell you, here is a thing that has never been brought out—the treasurer lives above the garage and he closed up that night and he said, 'I went home at two-thirty and read until three-thirty before I went to bed,' and then you know the plaster in that garage has been taken out . . ."

Now it was Johnson's turn to be nervous. Investigators from both the D.A's office and the LAPD had reenacted the start of the twelve-cylinder engine. They found the noise deafening, so loud in Smith's room that it was impossible not to hear something. If Smith had been reading, he would have heard the engine. If he was asleep, surely he would have awakened. Especially since plaster was both missing and chipped in his room. He would not have heard the engine, only if he was not home at that time, and he would have claimed not to have heard it, only if he had started the car himself. For some reason not yet revealed, both squads quashed that part of their probe. No one expected West to pry open that can of worms.

West was sweating from nervousness, but he had found an opportunity to cast suspicion on someone else for a change. He was ready to roll and expected his statements to be repeated in print and read by hundreds of thousands of newspaper subscribers who had already decided he was a murderer. He thought he could vindicate himself and had more to tell about the garage and Smith. But Johnson pulled the plug. He requested a temporary adjournment, and dropped that line of questioning.

As West left the courtroom he was mobbed by reporters who wanted to know more about the death garage and the mysterious treasurer. As West was about to speak, he saw Charles Smith standing alone, stern and glaring. Smith turned his back on West and West now had second thoughts about telling tales out of school. "No," he thought, "leave this for the men asking the questions. Let them figure this one out." West shoved past the mob, only remarking "No comment" at each question posed to him. He was unaware that he had said all he would be allowed to say in court about the twelve-cylinder engine.

After an hour and a quarter recess, the inquest resumed with West again in the witness box. In contrast to his demeanor in the morning's session, West now appeared confident and eager to face Johnson and his team head on. It was apparent that West naïvely believed he would be allowed to finish his statements about Smith. But, as before, when the round of interrogation began, Johnson was in complete control.

"Did you ever know of Miss Todd walking from the cafe up to the garage?"

"No." West was cautious, guarded, waiting for an opportunity to work Smith back into his testimony.

"That was a distance of three or four hundred feet?"

"Yes."

"And that was uphill all the way from the cafe?" It seemed apparent Johnson was guiding the line of questioning back to Todd's heart condition, a matter that West had repeated only as hearsay.

"Yes."

"And she was not one addicted to walking?"

"Never. In fact, I heard from several close friends . . . even Miss Todd herself that she had a bad . . ."

Johnson abruptly cut him off. "You will just answer the questions please, Mr. West." He paced in front of the witness box, then continued. "Did you know when you went to bed that the bolt on the door by which she would enter the place was locked on the inside?"

"I didn't know the door that she would enter from was locked. I locked the inside door. She had keys to the main door."

"Wasn't that also the key to the [out]side door?"

"No."

"Wasn't that the customary way for her to come in?"

"No, it was not the customary way for her to come in. She came in the other doors as much as the [out]side door. She never came in that door on Saturday nights." West was irritated that he was being forced to repeat statements he made in the morning. Obviously Johnson and his team were trying to trip him up. "It might sometimes be bolted at eight o'clock at night, and if the dog was taken out he was taken out that door because that's a dead entrance, and if the dog was taken out at two o'clock in the morning, Thelma would take him out by that door and bolt it again."

"When did you bolt that door Saturday night?"

"I bolted the door when I brought the dog in."

"About two-thirty?"

"About two-fifteen."

"The [out]side door was not bolted before you bolted it that night?" Johnson seemed to be making a statement rather than asking a question.

"Not that night, to my knowledge. I don't remember it being bolted, it just has a catch you open."

"What time did you wake Sunday?"

"I woke up when I heard the dog whining at three-thirty."

"You mean you were awakened, then went to sleep again?"

"I went to sleep first. I got up and examined the dog to see if he was uncovered. I covered him up and lay there a few minutes and heard water running in the other ladies' boudoir and figured it was Miss Todd."

"What was there in the way of partitions or doorways, if anything, between the bedroom you were occupying and the apartment of Miss Todd?"

"There were double doors with locks on both sides."

"Were those doors locked at night?"

"Yes!" West resented Johnson's insinuations.

"And when you ascertained it was three-thirty in the morning, you didn't make any particular inquiry to see if Miss Todd was in yet?"

"No."

Johnson paced and paused, then glanced over to the jury for effect. The move was well calculated to make West out to be either a fool or a liar. "And what time then did you get up for the day on Sunday?"

"I think I got up between nine and eleven."

"And you hadn't been awake or up or disturbed for any purpose since three-thirty that morning. Is that correct?"

"Correct."

"Then you got up Sunday morning and dressed. Did you find anything there regarding Miss Todd's whereabouts?"

"I went to see, opened the door, rapped, went out . . ."

". . . You went out where?"

"Out into the big room [main dining room] and saw she wasn't there. And then I went into the ladies' boudoir and examined the huge couch in there because she had slept on that couch and there was what I considered an impression on that couch. I thought she slept there because nobody else could have done it. I figured she had gone to her mother's."

"Then did you stay upstairs all day?"

"No. I finished my paper, rung for my breakfast."

"Until you went downstairs about one, you made no inquiry about Miss Todd?"

"Not until I got downstairs. I asked the boy that takes

care of Miss Todd's car which one she had used that night. He said he had been busy and hadn't checked. I told him I was buying a car for my wife and told him to go up to Smith's room and ask Smith for a check." West had just managed to work Smith back into the testimony. He hoped Johnson would ask whether the boy, Bob, who also worked as a cafe bartender, had actually found Smith in his room, but Johnson pretended not to notice the reference.

"Did you get any telephone messages on Sunday?"

West collected his thoughts before he spoke, trying to piece them together in the best order he could. "I was very tired, nervous for some reason, I don't know why, and about six o'clock the telephone rang and they said Los Angeles is calling and wanted Miss Todd. I said, 'Miss Todd isn't here,' and they said, 'Who is talking?' and on that phone, in the cafe, I always give the same answer. I told them, 'Mr. Schaefer, Miss Todd's manager,' and they said [to the caller], 'Do you want to talk to the party on the line? Miss Todd is not there.' They repeated the message and this man then said, 'Yes.' He talked to me and told me he was Mr. Skouras, and he said he had made a bet with Thelma that he would come to dinner that night [Sunday] and bring his family, eleven of them. I told him Miss Todd wasn't there but we were expecting her any minute. He said, 'Just wait a minute and I'll call you back.' In about fifteen to twenty minutes later he called back and said everyone was coming, there would be eleven between seven and seven-thirty.

"A little later, maybe five minutes or so, there was another call and I asked who it was, and he said it was George Baker [assistant director at Roach Studios] and I said, 'Miss Todd will be back in a little while.' He asked me to deliver a message, to call up North Hollywood, and I said 'What is the message?' He said, 'I am calling for Martha Ford, and Miss Ford wants to have her call her up.' I said, 'I will tell her,' then looked at the time and it was seven o'clock, and I thought I would go downstairs on account of the Skouras party coming." West paused to take another breath. "I really thought Miss Todd would have been back by the time the Skouras party broke up. With that crowd of eleven and the huge amount of food they ordered, I knew they would be there until eleven o'clock at night."

"Then you remained at the cafe Sunday evening, too?"

"Sunday evening, I stayed there until twelve o'clock, took the dog for a walk, then went to bed. I couldn't sleep and lay awake until about five o'clock Monday morning. I fell asleep around six o'clock and I was awakened by the house phone, buzzing very heavily. It was from Smith, who told me the maid had come from the garage and told him there was something terribly wrong with Miss Todd, that she was dead."

"And did you go to the garage then?"

"I put on a pair of trousers and a shirt and Mae Whitehead took me up to the garage. One of our employees saw us and thought Mae was taking me to the doctor because I was as white as a sheet. Do you want me to go on?"

"Yes."

"I come to the garage and rushed in the door and there was Miss Todd lying over there. I put my hand onto her face and there was blood and I wiped it off on my handkerchief and I then sent Mae to go up. She would not go through the garage, and I said, 'Get Schaefer and his wife as quickly as you can.' She sent them down to the garage and they opened the garage door from the inside, and I said better get the police and a doctor.

"I went in the car, I think through the other door. I don't know how I got this thought that the door had been mostly closed, but I found out now the door was open and I looked over there and I saw the switch. I saw the gas tank was almost empty and I knew from her position in the car she was trying to get out."

"The door was partially open?"

"It was wide open, not partially open. And the ignition was on, but the motor was off."

"You touched the body?"

"Yes."

"Exactly who was it that first alerted you to the death?"

"Charles Smith."

"And who phoned police?"

"Mae Whitehead. But . . ."

Johnson thanked West and strolled back to the group of investigators at his table. West's testimony contradicted police reports taken at the scene. According to those reports, Schaefer and Smith arrived at the garage moments before police. West had also told investigators that it was Whitehead who first told him about Thelma, and he upped the time of Whitehead's arrival by several hours. Was he confused, nervous, or lying? Had he really forgotten the details or was he deliberately altering the facts? Why did Johnson abruptly cut him off at the end of his testimony? The inquest that had been called to answer questions had actually stirred up further suspense.

The session was adjourned. Reporters dashed out of the courtroom and mobbed a line of black candlestick phones that had been set up as a temporary press booth in the hall. The wires hummed with "scoops," "hot stories," and "flashes" about the statements made by West just moments before. It was very clear that this was going to be the one of the most sensational stories in years. And no one yet had an inkling of its magnitude.

Chapter Three

By the time Mae Whitehead was called to testify, the focus of the investigation had shifted slightly from determining how Thelma Todd had actually died to who was at the garage when Whitehead discovered the body. Charles Smith's testimony was brief and concise. He remained firm in his statements that he was not initially at the garage when the maid and his boss found the body. The treasurer claimed he was in a deep sleep when the loud, twelve-cylinder engine was probably started, so deep, he claimed, it was possible he didn't hear the racket. Smith's wife, usually a light sleeper, was out of town (conveniently?). He then told the panel he was awakened by Whitehead's loud, shrill scream, and rushed to the garage to investigate. Clark, who took over this leg of the questioning from Johnson, pressed Smith on how he knew the scream had emanated from the garage—noises tend to echo and distort in the hills—and why, if the engine did not wake him, a mere scream would jolt him out of bed. Smith had no explanation for either question; and his testimony was now considered highly suspect, albeit unshakable at this stage.

Smith's answers directly contradicted West's, which came as no great shock to either the investigators or the jury. There was already a strong suspicion that West was either guilty of the actual murder or knew who had done it and was covering up for someone. His testimony was vague, rambling, and at times incoherent. But now it was Smith who was arousing speculation about his innocence in the death. Why was Smith unable to justify his actions? Authorities needed to grill the other members of the bizarre cast that had assembled near the garage on Monday. Rudy Schaefer was the third member of the party called to the stand.

Many of Schaefer's statements were similar to Smith's. He, too, was not aware of the death until he was awakened by Whitehead. But testimony he gave about Smith's arrival further muddled the case. He contradicted Smith's statement that he was already at the garage by the time Schaefer arrived. Schaefer claimed he saw Smith pace back and forth from the garage to the house at least twice, so it was possible someone who saw him only on a return trip would believe Smith had just arrived. Schaefer appeared to be in the clear, and Smith had definitely slipped into that terrifyingly elite group of central characters. Either West had perjured himself, or Smith had, or both. The jury hoped the next witness would shed some light.

Mae Whitehead was a gentle yet outspoken woman who often considered herself a second mother to Thelma Todd. She had been with the actress for more than five years, doing everything from light errands, housekeeping, and nursing Thelma through illnesses to offering advice and doing her best to keep Todd stable through rough times, which seemed to be cropping up with increased frequency toward 1935. In fact, Thelma had hired Whitehead on the advice of several friends who believed a maid (or in this case a maid/guardian) could keep a close watch on the untamed blonde. Thelma's mother openly resented Whitehead's influence; Alice treated Whitehead as a lowly servant and considered her both an interference and a possible wedge between her and her daughter.

One of Whitehead's duties was to drive the car from the garage to the rear of the cafe for Thelma, though Thelma quite often used a chauffeur instead of driving herself around town. (Thelma had a number of drunk-driving citations and accidents and had been cautioned against driving, especially at night.) Whitehead's duties, the car, and the position of Todd's body were the focus of the next round of questioning.

Friends remembered Whitehead's testimony as brief, with the interrogation handled by both Clark and Romero. Mae detailed how she arrived at the Carmen house that Monday morning, as she always did, just before ten o'clock, and opened the right door on the two-car garage. When she saw her mistress slumped between the wheel and the seat, on the driver's side, she tried to rouse her from what she believed was another night of partying and drinking. When Todd would not wake up, Mae started screaming, and ran down the hill to West's apartment. Those screams, Whitehead reportedly claimed, might have awakened Smith, who was already at the garage by the time she returned with West. The witnesses now appeared to be divided into two camps, both centered on Smith's whereabouts. Cafe treasurer Charles Smith was now a probable suspect.

Whitehead also introduced another, startling revelation that caught the investigators off guard and rang through the courtroom like a shot; that was the possibility of mob involvement in both the cafe and quite possibly the murder itself. Earlier, Smith had maintained the cafe was going broke, losing thousands of dollars a month, but he was at a loss to explain why. He stated Thelma herself had borrowed heavily from friends and was always deep in debt though she earned at least $2,000 a week at the Hal Roach Studios. He offered no clues as to who or what had been draining her money and bleeding the cafe dry. All he knew was that Thelma would have to sell out the following year, in 1936. (Is that what West meant when he testified that he would be in the cafe business? Could he have been juggling the books to squeeze Todd out?) Smith had carefully hinted that West might not be telling all he knew, and volleyed the ball back into West's court.

Whitehead was now offering a possible explanation for the financial difficulties of both the cafe and its owner. She said tough-looking men had been hanging around the cafe in the past few months. Thelma seemed to know them, though it was obvious she was frightened of them. Whitehead said she personally had no idea who these men were, but that Thelma became very nervous when she was asked about them. She said these men had also been seen around the Hal

Roach Studios, watching Thelma at work. Whitehead reportedly told Clark a "couple of mean-looking men" had approached her the day before, and threatened her if she testified about any mob involvement, or named names. When pressed by Clark, Whitehead backed off and refused to elaborate because she allegedly feared for her life. She would not continue and was released as a witness.

Clark, Romero, and Johnson were stunned. The jury watched in silence and the gallery of reporters sat quietly for the first time since the inquest began. No one had expected anything as shocking as ties to the underworld to surface in this case. Yes, there were rumors Thelma had been seen with mobster Lucky Luciano, the New York vice lord. But few anticipated a tie-in with the cafe and possible intimidation of a witness. Once again, the case swerved onto an unexpected course. The investigation not only had a life of its own, but apparently a mind of its own, and Johnson and his team had all they could do just to hang on. Each time they thought they had the direction of testimony plotted, a witness would steer them onto an uncharted road. This time that road proved dangerous, and possibly deadly.

As the day's session adjourned, the investigative panel scurried out the rear courtroom door into the judge's chambers to avoid reporters' questions. They had to figure out what direction to take next, to dig deeper into the alleged mob angle or swing the trial back on its previous course. Johnson phoned his boss, Buron Fitts, and requested an emergency meeting for 5:00 that evening. Fitts seemed reticent, unusually distant, but agreed to a brief session. When Johnson hung up the phone, he was reported to be confused by Fitts's sudden distance and reluctance to meet on such a crucial issue. The D.A's office had been looking into a far more serious, sinister, and diabolical scheme that involved the movie industry and two notorious mob gangs. Luciano's name had been mentioned as having a hand in the scheme. Johnson assumed his boss would be hell-bent on uncovering any scandal that could slam the lid on the mob. Such a chance, Johnson assumed, now lay before them. They might have stumbled on to evidence that could be used against Luciano in the movie probe. But Johnson had been brushed off, and not too subtly, by

Fitts. He had his first inkling that something was not quite kosher in the District Attorney's office.

The meeting was short, Fitts was curt. He stated flatly that Johnson was to proceed with the "Roland West angle" and forget about the other elements that Fitts called "loose hairs." Johnson reportedly told several close associates that Fitts seemed too quick to bury this new information, especially new evidence about Luciano's connection to the death. He knew about the string of muddled cases and the stream of bad press the D.A's office had received ever since Fitts took over. But he also knew that as Fitts's deputy, he had to follow orders. Johnson vowed to Fitts he would do his best to, as Fitts put it, stick to the facts at hand, but he would not go out of his way to suppress anything witnesses might want to bring up about threats, intimidation, or dealings with the underworld. And with Alice Todd due up next, anything could happen. Johnson had a strong suspicion that Fitts was either being paid off or threatened, or possibly both.

Alice Todd's demeanor changed once she stepped into the witness box. Outside the courtroom, she was smiling, friendly, and all too happy to answer reporters' questions about her love for her daughter and her determination to bring her killer to justice. Inside the box, she grew cold, hostile, and abrupt, as if braced for a test of wills against the investigators, especially Johnson. Those who knew her attribute her attitude to her not being in complete control of the questioning. She was a woman who was always in control of her life, and if she had her way, everyone else's.

"State your name."

"Alice Edwards Todd."

"And what is your relation to the deceased Thelma Todd?"

"I am her mother."

"And where do you live?"

"I stay, when visiting my daughter, in Hollywood. And I also maintain my home at 592 Andover Street in Lawrence, Massachusetts. I have also, on occasion, stayed at my daughter's apartment at the Sidewalk Cafe."

"When did you first arrive in Hollywood?"

"I first arrived about eight years ago, two years after my

husband died. I came out here to take care of my daughter as I had since she was born."

Alice knew why she had really come out to California in 1927. Thelma had just started her career as an actress and already seemed headed for trouble. Her first publicity photo for Paramount was still emblazoned in Alice's mind, and it was something she swore she would never forget. It was a picture of her beautiful, innocent, naïve daughter covered only in a loose drape, barely decent, definitely obscene in Alice's eyes. It was the first time she had thought of her sweet baby girl in a different light. It was not loneliness for her husband that brought Alice to Hollywood. It was to bring her daughter back home, so she convinced herself.

Alice never did bring Thelma back to Lawrence. A VIP tour of the movie studios, a taste of the champagne-filled night life, and all-night parties with movie stars changed Alice's mind. In a matter of months Alice began pushing her child into the arms of celebrities and movie moguls. She insisted on being invited as Thelma's chaperone, and demanded to be informed of all career decisions affecting her daughter. Alice had emerged as a greedy stage mother who was obviously living vicariously through her daughter.

"Was your daughter known to be unusually friendly, that is, in the sense of being improper or wild?"

"My daughter was always a proper lady. I saw to it."

Johnson smiled to himself because everyone had known about Thelma's reputation as a flirt, her flamboyant night life, her excessive drinking and drunk-driving arrests, her numerous engagements, and most of all her nickname, "Hot Toddy."

"Mrs. Todd, let's proceed to the morning your daughter's body was discovered. How were you notified of the incident?."

"I received a telephone call from Dr. Sampson, I believe. He told me that something was terribly wrong at the cafe and that I should hurry."

"And what time was that call?"

"Approximately ten-forty-five or so."

"And what did you do then?"

"I rang for a chauffeur, who drove me first to the cafe, then up to the garage on Posetano Road."

"What time did you arrive at the garage?"

"I believe it was shortly after eleven-thirty. I don't recall the exact time."

"And who was at the scene when you arrived?"

"Mr. West, Miss Whitehead, Mr. Schaefer, Mr. Smith, and several police officers."

"Did you make any statements indicating you might have personal knowledge about the incident?"

"I do not recall."

"Did you make the statement to the effect you believed your daughter was murdered?"

"I do not recall."

"Did you indicate you might have knowledge as to who may have had a hand in your daughter's death?"

A deadening, suffocating silence fell in the room. The jurors and audience waited for Alice's answer. Johnson fixed a stare directly into Alice's eyes. She glanced back, then looked at the floor as she spoke.

"Mr. Johnson, I was in an emotional state at the time. I do not recall any conversation to that effect."

Johnson knew he had lost a crucial round.

"Mrs. Todd, you were present at the Sidewalk Cafe the night of Saturday, December fourteenth. Is that correct?"

"Yes."

"Did you observe an exchange of words between Roland West and your daughter on Saturday night, December fourteenth?"

"Yes, I did."

"And how would you describe the tone of that exchange?"

"I would say, from what I heard, that Mr. West and my daughter were having a quarrel. Thelma was very upset, and I considered Mr. West's tone harsh."

"Do you recall the nature of the exchange?"

"Yes, they were arguing about what time my daughter should return to her apartment. Mr. West was insisting Thelma return at two o'clock. I told my daughter she was a grown woman and should stay out as long as she wished. As

I recall, he was very pushy, and I do not believe the fight was at all good-natured."

"What happened then?"

"Mr. Peters arrived, and we got into his car. Thelma and Mr. West were still quarreling. Inside the car, Thelma told me she was fed up with Mr. West's jealousy, that he was a dear friend but he would not let her live her own life. I told her she should stand up to him. Thelma hated to argue with anyone, she was so sweet. She told me she would try to be home by two and talk it over with Mr. West at a later time."

"Did you accompany your daughter to the Trocadero?"

"Mr. Peters took me Christmas shopping after he dropped Thelma off, then he drove me home to Hollywood."

Johnson paused, looked at the jury, then walked back to his table to review his notes. There were two options before him: He could continue along a standard line of questioning about what Alice might know about the last moments of her daughter's life, which would be only hearsay and subsequently inadmissible, or he could take the more perilous tack—he could ask if she had any knowledge of Thelma's association with gangsters, specifically Lucky Luciano. Johnson knew the first would be a waste of time and would only rehash old stories and stall the proceedings; the second choice could cost him his job. But the issue of gangsters had already surfaced and had been picked up by the newspapers. To drop the subject entirely would be certain to cast a shadow of doubt on Johnson's integrity. He threw his papers back on the desk and solemnly approached Alice Todd.

Searching for the exact words, Johnson proceeded. "Being a popular movie actress, your daughter was acquainted with a wide assortment of people. Is that correct?"

"Yes, of course."

"Both inside and outside of the film business?"

"Yes."

"In your daughter's association with the restaurant business, had she ever been approached by anyone offering to buy into the Sidewalk Cafe business?"

Alice was obviously uncomfortable with the question. "I don't know."

She thought about one of the last discussions she had had

with Thelma, about ten days before she died. Thelma was frantic and insisted on meeting her mother in her Hollywood home. Thelma drove herself and narrowly avoided rear-ending another car on the way. Alice knew Thelma had been seeing Lucky Luciano, and that he was trying to force his way into the restaurant. The restaurant had already been threatened with extortion and fire-bombing, but the police were unable to shed light on who had been making those threats. Alice had a strong suspicion that Thelma and Luciano were on the brink of some sort of personal disaster; either Luciano had threatened to take over the Sidewalk Cafe and had planted the threats as a scare tactic, or worse, he could have been seriously trying to muscle in on the restaurant, prepared to do anything and everything to get his way.

Alice suspected there was also more to the story than just the business with the restaurant. She suspected the problem was deeper and her daughter was in danger. She knew the books were being altered and had a hunch that either Smith or West was involved in some sort of underhanded dealings, with whom she was not sure. When Thelma arrived, she was hysterical and crying uncontrollably; she was thin and gaunt and visibly frightened.

Thelma confirmed at least some of Alice's suspicions. She told her mother how some of Lucky's thugs sat in the cafe every day, watching, not saying a word, though their intent to intimidate was apparent. Alcohol and food disappeared, money was being drained, and the books never quite balanced; the cafe was deep in debt. In the past few months, strangers would stop deliveries at the back door and rifle through the food. Thelma knew Lucky was orchestrating these events, hoping she would cave in to his demands. She said Lucky wanted to open a gambling casino on the then-vacant third floor, hoping to lure in celebrities by using Thelma's Hollywood connections and movie-star status. She had a hunch the gambling would be rigged at best. At worst, Luciano would use it as a means of laundering mob money and possibly as a front for drugs and prostitution, his main West Coast businesses. Alice believed her daughter had a clear idea of the monster she was fighting.

Thelma also told her she already had a scheme worked out that would not only freeze Lucky out of the Sidewalk Cafe but possibly put him behind bars. She never elaborated over the phone, telling her mother she was afraid that someone would overhear.

Alice looked back at Johnson and repeated her last statement in a distant voice. "I don't know. Mr. West would know more about that than I would."

"Mrs. Todd, let me ask you this. Now think carefully. Had your daughter, Thelma Todd, ever knowingly associated, in any manner, with any known criminals?"

"I resent your question!" A roar swept through the courtroom and the judge pounded his gavel.

"Mrs. Todd, I understand the delicate nature of this line of questioning. Please answer the best you can."

Johnson hoped this time Alice would open up. He knew it was his last chance to bring out any vague reference to Luciano or other gangsters and he hoped this time it would stick. One name could rip the inquest wide open if Alice would only say it aloud, in court, as everyone, especially Johnson, wanted. It was up to Alice, who appeared to be weighing her words carefully, thinking about her next answer, keeping everyone on edge.

Her mind drifted back twenty-nine years, to a hot afternoon in August. She had just returned from the hospital to a small brick home on South Broadway; a happy home filled with love between John and Alice Todd and for their new baby girl, Thelma, born July 29 and without a doubt one of the most beautiful babies in Lawrence. Her birth announcement gave a clear indication of the seemingly charmed life ahead of Thelma. The paper described her as "a little angel . . . bright blue eyes and a round cherubic face . . . a whole cornucopia of graces . . . her fairy godmother surely must have smiled upon baby Thelma."

From the beginning, she was a happy baby, alert and outgoing. Strangers were naturally drawn to her, had an uncontrollable compulsion to reach out to her, as if by touching the child, they could make of her striking looks and cheery personality brush off on them. From her first day in life, Thelma had a magical effect on everyone who met her.

The year 1906 was an important one for John Shaw Todd,

a handsome, stoic man who had worked his way up from street cop to lieutenant on Lawrence's police force. John was ambitious and cunning. He knew how to work with people and how to work around them. It was in this year that he first told Alice of his ambition to become a ward alderman. Both Alice and John knew that meant a hard and calculated climb, a struggle to eliminate political enemies and campaigns to gain the friendship of powerful cronies. Through his years on the force, he was owed favors by many of the politically "right" people, and in 1906, John Todd plotted his rise to power in the rough and often deadly circle of turn-of-the-century politics.

Alice thought it was fun and exciting at first, meeting new people, hosting parties and accepting impressive social invitations. It was a whirlwind life-style that Alice believed she could readily enjoy. But as John expanded his circle of friends, he withdrew from his family. He stayed out late, became secretive about his new associates, who smelled of cologne and stale cigars; men who schemed and contrived to control local industries and legislature; men of power. John charted his course very carefully and promised to be a powerful force whose personal ambition would be placed ahead of the emotional needs of his family. The happiness that Alice initially felt for her husband's success slowly faded away, and John drifted into his own world, shutting Alice out of his life. To compensate, she turned to her daughter and new baby boy, William, for comfort and companionship. Instead of becoming a friend to her children, Alice became overbearing and smothering, never understanding that the children needed to make their own decisions and live their own lives. The more they withdrew, the harder she pushed. Her children, especially Thelma, were never close to Alice as a result.

Alice always seemed to interfere with her children's lives, making decisions for them, and steering them away from so-called "undesirables" in the neighborhood. That left Thelma virtually without friends except for one neighbor, a dark-haired girl named Ann McMahon, whom Thelma called "Mac." Mac became a lifelong friend; they went to school together, went to dances together, and even remained close during Thelma's Hollywood life. Alice was jealous of their friendship, resenting any outsider's influence upon her daughter. Alice was also envious of the affection Thelma had for her father, an affection that became all too apparent to Alice when Thelma played with Mac.

Thelma emulated John, playing her favorite game of "cops and robbers." Thelma always played "the cop" (her father) and Mac the robber. Though the game was in fun, one time it became too real.

Thelma discovered her father's police revolver, which John kept in his bedroom bureau drawer. Thelma used to sneak upstairs when she thought Alice was not looking and get the gun, then chase Mac around the house or yard pretending to shoot at her. One day, Thelma squeezed the trigger, hard, and the gun went off, blowing a hole through the living-room ceiling. Alice took the gun away from Thelma, but did not unload it, leaving at least one more bullet in the chamber. Thelma could have killed Mac or herself, but oddly enough, Alice did not seem upset by the possibility. Alice sent Mac home and ushered Thelma upstairs to her room with a light scolding, more for appearances' sake than as a show of concern for her daughter.

That was not Thelma's last incident with the revolver. When she was in high school, she often took the gun out of the drawer and blatantly swung it at her side on her way to school, prancing, swinging her hips. She would make believe she was shooting at strangers or school pals. To Thelma it was just a game. But was she pretending to emulate her father, or was she closer to fantasizing herself as a "gangster's moll"? The two characters meshed frighteningly close in both her life and her mind. Almost everyone knew Thelma carried her father's police revolver; what they didn't know was that it was loaded the entire time she played with it.

It was the smell of the home that Alice remembered more than anything, the pungent mixture of strong cigar smoke and bay rum cologne, traces left after one of John's parlor meetings with his cronies. Alice knew that John had manipulated the demise of several men, and there were rumors around the neighborhood about John's "underhanded" dealings and his taking bribes to push laws through the legislature or swing city construction contracts to certain building firms. Alice was well aware that John's hands were not clean, and was made acutely conscious of the town gossip when friends and neighbors turned when she approached or whispered in low tones when they thought she was out of range.

She had little consolation in the fact that her husband was becoming increasingly aloof and withdrawn, even cold and hostile toward her and her children. Thelma's baby brother, William (younger by five years), was too immature to understand John's preoccupation with business. But Thelma understood her father's business only too well. She knew that her father's cronies, his gang, were men who commanded respect and controlled wealth and power. Even as a youngster, she was captivated and mesmerized by their authority; she was uncontrollably drawn to them and fantasized about them. She learned about the underworld literally on her father's knee, seeing power in action, witnessing bribe taking and corruption, and watching as gangsters shook hands and partied with police captains and politicians. She also saw how such dealings and corruption paid off.

By 1915, John Todd was one of the most important men in the East. He was appointed Massachusetts director of public health and welfare, a job that gave him carte blanche to write checks and approve construction and medical contracts, offer political positions on high-paying state committees (most as repayment for favors), and pass funding along to hand-picked organizations and charities. Many believed he lined his pockets on more than one appointment or contract. He saw a very bright, very powerful, and very lucrative career ahead of him. Most important, he was in favor with the people who could open doors, for the right price. These people devoured his time, leaving fragmented moments for what affection he felt for his two children and wife.

Thelma may have believed that by winning the love of one of these "men of power," she would win the love of her father. It is possible she was searching for a substitute father. In any event, throughout her life, she had an uncontrollable compulsion toward rough, powerful men who were usually on the wrong side of the law. It was a compulsion that dragged her through the depths of drugs and the underworld; a compulsion that threw her into the arms of one of the ugliest, most bloodthirsty criminals in history, a gangster whose name would be synonymous with the devil. It was a compulsion that would slam a charmed life into the gutter, and end it with a sickening thud one night in a cold, damp garage.

Alice laughed to herself. Did her daughter knowingly associate with any known criminals? She could not recall a time when she had not.

Chapter Four

Thelma never wanted to go to Hollywood; she never dreamed of becoming famous and had a complete disdain for the motion-picture industry. She thought of Hollywood as a ramshackle dustbowl, crawling with lecherous men and tawdry women who bargained away their morals for a chance at becoming bit players in a crude and vulgar business. But Thelma had no choice. She never had a choice when it came to her own life; there was always someone else ready and eager to shove her this way or that, telling her what to think, what to do, where to go. The first of those self-serving advisers who magnanimously guided Thelma's life was her mother.

Alice was aggressive, bossy, domineering. Her obvious ambition was to be "somebody," and she used her husband and her daughter as pawns to buy into the elite realm of celebrity status. Though John grew cold, she made a public posture of presenting herself as the adorned and adoring housewife with a perfect and happy marriage. She flaunted John's power around Lawrence, using her position as "the health director's wife" to push ahead of the line in stores, get better seating in restaurants, and worm her way into upper-crust social circles. Alice wallowed in her husband's prestige, she surrounded herself with it, lavished every benefit she could upon herself with little regard to anyone else's opinion. John was too busy and probably far too indifferent at this point to care. When Alice saw her daughter's flamboyant beauty and popularity emerge, she knew she had yet another passkey to center stage. And she knew exactly how to make the most of it.

Even as a little girl, Thelma followed orders and did as she was told. She never spoke out against her mother's domineering nature, but seethed quietly inside. No matter how hard her mother pushed her, she smiled and obeyed, letting few know how suffocated and frustrated she really felt; she was a convincing actress even as a child. She carried that talent to Hollywood, smiling and cheerful when producers and friends blatantly used and abused her, ordered her to sign contracts that were ultimately harmful to both her well-being and career, and pushed her into the path of evil men who used her for her movie-star status and beauty. It was a trait that eventually forced her to seek refuge in drugs at the end of her all-too-brief life. But Thelma fought back against her mother's influence in her own way, establishing a style that she knew her mother could never steal from her. As a young girl, she found the one thing she could make her own, her one form of rebellion. That was her "look," which earned her the nickname Hot Toddy. As an adult, she turned both the look and the nickname into her trademark.

She piled her blond hair into big scoops of curls when the rest of the children wore long sausage curls. Her vanilla-ice-cream locks immediately set her apart from the other girls in Lawrence, who were far more conservative in appearance but probably more independent in fact. She stood out from the crowd.

Thelma also dressed very flamboyantly for the times; she wore short-shorts and flimsy blouses that were considered very risqué for the second decade of the century, and especially decadent for the conservative industrial town. She flirted, made "innocently suggestive" remarks to older men. She also played the part of the town tomboy, doing acrobatics and tumbling, showing off on the front lawn when the other girls were told to conduct themselves as "proper young ladies."

As she grew older, she went braless and wore clingy satin clothes and long flowing scarves. She wore perfume and was an expert at putting on makeup before the other girls even considered such things. She originated the sultry, sexy-innocent look long before Jean Harlow made it famous in Hollywood. She loved to shock people and enjoyed seeing the reaction her revealing, sensuous clothes drew from strangers. She was, by the time she entered her teens, Hot Toddy, and lived up to everything the name implied except for one; she teased, flirted, and led men on but she had yet to experience her first sexual encounter.

Almost everyone who knew of her assumed she was sexually active, but Thelma had a deep-seated fear of getting close to any man, most likely because of the emotional restraint she felt from her father. She idolized him, and even as a teenager based her standards for men on qualities she thought she saw in her father. Of course, no teenage boy could even come close to the tough, polished "men of power" Thelma knew and desired at that age. As a teenager, she had no suitors, but enjoyed the notion that others thought she was "hot." In fact, one afternoon she confessed to Mac that she had a secret desire to be a madam at a brothel. She even sent letters to Mac, years later, signed "The Madame." Thelma fantasized about sex and was almost uncontrollably preoccupied with sexual fantasies, but had yet to walk on that other side of life, something she would more than compensate for in just a few short years.

She was an anomaly, different from the other girls her age, more mature, more sophisticated, and more calculating. She was also a paradox, looking like the epitome of a perfect lady, yet acting like a rough-and-tumble back-street urchin. She appeared sexy and lustful, but remained a virgin throughout her teens and teased men from a distance. Her ultimate charm was that she was very likable; innocent and sweet and not vain about her looks. To older women she was the perfect daughter; older men found their egos bolstered by the attention Thelma gave freely to them. Together, these characteristics captured the attention of every man and woman who knew her. They also made her somewhat of a loner because most girls her age were openly jealous, and boys too shy or intimidated to approach her. How ironic that the one thing she chose to mark her independence, her escape from someone else's domination, was her sexy, flamboyant Hot Toddy image, an image that was the exact opposite of the real Thelma Todd: a frustrated, lonely person who believed she was never really loved by her parents or anyone else throughout her brief life. No one understood that her image was really a plea for help, help to break the emotional barrier she had created that blocked her from finding and feeling real love.

Not surprisingly, Alice never interfered with Thelma's obvious struggle for identity, most likely because she realized her daughter's erotic clothes, tomboy actions, and sexual teasing caught the attention of the neighborhood and created a bit of whispering around town. For Alice, any attention was eagerly accepted, and expected.

Thelma's only desire was to go from the Packard Grammar School in Lawrence to Lawrence High School to the Lowell State Normal School, a teachers' school that was considered one of the best in the East. Mac and Thelma both enrolled as freshmen in 1923 and both did well academically, averaging As with a few Bs, thanks to some help in chemistry.

Thelma was poor in chemisty, to say the least; no matter how hard she studied and how rigorously she drilled, she fared no better than Ds—until she turned on the charm. She flattered and flirted with the smartest boy in the school, who was more than happy to stay up till all hours of the night doing Thelma's homework and coaching her for tests. When it came time for the big senior-class chemistry final, Thelma passed with flying colors, a B+. Unfortunately for her "coach," the long hours of helping Thelma left him too exhausted to concentrate. He failed, which did upset Thelma, who felt obligated to date the boy for a good part of the summer until the "romance" faded on its own.

During the summers, Thelma worked as a part-time fashion model for shows at the local theater, called The Empire. The pay was low, but Thelma enjoyed the work and the notoriety; the shows got her noticed around town and she began receiving a steady stream of offers for other modeling jobs, as well as a few proposals of marriage and offers to move to New York or Hollywood to star in silent pictures. Most of the offers were brought about by the theater manager, who was in love, or at least in lust, with Thelma, and thought he could win her affection by pulling a few strings with talent-scout friends. Thelma was completely indifferent to the movie offers and the manager. They were from small-time producers, most of questionable repute, and Thelma had her life planned in Lawrence as a teacher. She politely declined and continued her work.

Thelma knew how to gain attention everywhere she went. When it came time for neighborhood socials, summer dances, she made a point of asking the ugliest, homeliest, and most awkward boy in town as her escort. She did it for fun, knowing that most every head would turn and whispers would begin when the others saw her date. She also did it because no one else ever asked her; most of the other boys assumed she had a line of suitors, which was far from the truth. Though she chose her date for fun, she was never mean. She stayed with him throughout the evening, danced every dance with him, and kissed him good night on the cheek after he walked her back home.

After two years at Lowell State, aspiring teachers vied for a position with the Hood Practice School, a small, prestigious institution that gave new teachers on-the-job training. Hood drew applicants from all over the country and had tough enrollment requirements. In addition to meeting grade-point and achievement restrictions, potential students had to pass a tough round of interviews given by the Hood faculty. There were only twenty-five openings for the class of 1925, and nearly one hundred applied, including Thelma and Mac. Fifty girls did not meet the required A— grade-point average, but fifty were given appointments for interviews.

Thelma was sure her chances were poor, at best. Her employment record was questionable, her only job a disaster. She had been hired as a salesclerk in a neighborhood department store, and she was fired after only one day on the job. The manager claimed she disrupted business and turned the entire store into a madhouse. The problem lay with Thelma, true, but it was not due to any incompetence on her part.

She had talked her way into the job, charming the manager, a gruff older man who had not been flattered by any woman in years, let alone a good-looking blonde. Most of the other clerks were middle-aged housewives who were all business. He put Thelma behind the cosmetic counter. Wearing her Hot Toddy outfit of clingy, revealing blouses, she flirted, laughed, and enticed a sizable crowd around her counter. The problem was that the crowd was all men and the cosmetics were for women. Within three hours, the area was jammed with men, talking, getting their egos massaged, and unfortunately not buying anything. The store was soon out of control, with a bottleneck that triggered a mass of pushing and shoving by irate wives and customers unable to pass through the area. She was paid $1.50 and told to be on her way.

Thelma believed she was not the type of girl Hood wanted teaching young children, no matter how much she loved them and wanted to become a teacher. But fate was with both girls, and Thelma and Mac were accepted in the 1925 class. However, 1925 proved the most important year in Thelma's life for other reasons. It was a year mixed with tragedy and personal disaster, a year that jolted her onto a rollercoaster ride from which she was never able to escape. Just ahead were three consequential events that would forever alter her life.

The summer of 1925 began on a happy note. John had fallen out of political favor, reportedly over a dispute about a construction contract. The details are not clear, but by 1925, John Todd was more of a political adviser to local legislators than someone who carried any personal clout. He began to mend the rift between himself and Alice, and the two were increasingly seen together in public. Both John and Alice thought a family vacation would pull the family back together. Unfortunately, it did just the opposite.

The Todds went on one of their first family trips in years, and spent a week at a friend's farm in northern Massachusetts. John set the week aside to relax and get away from politics, Alice to take a break from her social pressures (though self-imposed) in Lawrence. For Thelma it was a break from part-time modeling jobs and a fresh start before entering Hood. For William, who was ten, it was to be a summer vacation of playing with animals, running through fields. The Todds locked up their home, and headed out for a week of rest and relaxation.

Several days after they arrived at the farm, William met a group of boys who lived on other farms in the area. They had grown up with farm equipment and knew how to play around the machinery without being injured. But William had never seen such things as silos used to store grain, and grain elevators used to transfer grain to the silos. He eagerly and naïvely thought a ride on the grain elevator would be fun, and climbed on top of the conveyor belt, on a dare, after goading from the other boys. Slowly the elevator chugged and creaked, the conveyor belt inched toward the silo in slow, jerking motions.

The gang thought it was great fun to hear William, a "city boy," scream for help. They thought he was merely scared, in no real danger, and laughed uncontrollably as he screamed louder and louder. They assumed William knew enough to jump off before the belt dumped him into the elevator and through the grain-crushing equipment. But William was petrified, too terrified to jump. The boys shouted after him when he got to the edge of the silo, but they could not coax him off the conveyor belt. Then they no longer heard his screams and knew something was wrong. When one of the boys shut down the elevator, there was no sign of William, just a slight trickle of blood seeping out from the bottom of one of the grain-storage bins.

Local authorities believed the youngster had first suffocated in the grain, then been crushed. They never found the body. They tried to console the Todds by telling them he had died instantly in the accident, that he had felt no pain. There was no way to ease the horror of the accident for John, Alice, or Thelma. They packed their bags the next morning and drove back to Lawrence in a long, silent drive. The family never discussed the accident with one another or with friends, but the tragedy had a marked and obvious effect upon the Todds. It widened the rift between Alice and John, shattering forever what bonds remained between them, and it was apparent to almost everyone in town. The delicate thread that held the two together had abruptly snapped. Though they continued to live in the same house, the icy barrier between John and Alice would never again thaw.

William's death had the most significant effect upon Alice, who turned to Thelma as her only purpose in life. She swooped down upon Thelma like a hungry vulture, watching her, ordering her, "guiding" her every step. Alice seemed to be everywhere, lurking in the shadows, and she made Thelma accountable for every action. If Thelma laughed too loud, Alice was within earshot, reprimanding her for unladylike actions. If Thelma came home late, Alice interrogated her and made her account for every minute. She slowly strangled the life out of her daughter. What little freedom Thelma had had before her brother's death was now completely buried. From that day forward, her life would always be under the scrutiny of her jealous mother, and Thelma would expend most of her energy trying to get out from her mother's influence the only way she knew how—by running into the arms of men who were ultimately destructive.

Her homelife was now a shambles, her parents cold and aloof toward one another, her father abrupt and distant from her, her mother unbearably domineering. All Thelma could think of was how to run away. She was on the verge of a breakdown and felt old and tired, though she had lived only twenty years. She believed her only chance at getting away from her mother was to earn her teaching credentials and find her own place to live. She looked forward to the end of what seemed to be a brutally endless summer. What she did not yet know was that the second major event in her life was already in motion.

In late August of 1925, Thelma received a telegram announcing that she had been chosen as a finalist in the Miss Massachusetts beauty contest. She was sponsored by the Lawrence Elks Lodge 65. She thought it was a joke. She had never even heard about the contest, let alone entered it. She did not know that one of her high-school chums, one of the "ugly" boys she had taken out, had clipped her picture out of the high-school yearbook and submitted it under Thelma's name. She threw the telegram in the trash and said nothing to anyone.

When there was no response to the first telegram, the pageant board sent a follow-up letter. This time Thelma took it seriously and wired a reply that she was not interested. Alice found out about the contest and the telegram, intercepted Thelma's letter, and substituted her own, a letter stating that she was thrilled at being selected and would indeed appear at the Empire Theatre as requested. When she found out about Alice's underhanded actions, Thelma exploded into rage, lashing out at her mother in what turned out to be the only time she stood up against Alice's demands. For Thelma, the contest was a lark, but its repercussions could be severe. It could once again set her apart from the other girls in town, already jealous of her beauty. It could also spell the end of her practice teaching at Hood. Winning the contest meant tours, road trips, and public appearances, leaving little time for a career. Thelma knew she had a good chance of winning, and was desperately opposed to putting off her career for a year, especially for something she perceived as silly and frivolous.

To Alice, her daughter's winning the contest meant one notch higher in her accomplishments as a mother, one more claim of "one-upmanship" against the other women in town. She would not hear of Thelma's turning the contest down. It was a long and bitter quarrel. Alice, being the stronger-willed, won. Thelma agreed to show up for the final selection in a contest that she despised and that she had not even entered, a contest that she saw as holding the potential to destroy her life. But its full impact had not yet been felt.

Thelma showed up at the Empire Theatre, smiling and outwardly happy. She was familiar with the stage; it was the same stage, the same runway she had walked down so many times before that summer, modeling clothes. The theater was a refuge then, a friendly, safe place to kill some time and earn some money. But now it seemed hostile, a cold, dark room filled with lusty, dirty, dour men and women given the power to decide someone else's future.

It was no surprise to anyone when Thelma was named Miss Massachusetts of 1925. She made the usual obligatory motions of gratitude when she was handed the crown. No one in the theater, especially Thelma, had prepared for the next event, the second card dealt by destiny.

The day after the contest, a man rang the doorbell of the Todd home. Alice answered, chatted with the stranger for a few moments, then invited him in. Thelma had been outside with her friends, laughing and talking, when Alice excitedly called her inside. Thelma now stood face to face with the man who represented both a much-needed chance to escape from Alice, and the end of her dream to become a teacher. The stranger was a talent scout from a movie studio, who had been asked to take a look at Thelma by a man named Napoleon DeMara, the manager of the Empire Theatre. The talent scout was in the audience for the Miss Massachusetts contest and liked what he saw. This man represented Paramount and the Famous Players-Lasky Studios, which had merged under an agreement eight years before between Lasky and aggressive filmmaker Adolph Zukor. The films were being distributed by Paramount, the parent company, which had been acquired by Zukor in a takeover coup shortly after the Famous Players-Lasky merger. It was the most prestigious studio in the country, with offices in both California and New York, and it was prepared to make Thelma an offer.

The offer required that Thelma first submit to a screen test, which would be conducted at a small film studio in Boston. If Thelma proved photogenic, she would be invited to join an experimental group that Paramount was in the process of forming. The group would eventually become the first film actors' school in the country, a novel idea for 1925. Prior to the founding of the school, actors were either taken from the stage or hired on as "favors" to studio executives or motion-picture stars who lured eager teenagers onto the movie sets with the intent of finding another bed partner. An official actors' school gave the studio a chance to groom and develop talent and add an air of legitimacy to the hiring process.

Thelma had mixed emotions and was torn between finding that elusive escape and turning her back on teaching in Lawrence—leaving behind her friends and what had been the only life she had known. It was a serious step, and a frightening move into the unknown. She knew Hollywood often devoured innocent girls, and though she let strangers believe otherwise, she had little "real life" experience outside her hometown. In some ways, she was hoping she would fail the test, thus giving her an out, letting someone else make the decision. In other ways, she hoped she would succeed. Again someone else would call the shots, forcing her to leave home.

Both John and Alice, for their own reasons, encouraged their daughter to accept the offer. John believed the experience and the chance to live on her own for the six-month duration of the school would be an excellent opportunity. He felt that when the class was finished, if a movie contract was offered, Thelma could decide her own fate. If not, she was always welcome back home.

Alice seized upon the idea for another, more personal

reason. For Alice, it was not only a chance for her daughter to mix with the monied movie crowd, but her own opportunity to boost her reputation. She needled, goaded, connived, and coerced Thelma until she gave in and agreed to the screen test, which she easily passed.

Once in Boston on her own, without the pressure from her parents, she began to look at the opportunity in a different light. The idea of traveling alone, meeting new people, doing as she pleased and establishing her own identity— away from Alice—excited her. A heavy burden lifted, and for the first time in her life, she made up her mind she was going to have fun. She was going to be wild and free, live life as she had always dreamed. It was almost as if she suddenly had an inkling of what lay ahead of her, and she knew she had to cram a lifetime into her remaining ten years.

She eagerly signed the contract with Lasky. She was now, officially, a member of a group of sixteen aspiring thespians, soon to be formally known as The Paramount Players School—Stars of Tomorrow. The talent scout who judged her screen test attached a note to the contract her first formal order from the studio. She was to lose ten pounds of "baby fat" within one month from the day she would arrive at Paramount's Astoria, New York, lot. There was no indication that the contract would be canceled if she failed to lose the weight, but even before she set foot on the lot, Thelma understood the firmness of the directive.

When she returned to Lawrence to pack her suitcase, she went on what was to become the first of many brutal crash diets that quickly led her into pills and later into hard drugs. She refused to eat for days, literally starving herself thin for her arrival in New York. She lost the weight, but she looked tired and drawn, without nearly enough energy for the rigors she was soon to endure at the studio. She looked to the next six months as a glamorous vacation, but it turned out to be the beginning of a psychological, almost schizophrenic, split between Thelma Todd, the "good girl" from Lawrence, and the sensuous, sexy, sultry blonde called Hot Toddy.

Thelma boarded the train for Astoria with one suitcase and fifty dollars in cash, anxious but bubbling with dreams and ambition. She was a virgin piece of clay, ready to be molded by tyrannical studio bosses, greedy men, and fortune hunters thinly disguised as friends.

Chapter Five

Astoria was a far cry from small, industrial Lawrence. On the outskirts of Long Island, the rural, picturesque town consisted mainly of the Paramount/Famous Players lot. It was surrounded by trees, lakes, and open fields. There was an abundance of room for outdoor movie sets, chase scenes, and expansive brick offices. If not for the bitterly cold, snowy winters, Astoria in 1925 would have been the ideal setting for a long escape from reality and the first test of independence and freedom. It was nonthreatening, calm, and serene.

As Thelma stood outside the studio's broad iron gates, she took a deep breath and smiled. She liked what she saw. She had a sense of lightness, of release from her past and her family. She immediately forgot about teaching; her soul soared. This, she believed, was going to be fun.

Thelma presented her introductory papers at the gate. Exhilarated, she took her first step onto the compound. Here suddenly was a new world, an exciting world. Stagehands wheeled cameras and equipment across the pavement, men and women dressed in costumes ran across the sets. Boys with scripts chased after tough, arrogant men who must have been directors or producers. She was wide-eyed and fascinated. She had never seen anything like this in her life.

As she walked across the lot, she saw odd-looking single-story buildings with only three sides; some were decorated as living rooms, some as bedrooms, with old, cheap furniture and what was supposed to be artwork literally painted on to the walls. On closer inspection, the walls were nothing more than canvas, with wallpaper slapped across and wood paneling slathered on with a roller. "So this is what moving pictures are really about," she wrote friends back in Lawrence, ". . . all fake . . . unreal." She had yet to realize how accurate her initial impressions really were.

As she wandered toward the back of the lot, the area designated as the new players' school, she saw her first movie star. The woman was surrounded by an entourage of hairdressers, makeup men, wardrobe girls, script readers and lackeys, fawning over this woman who seemed a bit too regal and haughty. She ordered her acolytes, barked commands at them, scolded and humiliated them for mistakes in a loud and definite tone. Thelma stood at a comfortable distance so as to avoid getting swept up in the commotion, but she was close enough to get a glimpse of the queen commander, now, through her recent marriage, the Marquise de la Falaise de la Coudray, but still known to millions of movie fans as Gloria Swanson. (Marrying royalty of any sort was the thing to do in the mid-twenties; actual wealth was unimportant, as long as a title came attached to the wedding ring.)

Gloria Swanson was Astoria's first and only real remaining star. The others, Pola Negri, Rod La Rocque, and Leatrice Joy among them, had long since fled to Hollywood, the new boomtown of the motion pictures, leaving the Astoria lot a near ghost town, the crumbling remnant of a once bustling studio. Paramount's Hollywood (Famous Players-Lasky) studios was the new hub of production for the company, and the two locations were in competition for top features, though they were branches of the same studio tree. For Swanson, New York was far more cultured, far more sophisticated than the bawdy cow town of Los Angeles, and she had enough clout to force New York/Astoria production of her movies after she packed up her bags and settled on the Astoria lot in 1923, for what she thought was a permanent move. Other stars, directors, even studio officials had to come to the mountain named Swanson; the mountain never moved, except when it wanted to.

Thelma was awestruck; she had never seen anyone as beautiful, anyone as rude as Swanson. She froze in her steps and stared, probably a little too long, which caught the attention of The Star.

"You! Come here!" Swanson gave Thelma a cold glare. She later told friends she was completely intimidated but did her best to act unimpressed with Swanson.

"Who are you? I've never seen you here before. Wardrobe? Script?"

It was probably Swanson's accent, just a bit too cold and refined to seem natural, or the aloof manner in which she addressed Thelma, as if assuming she was just another of the queen's servants, that put Thelma off and gave her the spunk to speak out.

"My name's Thelma Todd. And I will be your co-star one day. Who knows, you might even appear in one of my films!"

She thought to herself, "Did I really say that?" She did not know whether to laugh or run, so she braced herself for an explosion. It never came.

"I'm Gloria Swanson. You have a lot to learn, my dear, but I do hope you succeed. Just starting?"

"Yes. The Players School."

"Just don't let them get to you, dear. Keep them at a distance and let them think you've got steel claws and sharp fangs." With that, Swanson turned back to her clique, almost fading out of sight, enmeshed in the cortege.

Thelma had yet to understand the meaning of Swanson's message; she was still too eager, too impressed with the newness of the studio to understand the vultures lurking just below the surface glamour. She felt elated after the exchange. She smiled and proceeded to the school bungalow, her home for the next six months.

The first sixteen students of the Paramount Players School were put through a tough, grueling schedule of classes. They were divided into groups of five for some classes such as dancing and speechmaking and etiquette, trained on an individual basis for horseback riding and swimming, and as a complete group for acting, from comedy to drama, from pratfalls to passion. Among Thelma's classmates were Charles "Buddy" Rogers (soon to star in the first picture to win an Oscar, *Wings*, later to marry Mary Pickford), Josephine Dunn (who became a successful silent/early talkies screen star before retiring), and a mixture of others of various ages, backgrounds, and talent, most of whom never rose to be more than bit players. Clearly Thelma and Rogers were the leaders of the group and showed the most early promise.

The group quickly became close-knit, and Thelma seized the opportunity to take charge and lead the others into good-natured trouble. Her devilish side was raring to escape and found its chance. One night, after the studio curfew of ten o'clock, and after some encouragement from a now-mischievous Thelma, some of the gang sneaked out of their rooms, which were tucked way in the back near the school bungalow. They had all gotten a taste of Gloria Swanson's haughty command, and thought it would be fun to play a joke on the Great Lady.

The young actors broke into one of the sets where Swanson was filming her new silent comedy, *Stage Struck*, which turned out to be her last big hit for Paramount. Swanson played a waitress whose boyfriend was wild about the theater, especially beautiful actresses. As a means of getting his attention, she became an actress by taking mail-order lessons. The "restaurant" was still set up, ready for the next day's shooting.

Taking a cue from the title, and making a play on words, Thelma devised what she thought to be the perfect gag. Turning *Stage Struck* into stage "stuck," the gang rearranged the set, glued plates and drinking glasses down to trays, nailed chairs to the floor and tightened hinges on doors. Thelma also thought the title of the picture naturally lent itself to a bit of chicanery in that the group was itself very much "stage struck." Making sure no permanent damage was done, the gang trotted back to bed, giggling, snickering, acting out how the "Marquise" would walk into mispositioned props, strain to open doors, and yank the glued-on glasses and plates from the nailed-down tables. Thelma did riotous impressions of the regal Miss Swanson blowing her cool, screaming for the propman, screeching at the director, and storming off the set.

The next morning, the culprits got up early and eavesdropped on the beginning of production. Swanson entered, the director, Allan Dwan, shouted "Action," and the cameras whirred. When Swanson grabbed her huge waitress's tray and tried to give one of the "customers" a glass, she found it stuck tight. When she tried to open the restaurant's kitchen door, she found she could not, because the hinges were screwed down tight. Swanson did a very slow burn, her eyes flashed with fire and she looked around the set, but she did not lose her temper. Dwan yelled to stop the action.

Swanson looked around and huddled off to the side with Dwan. They chatted in whispered tones for several minutes. Swanson called two stagehands over, spoke to them, and sent them off. Dwan ordered the production moved to another location, a different set for another scene. The incident seemed to blow over without fireworks, much to the disappointment of Thelma and her cohorts, who could not figure out why the volcano failed to erupt.

That afternoon, they got their answer. They were handed scripts and told they would be performing on one of the stages and critiqued by one of the studio's performers. The sixteen were each assigned parts, some as actors, others as crew. Thelma received the starring role. When she looked at the script she noticed an all-too-familiar title *Stage Struck*. She had Gloria Swanson's part. When they trooped down to the set, they realized they had met their match. Swanson sat in a canvas director's chair, stern and serious, off to the side, notebook in hand, ready to evaluate their performances. Thelma and Swanson exchanged long, hard looks, but no mention of the "prank" was ever made. The students acted from the script, and did their best to work around the glued-down set. The performances were disastrous, with the group walking into tables, unable to sit in chairs, making a shambles of the story. Thelma had the most trouble trying to perform the impossible tasks of handing out drinking glasses and opening doors. Thelma knew she had been had. The point was made by Swanson, who rose from her chair and left after the scene was finished. That lesson also finished any other pranks during the six-month term.

The incident changed Thelma's opinion about Swanson and movies in general. She wrote that Swanson was "an okay lady after all," and she realized that "moving pictures is a serious business," not the holiday she had anticipated. She also discovered the power of a studio to completely control a starlet's life.

During the six-month course, Thelma had become romantically linked with another student, a dark-haired boy named Robert Andrews. The two quickly became an item and set studio gossips' tongues wagging. Though no one knew the details, most assumed the two were sexually involved—something the studios frowned on, though almost every star, producer, and director on the lot was involved in some sort of dalliance at one time or another. It was really nothing more than a flirtation, but Paramount slammed its iron fist down hard on any such romantic entanglement. The studio wanted to avoid any scandal with its fledgling stars no matter how untrue or minor, and maintain a pristine reputation for its school.

Thelma made light of her romance with Andrews, but not so the studio bosses, who put out a bit of publicity with neither Todd's nor Andrews's consent or prior knowledge. Thelma found out from one of the other students that she and Andrews had become "engaged," that "love as well as talent are blossoming on the Astoria lot" (according to a press release). Thelma cried and sulked in her room for several days, and Andrews avoided the rest of the group, withdrawing for a time as a loner. What might have developed into a friendship, if not an eventual romance, was destroyed by the studio.

The fun-loving spark Thelma had felt upon her arrival in New York was now extinguished. She was cautious about getting attached to any man after that. She was also determined to fight back, and her Hot Toddy image resurfaced, partly to show her studio bosses how uncontrollable one woman really could be (or appear to be). When the bosses were within earshot, she went into her sexy blonde act, but among friends she remained a fun-loving, sweet girl. She was sensational at switching characters in a snap. The split between good girl Thelma and the sensuous Hot Toddy was now evident and frighteningly real.

Toward the end of the course, Paramount issued a new directive for the class; it was to concentrate on speech, diction, and singing. The studio had already released some films with sound, not yet quite "talkies" but films with some sound effects and musical inserts. Audiences yawned at the experiment as gimmicky; many claimed the scratchy "noise" interfered with the film and distracted from the plot. Other studios had tested the new toy with similar, unimpressive results. But Zukor, who was now the ruler-supreme of the industry, took no chances. He saw sound on the horizon and made sure his new, expensively trained "junior stars" were able to conquer anything and everything that might spring up in the next few years. All were drilled in diction, forced to lose native, regional accents, and made to sing whether they had the voice for it or not. As the course progressed, it was all too clear that some of the "Hollywood Hopefuls" were doomed before they got out of the door.

The school's graduating assignment was to star in a Famous Players/Lasky production titled *Fascinating Youth*, a corny melodrama released as a silent feature on March 17, 1926. The class, now finally dubbed "Paramount's Junior Stars of 1926," was cast with Paramount regulars Richard Dix, Adolphe Menjou, Clara Bow, Chester Conklin, Lewis Milestone, and Malcolm St. Clair, who played hotel guests registered under their own names. The plot was simple; the son of a wealthy resort hotel owner falls for a Greenwich Village artist from the wrong side of the tracks. Though the boy's father favors a society girl, he will allow his son to marry the girl of his choice if he can make a go of the resort. As a publicity stunt, the boy drums up an iceboat race, then advertises that movie stars will be attending. When the stars back out, the boy's friends disguise themselves as the celebrities, only to find the Greenwich Village girl knows the stars through her drawings and saves the day by bringing them to the resort. Buddy Rogers played the leading role as the son, Thelma a lesser part as the sister of the society girl.

The students were paired, according to the location of his or her hometown, and sent out on their first publicity tour, promoting the film. Thelma and Greg Blackton (who was from Boston and had a minor role in the film) covered Massachusetts; the first stop was a splashy premiere in Lawrence at the Palace Theatre, the swankiest movie house in town. Thelma was wined, dined, and welcomed with a whirlwind week of parties, speeches, grand openings, and an odd public appearance at a joint meeting of all the service clubs in Lawrence.

The meeting was in the Boys' Gymnasium, a huge, stuffy complex in the center of town, which served as both a recreational facility and a town meeting hall. The focus of the meeting was to decide the fate of a neighborhood sandlot. A conglomerate wanted to pave the lot and build a massive hotel. The group wanted to discuss the ramifications before making a decision. Thelma was invited as the "movie star/guest speaker," and she felt completely out of place. She surprised almost everyone when she spoke out clearly in favor of the hotel. In fact, she told the audience that she would always consider herself "Thelma Todd from Lawrence, no matter how big a star" she became, and that her dream was to sign the hotel register as such.

Her speech swayed the crowd in favor of the hotel much to the shock and disappointment of many Lawrence families who had considered Thelma more "family oriented," and assumed she would push for a playground for children. She received a stream of flowers and thank-you notes from men involved in the construction deal. She became a symbol of progress, of the future of Lawrence. But Thelma was not happy with the result, and was disgusted with herself. She confided to friends that she had "sold out." As it turned out, her father had a significant stake in the hotel, both in financial kickbacks and personal favors, and many of the men involved in the construction were business associates. Her father had bluntly pointed out the value of the hotel and the wisdom of making others see that value. Once again, Thelma had crumbled under pressure from her parents and buckled under the force of powerful men, a force that she never did learn to overcome.

John Todd was a businessman, and he knew the meaning of payment for favors, those granted and those received. He knew he owed his daughter for her cooperation on the deal, and called in every IOU, his markers, for repayment of the debt. During the film's week-long run, he made sure every newspaper and radio reporter gave the film rave reviews, highlighting, of course, his daughter as the next big Hollywood star. He gave his daughter reams of press clippings to take back to her bosses at Paramount, hoping the publicity would help win a more lucrative contract.

Once again, Thelma was a pawn in someone else's game. She was not there to enjoy her own success, but rather to be used for someone else's profit. She traded her integrity for a handful of newspaper columns, but she was not one to say no. This was the last time John Todd affected his daughter's life. He had allowed her to peek through the curtains of political manipulation, to see sweet-smelling power games, to enjoy attention and lust after adulation. She savored the taste of the "other side of life."

Thelma left for Boston after the premiere week in Lawrence. Bulbs flashing, bands playing, crowds cheering, Thelma and Blackton climbed on board the train and waved farewell. She kissed John and Alice good-bye after the prearranged, well-publicized send-off at the station. It was the last time she saw her father. John Todd died of a massive heart attack three months later. Now fate was about to play its third hand, the last of three scenarios to affect Thelma's life.

Upon returning from the *Fascinating Youth* tour, Thelma was ordered to audition for a new release, to be shot at the Astoria lot. The film was in Technicolor, a process considered quite new in 1926. Titled *The American Venus*, it was an eye-popping comedy filled with beautiful women in very revealing costumes. The plot was thin, centered around rival cosmetics manufacturers and the Miss America contest. It was meant more for its titillation than its production values. Thelma had already caught the eye of the director Frank Tuttle, who recommended an audition—in costume.

Thelma did not get a part in the film (which was no tragedy because she had already been put to work in another film, *God Gave Me Twenty Cents*, which Paramount used as its feature attraction to open its new Times Square Theatre), but she received her first real publicity photo. And what a photo it was! Thelma posed in a very clingy body stocking, making it appear as if she wore nothing except a loose drape. It was an innocent gesture on Thelma's part; to her it was nothing more than a photo, a memento to send her mother for her amusement.

Alice was not amused. She took one look at the picture,

which she deemed obscene, packed her bags, and hopped the first train to New York. She was certain the studio had turned her daughter into a tramp, and she was hell-bent on ferreting out the man who had tainted her daughter and stained the Todd name. She raged into the head offices and spewed out a venomous series of accusations and threats against the studio, denouncing it for dragging her daughter to ruin, destroying her morals, and corrupting her innocence. Thelma was proving more bother than she was worth to the Astoria managers, who finally found what they perceived to be the ideal way to get even with their Hollywood/Paramount counterparts. Paramount's king, Adolph Zukor, was high on Thelma Todd (and some of the other graduates), so Astoria knew canceling her contract was impossible at this point. So they went one better. They threw the problem of Alice Todd right on Paramount's doorstep.

A contract with a movie studio was a mixed blessing; a starlet was continually enticed into following studio whims by the promise of stardom. Those who disobeyed found themselves out of work, had their contracts dropped, and were blackballed from other studios. It was a small, incestuous group, though backstabbingly competitive both among the actors and between the studios.

As the movies grew into a formidable force of entertainment, so grew the power of those who pulled the strings at each studio, a power that was exercised on those who happened to land on the next underlying tier. To someone on the outside, a stagehand, script girl, even studio gofer was a ticket inside the ominous fortress. To those on the inside, the pecking order was clearly defined—stagehands paid homage to stars, stars to producers (and in some cases directors), who in turn ate humble pie in front of production heads and studio heads, who all bent in terrified reverence to the supreme power of Adolph Zukor, Sam Goldwyn, Carl Laemmle, and Louis B. Mayer. It was a rare occasion when a mogul considered a star anything more than chattel. No one questioned their authority. Those who did either skyrocketed to the top because of their spunk and tenacity or were out of work because they could not keep their mouths shut.

Though Thelma, through Alice's actions, had inadvertently crossed the powers at Astoria, she was given one last chance to learn her place and her lesson. She was given four days to relocate to Hollywood. Her ticket was already made out when she received the orders. Thelma boarded the train west, and Alice headed back to Lawrence for a respite from her daughter's career, a postponement that was sadly too short to help Thelma regain the sense of independence she had only begun to experience.

Thelma's next stop was Hollywood, a town she had only heard about from others on the Astoria lot; they told bizarre tales of drugs, free sex, and fortunes earned and lost overnight. It was a life she knew nothing about and for which she was not in the least prepared. And Hollywood was eagerly waiting to carve up its next victim.

Chapter Six

Hollywood in the late twenties was a town filled with seedy people desperate to cash in on get-rich-quick schemes, whether through the movies or through real-estate sales and swindles. It was a gaudy, glimmering boomtown, crowded with down-on-their-luck movie moguls looking for that one picture to get them back in the chips; men who talked of past glories that existed only in their minds, enticing newcomers to listen to their fantasies and join the rest of the dupes who were desperate to hitch a ride on the gravy-train express called stardom. There were studios galore, big and small, from the well-known—Fox, MGM, Warner Bros., and Paramount—to those built on the egos of stars and directors such as Hal Roach, Thomas Ince, Charlie Chaplin, and Mary Pickford and Douglas Fairbanks.

In 1924, the population of Hollywood was 100,000. It had nearly doubled each year after that, swelling 850 percent in ten years, suddenly too crowded to be considered a sleepy, picturesque village in the foothills. Land hucksters sold dried-up orchards and useless hillside properties to out-of-towners who plunked down ready cash for a plot of land in the sunshine. Many sold out of tents and shacks, and were gone as soon as they seized their fortunes. Sprawling orange and citrus groves were plowed under and covered over by greedy contractors who slapped together ramshackle homes as fast as cheap labor would work.

The once-quiet streets were paved over with inferior cement that cracked and crumbled, oddly reflecting the decay of the town itself. The roads were soon glutted with Packards and Stutzs, choking out the workingman's Fords and Chevys. Expensive mansions loomed snobbishly in the hills, overlooking the minions who worked hard to pay for their idols' indulgences. Nightclubs and movie palaces sprang up overnight, one more opulent than the next. Those who had money spent it with wild abandon, flaunting their newfound wealth before those who were only allowed to look through the gate and dream. The eyes of the world were riveted on Hollywood, along with the dreams of those who believed their ticket west would be the key to a better life filled with fur coats, mansions, and money to burn. "Hollywood" became the irresistible cry that enticed victims to ruin. Movie fans around the country could not get enough gossip about their fantasy town, and devoured every tidbit of information, no matter how untrue or unsavory, just as long as it offered the "inside dirt" on a star.

It was *The Day of the Locust*, with thousands of naïve, young men and women pouring into the city each month hoping to catch the eye of a movie star or casting director, who, they heard, were always within arm's reach on the streets or in the stores. Most ended on the trash heap, involved in drugs or prostitution to make ends meet, living in squalor but never giving up hope that they would be discovered. Local tabloids and national newspapers ran full-page ads warning youngsters to stay away, that only one in ten thousand ever became famous, that the city was a plague, eating away at the moral fiber of America. But to eager hordes who saw only fame and fortune, those ads meant that as long as one could succeed, they would hold out to become that "one." High-school beauty queens and handsome boys-next-door clamored to hop the thrill ride and grab the brass ring, but the pain usually outweighed the promise.

These years were still the tail end of the Jazz Age, the Roaring Twenties. As hungry young women flooded into the town, willing to do anything to "get in the movies," men waited at the door knowing the farm girls were easy game. The twenties roared loud and long in Hollywood, and most went there knowing full well what was expected of them if they wanted to crash into the movies. Sex ran rampant behind the sets, casting couches got their workout, and homosexuality became the "in" thing among men and women, stars and extras, who experimented for the fun, the curiosity, the excitement. Hollywood already had a long and seamy reputation, filled with scandal of monumental proportions that made the rest of the country seem stagnant and out of step.

Hollywood began its descent in 1920, when Olive Thomas, considered by many to be the most beautiful girl in the world, was found dead in a Paris hotel. She was married to Jack Pickford, brother of movie star Mary, and they were considered the ideal couple, until stories of brother Pickford's heroin addiction seeped to the surface. And there was gossip that Thomas, the Ziegfeld girl who adorned the cover of every fashion magazine in the world, was herself an addict. Then things got worse.

Bobby Harron, the young boy in D. W. Griffith's epic *Intolerance*, shot himself in New York, despondent over losing the role in Griffith's new film *Way Down East* to Richard Barthelmess. Insiders whispered about homosexual liaisons on the Griffith set, that Harron was involved in a triangle that did not include women, that many women on the lot were involved in lesbian relationships.

In 1921, the Fatty Arbuckle scandal erupted, causing a worldwide furor. Arbuckle was accused of murdering Sennett studio starlet Virginia Rappe, a virtual unknown who skyrocketed to fame only because of her disgusting death.

Arbuckle and his pals drove up to San Francisco to celebrate his new three-year contract with Paramount. Among the guests was party girl Rappe, who imbibed bootleg booze with the Arbuckle contingent and headed to a suite with the roly-poly comedian. Several hours later, friends heard her screaming, and saw her lying in a pool of blood in a room that was literally bashed to pieces. According to witnesses, Rappe claimed Arbuckle tried to rape her, then stuffed a champagne bottle into her because he found himself impotent from too much drinking and drugs. That, prosecutors tried to prove, killed the girl.

Other facts came out, among them that the Sennett studios had to be shut down and fumigated several times after an outbreak of venereal crabs, passed among the crew by none other than Miss Rappe. Fatty himself testified he was only tickling the woman, and she started bleeding after he accidentally jammed his knee into her stomach. An autopsy showed her internal organs were inflamed and infected from several sexually transmitted diseases. Three trials could not convict the comedian. But no matter. He was blacklisted, organizations across the country boycotted his films, and Hollywood had a big black eye that never faded. Paramount became the focus of ridicule because of that scandal—and because of another one that broke the following year.

Director William Desmond Taylor was found shot to death in his bungalow, and Paramount stars Mabel Normand and Mary Miles Minter, and Minter's mother, were considered prime suspects. Soon after the murder was discovered, Paramount studio officials entered the bungalow and destroyed evidence and personal effects, in an attempt to quash scandalous rumors that involved all three women. Zukor paid authorities handsomely to cover up the killing, but the attempt blew up in his face. Not only was the studio linked to the murder through its stars, but rumors of homosexuality between the director and his houseboy also cropped up. By the time Paramount's biggest star, Rudolph Valentino, died in 1926, it was almost common knowledge in the industry that he was gay, or possibly bisexual, though the studio did its best to cover up the obvious. Toward the end of Valentino's life, newspapers began to hint at the "powder puff" that was Rudy. Paramount was linked now to murder, and to sex, both straight and gay. But that was not the end.

Newspaper reporters also learned of Mabel Normand's $2,000 a month cocaine habit, a habit started in her early days at Sennett, a lot literally run on cocaine handed out by a studio supplier named "The Count," which she continued at Paramount. That same year, Paramount's top male star, Wallace Reid, billed as "the King of Paramount," was shipped off to a sanatorium for severe heroin addiction. When he died, Zukor knew he had a disaster on his hands. A little digging and backtracking turned up widespread cocaine use among other stars, with on-lot dealers and pushers at most of the studios.

In 1926 Barbara La Marr (billed as "The Girl Who Is Too Beautiful") was to die a junkie, soon followed down that path by other stars.

Then, in 1924, director Thomas Ince was shot to death on board William Randolph Hearst's yacht. Though there were witnesses (including such major stars as Charlie Chaplin, and movie and newspaper people noted for their excellent recall), they conveniently forgot what they had seen after a word from Hearst and a bit of questioning by authorities. No one dared cross the most powerful man in America. The body was immediately cremated, the death clouded in confusion and mystery. Those who kept quiet were rewarded with promotions or financial backing.

The industry was running amok, speeding down the road to its own ruin. Stars were determined to outdrink, outdrug and outparty one another in a sadistic game of one-upmanship. The Hollywood dream factory was producing a macabre nightmare. Cocaine and heroin were easily accessible and even paid for by some studio bosses who encouraged drug use to keep stars thin, awake when needed and sedated when necessary. Those who were not addicted to drugs were hooked on booze, a habit developed during Prohibition when taking an illegal drink proved far more intoxicating than the alcohol itself. Somewhere things had gone haywire. The other moguls stood by in silence, content to let Zukor take the fall. Paramount's reputation was in serious trouble, and seemed to reflect the downward spiral of the rest of the industry, an industry that needed serious help not only in cleaning up its mess, but in keeping it hidden from the general public. The man chosen for the task was Will Hays, a former postmaster general, who was hired as president of the newly formed Motion Picture Producers and Distributors of America. This on-paper group was slapped together by various studio heads to give the impression the industry was taking care of its problems.

Another important man, Buron Fitts, entered the scene as a hungry, aggressive, aspiring deputy district attorney. While in office, he successfully defended his brother on an unusual murder charge, one that raised many eyebrows in the state's legal department. His brother was accused of killing a rival cement contractor. It was later learned that Fitts's brother was involved in questionable dealings in his cement and construction business and had allegedly won a number of government contracts through underhanded means. It was always assumed, but never proved, that he had underworld ties. That case ended with a not-guilty ruling, just one of many victories Fitts claimed during his term.

In return for his tough, hammer-slamming convictions, he was elected lieutenant governor of California, serving the state in the mid-twenties, a volatile time when the Mulhollands, Dohenys, and Huntingtons were buying up water rights, expanding their empires, and swallowing up acres of valuable land for development and mass-transportation rail systems. Fitts really made his reputation as a man of action when he successfully convicted District Attorney Asa Keyes on bribery charges. In fact, he was called into the case as "special prosecutor" by the Justice Department while he was serving as lieutenant governor. Because of the Keyes conviction and other sensational cases of political corruption, Fitts was viewed as the "white knight" of the righteous, the crusader who kept Los Angeles honest. The rich and prominent needed a strong, political ally to kick open doors and knock down opposition.

Buron Fitts always obliged and made himself readily available to those with money, power, and big dreams for the future. He knew which teams to back and made his quest for power obvious to everyone politically aware. His position as lieutenant governor made him well known among the leading families of Los Angeles. He also knew who could put him in the position he wanted. He viewed the District Attorney's office as the catbird seat, a nice spot from which to wield influence and play the legal cards necessary to make or break laws and dredge up or bury evidence to suit the highest bidder. The office already had a reputation for corruption even before the bribery conviction of Keyes, and Los Angeles was a city that was still wide open and teeming with greedy land developers and crooked politicians. The city was too busy trying to deal with a population boom and other problems to notice who was stuffing Fitts's pockets at the taxpayers' expense.

Fitts also knew how much power and influence were held by studio heads, and made a point of ingratiating himself with the likes of Zukor, Laemmle, Mayer, and Goldwyn. He knew of the turmoil and trouble in Hollywood, the scandals and the desperate need for someone to run interference for the studios and keep the lid on goings-on that were better kept secret. As the twenties wound to a close, Fitts increasingly attached himself to those in his old stomping grounds. The Taylor case, the Ince case, and a host of others were slammed shut, declared "unsolved" (Taylor) or death from natural causes. (Though the San Diego district attorney handled the Ince investigation, those who remembered the incident maintained Fitts played a very strong and obvious hand in the dubious outcome because Hearst was L.A.-based.) When drug overdoses could no longer be hidden, they were made to appear as "tragic consequences of overwork and association with bad company," playing upon the public's pity and dolled up to seem the exception rather than the norm. Fitts proved a pliable champion with a ready ear for the studios, especially Paramount and Zukor, who still dictated to the influential and still took the brunt of the heat in town. Zukor owed Fitts in a big way.

In 1928, Fitts got what he wanted; he won election as district attorney, to no one's surprise. Many believed the way was already paved, by those in position to sway the vote, as payment for his assistance in eradicating ordinances and laws that prevented the wealthy from expanding their businesses (including the control of water rights for the entire county of Los Angeles and establishing the only streetcar system in town). Fitts also helped get unsavory evidence expunged from official records that would have cast a damaging light on movie stars and studios involved in sex and drugs and murder.

Right when Hollywood was trying to claw its way out from under an avalanche of scandal, it was faced with another explosion, one that was both a blessing and a calamity; it was the advent of sound.

By the mid-twenties, movies were playing to half-empty houses. Audiences were noticeably bored with voiceless strangers overacting in exaggerated motions. Many were fed up with stars who flaunted riches as their fans starved. The country was growing tired of the same old stories about good girls gone wrong. Families were staying home, listening to their radios, which, though still uneven and filled with static, were becoming a far cheaper source of entertainment, available without leaving the house, on the air at almost any time of the day. Movie attendance was plummeting from its 1920 high of 40 million tickets sold per week to less than half that by 1926. The motion-picture industry was in serious trouble.

Small, independent studios and producers folded, bankrupt, unable to finance cheap one- and two-reel comedies, or if they could, unable to compete with bigger studios to pay theaters to show their wares. Many of the majors also drove out competition by buying up theaters or building their own plush exhibition halls, forcing the independent exhibitors to the sticks. At least the major studios felt somewhat safe in that they always had a place to run their films, but even this peace was short-lived. The Federal Trade Commission began investigations into charges of unfair monopolies in the cinema, the first round in a long battle that would end more than twenty years later, with the studios forced to open distribution and exhibition, and eventually sell their theaters. The studios were running scared.

By 1925, the only studios making any money at all were Fox (which was cranking out eighty-three films per year), Universal (already stereotyped for horror films with its *Hunchback of Notre Dame* and *Phantom of the Opera*), MGM (which boasted nearly $5 million profit), Paramount (which raked in $1 million more than MGM), and the up-and-coming new guy in town, Warner Bros. Of the group, Universal owned no theaters and focused its releases on rural movie houses and Europe. Warners owned only one.

Though the major studios were talking in terms of million-dollar profits, they still saw those millions slowly diminishing. They needed a new gimmick, something that would draw audiences out of their homes and back into the theaters. Crystal chandeliers, velvet chairs, tapestried walls, and indoor fountains were not enough. After one look, the fantasy wore off. Some of the higher-class cinemas staged special "prologues," half-hour vaudeville acts or musical numbers offered as added enticement to pull audiences in. The gimmick was old and stale, and for most, too costly to continue after a few years.

Several of the studios had been experimenting with a new draw, something they were sure was nothing more than a flash-in-the-pan publicity stunt, but one that would create a stir nevertheless. It was sound. Edison had experimented with amplification in 1887; Lee De Forest (who invented the audion tube for radio and gramophone) found a method of running a sound recording along with film, the first real "sound film," in 1906. His idea was quickly stolen by Victor (later RCA/Victor) and Bell Telephone, which perfected the method of running a phonograph record (recorded at a later date, usually containing only music) along with the film. RCA then went one better and physically recorded the sound track at the same time the film was being shot, and this system eventually became the basis for Fox/Movietone Films, and the grandfather of current motion-picture sound tracks.

These early sound films were crude and rough, and quite often the sound slipped out of synchronization with the film, which was embarrassingly noticeable when dialogue was added to enhance specific scenes. Instead of a boon, sound became the joke of the industry. William Fox owned the major patents and had a clear edge over the competition, but he was afraid to put out the $10,000 to $30,000 each to wire all his theaters for the stunt, which he was positive would fade away. He let a bonanza slip through his fingers.

Zukor, quick to outbid competitors for theater chains, film stars, and new inventions, bought the experimental system from De Forest, called it DeForest Photophone, and put voice to one film in 1923. The test film was a Pola Negri silent, *Bella Donna,* which played only in the Rivoli, Paramount's New York theater, and it was a disaster. Negri's heavy accent was made even worse by the squeaky, scratchy recording, and it drew hisses. Zukor pulled the plug on the noise and wrote off the experiment.

Because Warners owned only one movie house, a theater in New York just down the street from the Rivoli, the brothers desperately needed something to pull their outfit into the big leagues. Warners took its turn with sound, and premiered its epic *Don Juan* with John Barrymore in August 1926. It was a solid film, with music and sound effects but no dialogue, complete with an opening address, on disc, by Will Hays. The film was the unveiling of Warners' Vitaphone "synchsound" system. It did not light a spark among moviegoers who had already passed on the gimmick from Paramount. But Warners did not give up.

With $500,000 to spend, it again invested capital in the Vitaphone system, this time pulling out all stops, synchronizing not only music but limited dialogue on disc, to run with the film. Amid ridicule and sneers from competitors, Warners opened *The Jazz Singer*, starring Al Jolson, on October 6, 1927. Audiences flooded theaters all over the world to hear their favorite crooner not only sing but speak, and Warners made $3 million profit on the "freak" film, enough to buy up independent theaters and give other studios a real run for their money. Paramount's supreme position as the top moneymaking studio was now threatened.

Though Zukor had seen it coming, and trained his Players' School students for speaking roles, he had not equipped any of his theaters for sound. Because his Photophone system drew yawns, he assumed the boom was several years off. Suddenly, the other studios scrambled to catch up, completely caught off guard by the popularity of the Jolson film. Crude sound systems were installed in major theater houses from coast to coast. Though the sound quality was still poor at best, unbearable at worst, audiences could not get their fill. They were riveted, stunned at actually hearing their idols speak! Fox countered with his Fox/Movietone system, a sound-on-film system different from the sound-on-disc system Warners had used. Zukor saw this as the more reliable of the systems and chipped in to get it off the ground.

Silent films were pulled back and rereleased with the new synchsound. Films still in the can were reshot and reedited for the new technique. Films that had seemed so advanced and wondrous were rapidly tossed on the scrap heap as outdated and useless. The studios spent fortunes on sound, and lost fortunes revamping and destroying old stock.

All hell broke loose in Hollywood. The big studios hauled in gold as fast as they could count, profits soared into the tens of millions, and the money faucets were flowing once again. Theaters shot up in every neighborhood in every city in every state in America. Hundreds of millions of movie tickets were sold each week for five, ten, and even twenty-five cents to people who earned less than that an hour. Talkies were the only thing that made the average workingman gladly part with his money.

Along with the wealth they had always envisioned, the

studio heads regained the edge they had lost when film players became "stars"—the power to control the lives and destinies of those who received public adulation while the bosses remained anonymous. The moguls could finally take revenge against their too-successful stars. Everyone under contract at any major studio was ordered to face that dread menace, the microphone. Those who passed the test were assured even greater stardom; those who failed were ruthlessly tossed on the Tinseltown trash heap.

The studios used the get-even method without hesitation. It was a golden opportunity to unload expensive stars with previously ironclad contracts, among them screen god John Gilbert, who was set up as the sacrificial lamb to teach the other stars a lesson.

Gilbert was Hollywood's highest-paid star, earning $10,000 a week from MGM, with a following that was solid, an attorney who was powerful, and a contract that was unbreakable. MGM knew if it let Gilbert go, another studio would grab him, but it did not want to fork over the megamoney Gilbert demanded. He was put in his first talkie, *His Glorious Night*, which turned out to be his least-glorious opening. The sound engineer was ordered to turn up the treble, giving Gilbert a shrieky, tinny voice that sent audiences into hysterics when he spoke romantic lines of love. His star plunged from the heavens, he was snubbed by other studios, and his subsequent films were ignored by once-adoring fans. Gilbert took to drink and died of a heart attack a short time later. Other stars, such as Norma Talmadge, Pola Negri, and Emil Jannings, found themselves Hollywood has-beens. The studios cleaned out their stables of big-bucks stars, and others who hoped for fat contracts were best advised to take what they were offered . . . at first.

Thelma and the others in the Players' School passed the test because of rigorous voice training on the Astoria lot, so their futures were secure. After Thelma's test, she was offered a five-year contract from the studio. Her starting salary was $75 a week, considered a player's salary, nowhere near a star's. That amount was gradually increased to $500 a week in the final year. Part of the agreement called for loan-outs, a studio moneymaking scheme that rarely benefited the stars but earned the studio huge profits. The loan-out system was nothing more than the buying and selling of actors for a fat fee—paid to the studio while the star earned his usual contract salary. Paramount wanted Thelma to appear in any picture it arranged, without any additional pay, and without any say by Thelma. Though it was standard practice (and one later successfully fought by James Cagney and Bette Davis at Warners), Thelma rejected the arrangement. That, of course, did not sit well with Zukor, studio chief Jesse Lasky, or Alice Todd.

A meeting was arranged to sit Thelma down and explain some basic facts of life—the studio owned the star and the studio called the shots. Zukor even told Thelma that she "owed" them for the six months of training, given to her free because of her potential. The guilt trip did not work with Thelma but played well to Alice, who, of course, came straight out from Lawrence and wormed her way into this and every subsequent meeting affecting her daughter's career. Alice saw the studio's reluctance to put up with another temperamental star, and sensed Paramount was inclined to write Thelma off rather than negotiate any special favors. Speaking for her daughter, Alice agreed to Paramount's offer. Thelma was put to work in an assortment of films from Westerns to melodramas to comedies, where she really shone. She bounced from Paramount to Warner Bros. to First National to Columbia before she found a spot that would soon become her home—the Hal Roach Studios.

Talent scouts staked out theater and vaudeville, eager to sign stage actors, who already knew how to speak. Though movies were considered "low class" to theater people, many hungrily signed for a chance to dip into the pot of gold. Paramount soon rivaled MGM's star-studded list, with Fredric March, Claudette Colbert, Walter Huston, Carole Lombard, the four Marx Brothers, Gary Cooper, William Powell, Clara Bow, Richard Arlen, Buddy Rogers (fresh out of the gate and one of the studio's brightest because of his success in *Wings*), W. C. Fields, Mae West, and Richard Dix.

The sound explosion breathed new life into the studios and created bigger stars than the studios, or even the actors themselves, had ever anticipated. Within a year, the actors were back in control, signing short contracts (as opposed to the lengthy multiyear deals they had previously been accepting), knowing their popularity would steadily increase, along with new demands for higher pay. The studios were once again operating on a star system, with a clearly defined pecking order among the actors; there were stars who made demands, and bit players who took what they could get. The two rarely mixed. Studio raiding became popular, with agents hired specifically to keep tabs on lapsing contracts and peddle clients to rival studios the instant the star was unattached. Paramount and MGM were the top raiders, but Warner Bros. managed to keep up with the pack and stole names like William Powell away from Paramount.

The money poured in. Many believed the flow would never end. But the 1929 Wall Street crash caused Hollywood's heart to skip a beat. Actors and moguls who had bought stock on margin were broke; others who had invested every dime in stocks were bankrupt. Millionaires became paupers overnight. The Great Depression took its toll on the studios. Paramount, which had expanded its holdings through stock offerings the studio guaranteed to repurchase at a fixed price, was hit hard when creditors demanded payment at now inflated prices. Losses kept mounting into the millions for the major studios; production managers were fired and salaries were cut. Contracts were bought out or sold to other studios. Paramount ousted Jesse Lasky, then went into receivership. The only money the studio made was on the strength of such stars as Mae West, W. C. Fields, and the Marx Brothers. Studios quickly became stereotyped for their films, with all but one offering escapism. Paramount had comedy; Universal, horror; MGM, splashy features; RKO, tap-dancing, Busby Berkeley musicals; and Warner Bros., a new genre that frighteningly reflected the real world, gangster films.

As 1929 wound to a close, Thelma Todd found herself out of work, with most of her money spent for clothes (which the studios insisted even bit players buy to keep up appearances), cosmetics, and rent. She grew despondent but had enough self-reliance to knock on doors to find work. And for once, the loan-out she had so bitterly opposed saved her. Friends she had made during her brief stay at Paramount helped open doors at other studios. People she met at other studios remembered her, mainly for her striking looks and bubbly personality, rarely for her acting ability. She landed a job as a

contract player at the Roach Studios, and her career as a comedienne was now cast in stone. She hated it. She wanted to
be a dramatic actress but found she had no choice. A job was
a job, no matter what.

As for Hollywood, once the initial furor of the Depression
died down, it found it had itself another gold mine; the box
office was stronger than ever. Depression audiences desperately needed a diversion, and Hollywood provided just that.
Films were more spectacular than ever, with lavish sets, beautiful girls and handsome men singing and dancing about pros-
perity just around the corner. There were more movie houses
than banks, with more than 9,000 theaters equipped for
sound. More than 110 million tickets were sold each week, the
highest number in history, with no end in sight. Hollywood
now represented the Great Escape. Once again, it quickly became full of itself.

Stars indulged in drugs and booze, only more openly
than before. They flaunted their wealth in newsreels, which
conveniently ran before feature films and showed Middle
America just how decadent their idols could be. It was play-
time for the rich as the rest of the world starved. But along
with millions of jealous movie fans, two others had been
watching, keeping an eye on the filmland gravy train for some
time. They were two of the era's most bloodthirsty killers:
Charles "Lucky" Luciano and Al Capone.

Chapter Seven

" Ninety-nine percent of the men of the world are suckers, totally at the mercy of the other one percent, the men of power." For Alphonse Capone, those words were more than armchair philosophy; they were the foundation upon which the world's most notorious gangster built his bloody empire. Street-smart and ruthless, calculating and almost completely devoid of any emotion, Capone knew how to size up a victim, find his weak spot, and home in for the kill. He had an insatiable lust for power, a gnawing greed for money, an uncanny instinct for people, and he knew exactly how to seize what he wanted. No one stood in Capone's path, at least not in the late 1920s.

Capone amassed his initial fortune and established his power base in 1920, when the Volstead Act was signed into law. Prohibition was on, and bootlegging and speakeasies became the symbols of rebellion. Those who made the illegal hooch dictated to those who peddled it. People went insane from the grain alcohol-formaldehyde concoctions that were bubbled up in bathtubs and drained into bottles marked gin or vodka or pumped into beer with needles. No one knew just what they were drinking, and no one cared as long as it was cheap, inebriating, and illegal.

Beer, once the American workingman's drink, soon became the focus of all-out gang violence. Hijacking beer trucks, knocking over rival breweries led to machine-gun shootouts in broad daylight; bloodied bodies sprawled along gutters were soon commonplace. Beer Baron gangsters were crowned kings of the major cities. Detroit had its Purple Gang; New York had Lepke's Murder Incorporated, Dutch Schultz's boys, and Lucky Luciano's mob; Chicago was divided and fractured with at least twenty-two street gangs vying for power. Bugs Moran fought Dion O'Banion, who fought the Terrible Genna Brothers, who hated the O'Donnell clan, who all hated a big fat man with two knife-gash scars, Al Capone.

Capone was born in a small village near Naples, Italy. He learned to steal almost before he learned to walk; he pimped for young girls before he himself reached puberty. When his family emigrated to America, he continued his crime career on the streets of Brooklyn, joining a gang called the Five Pointers, one of many that overran and terrorized immigrant neighborhoods. The gang was named after a Lower East Side Manhattan intersection near Broadway and the Bowery, the training school of sorts for the Dead End Kids. Those who made it out alive rose to the top of the crime world. Most ended up in the coroner's meat wagon before they reached adulthood. It was while knifing rivals and robbing stores that Capone met another hood, someone who was even more coldhearted and barbarous, a steely-eyed Sicilian of whom even fellow gang members were afraid, Salvatore Luciana (later to be known as Charles "Lucky" Luciano).

Luciano and Capone quickly developed an intense, seething hatred for one another. Luciano thought Capone a braggart, loud-mouthed and slow, who did more talking than killing and spent too much time trying to play diplomat to factions within the gang. Capone, who was frighteningly quick at sizing up a man, knew Luciano was trouble. He saw him as hot-tempered, too eager to kill, someone who would murder even a close friend if he stood in the way of something Luciano wanted. It was all too obvious that Luciano enjoyed killing. For Luciano, murder was a catharsis.

Luciano and Capone were also enemies by nature of birth; the Sicilians had a centuries-old hatred for the Neapolitans. The Sicilians were the leaner, colder, more calculating, those from Naples, more gregarious and jolly. The Sicilians had developed a reputation for being quick to fight, quick to kill. The Neapolitans were known as talkers, negotiators, who would try to win an enemy over before reaching for a gun. Luciano and Capone were true to type, and therefore adversaries.

The difference between the two reached the crisis point one summer afternoon while they were out on patrol looking for rival gangs. Two boys from another gang were running through an alley, breaking into stores in Five Pointers' territory. Capone and Luciano drew their knives and brass knuckles, ready for a fight, something Capone looked forward to as nothing more than recreation and exercise. Luciano, though, took the game seriously. While Capone was busy duking it out, Luciano grabbed one of the boys from behind and slashed his throat. Then he jumped Capone's "sparring partner" and did the same. Luciano wiped the blood on his shirt and laughed, calling it "slaughter time for the pigs," as his two victims lay on the cold pavement, blood spurting from their necks. Capone was obviously shaken. It was his first real encounter with murder. Luciano turned his lethal knife on Capone, threatening to kill him if he tried to leave Luciano holding the bag.

The murders were pinned on Capone, who unwillingly took the fall. He let the group know he played the dupe. He vowed a vendetta on his dead father's grave. Though the arrests remained on his record, he avoided conviction by using something that eventually helped him rule over Chicago as the nation's number-one gang lord: bribery. During his arrest, it seemed obvious to Capone that the police were after something besides tossing another punk in the clink. It did not take him long to figure out what they wanted. He handed over some money, then more, until they, in Capone's words, "bled the kid dry," taking his last bit of pocket change.

It was this incident that nurtured young Capone's distaste for and spite against the police, and he learned to keep a little extra money hidden under his belt or in his shoe. To him, the police were whores who sold out to the highest bidder. But the experience taught him a lesson that he quickly turned into his code: *Una volta corrotto, sempre controllato,* "Once corrupted, always controlled." Capone learned that anything can be "fixed" with the right amount of money, and once someone took a bribe, Capone knew he would always be his slave.

It was during his time with the Five Pointers that Capone met another, older hood, a big shot named Johnny Torrio. He was a smooth-talking gangster who was well-known in both New York and Chicago, more or less the senior crime adviser to the gang, and later Capone's mentor. Torrio had a rich and powerful uncle, Big Jim Colosimo, who in the early 1920s was the top gun in Chicago's gangland.

Colosimo ran a booming night-club business and was rich far beyond the dreams of the average workingman. He wore diamonds and smoked expensive cigars. Vaudeville performers and famous singers always paid their respects to Big Jim whenever they were in Chicago. Their visits drew other customers, who hoped to see their favorite stars. Torrio saw a fortune ready for the taking and quickly worked his way into a silent partnership with his uncle. While Colosimo greased the wheels with politicians and police, making sure rivals were closed down and property assessments kept to a minimum, Torrio kept busy learning the ins and outs of Chicago politics. That lesson conveniently came with a handwritten list of those "on the take" and those considered "untouchable." The names on the first list ran past the mayor to the governor to some White House officials, stopping just short of President Wilson. Torrio was quick to catch on to how to use those names to keep the law from looking too deeply into his businesses, whether it was through bribery, blackmail, or outright murder. He passed his wisdom along to protégé Capone.

As for Capone, his career had taken a turn for the worse. His two early murder raps made him a target for police harassment, something the Five Pointers did not welcome. His hatred for Luciano was also obvious, and the two were commonly at each other's throats with knives as well as verbal assaults. Luciano was openly vying for rule of the gang against the ambitious Capone. Worse yet, the gang had started to sway in Luciano's direction, mostly because they were afraid not to. In fights, it was always Capone who was held back by other gang members, never Luciano, who was allowed to say what he pleased and do as he pleased and dared anyone to stop him.

The final break came when Capone got into a barroom knife fight with another thug, who happened to be the son of a politician. The fight happened while Capone was working as a bartender/slugger for the Harvard Inn, run by Frankie Yale, who formed the Unione Siciliana, the first official organized-crime racket. It was a club offering "protection" for fellow Italian immigrants badgered by crooked cops or street gangs, and it also kept the lid on simmering hatred among the Italian gangs in New York and Chicago.

The fight earned Capone two deep gashes in his left cheek and an unbeatable murder conviction if the thug died of stab wounds. Capone had just gotten married and needed quick cash, which seemed to be just out of his stubby-fingered reach. When Torrio wired that he needed a bodyguard, Capone did not wait for a second invitation. He and his new bride, Mae, fled to Chicago, where his future, and history, awaited.

"I spit on your grave," Capone vowed to Luciano as he packed his arsenal of knives, guns, blackjacks, and brass knuckles. He also swore he and Luciano would meet again, next time on Capone's terms. Luciano sneered at the thinly disguised threat and taunted his obese opponent for what he perceived as running out on the gang, folding when the heat was on. From that moment on, Luciano pegged Capone as a coward and weakling. But Luciano's feeling of superiority would eventually be his undoing; blinded by his own conceit he grossly miscalculated the determination and cunning of the one man who would figuratively castrate him before the entire underworld, making him a laughingstock and sucker. Though Capone left New York, he never let go of his obsession with Luciano, the punk he called "dago slime." The day of reckoning was still fifteen years in the future.

When word got out that the Volstead Act was soon to become law, breweries began closing up and selling out across the country. There were few takers for operations that had no future. But Torrio and Capone looked ahead, knowing that they of all people were far above the law, as long as they had money. They drained the profits from Colosimo's place to buy the Malt-Maid Company, as well as taking out options on other, smaller Chicago breweries.

When Volstead went on the books, Torrio and Capone

renamed their business the Manhattan Brewing Company; they were now officially bootleggers, something old Gentleman Jim despised as low class. He ignorantly assumed he was still the Big Boss and tried to put the kibosh on the power-hungry pair.

When Colosimo refused to expand his business into the newly lucrative bootlegging/brewery empire, Torrio ordered Capone to eliminate his jolly patriarch. Though he was never convicted, most likely because the bulk of the Chicago Police Department was in Torrio's pocket, it is believed the double-shot-through-the-forehead gunning of Big Jim was Capone's first big contract killing. It was on Tuesday afternoon, May 11, 1920. Prohibition had been in effect less than four months. Big Jim was Prohibition's first casualty, Capone its first killer.

It was Irish rival O'Banion who said, "There's thirty million dollars' worth of beer sold in Chicago every month and a million dollars is spread among police, politicians and federal agents to keep it flowing." Gin, whiskey, and wine sales were easily twice that amount. Bootlegging was no penny-ante poker game, it was the biggest business in the United States. Divvied up among the various crime "families" of Chicago, bathtub gin and needle beer made overnight millionaires of common thugs who now openly defied the law, brandishing guns, flaunting fancy cars, and parading in custom-made suits. Police and politicians were too greedy, too corrupt, or too scared to defy them, and they knew it.

With a ravenous appetite for money and power, the Torrio-Capone combine continued to expand, swallowing up more and more breweries; and when they could buy no more, the pair closed in on other businesses. Soon they owned linen-supply and cleaning operations, bottling plants, food-processing mills and dairies, packaging companies and warehouses. Capone openly bragged to gunslinging pals that by the time he was through, "any business relating to booze" would be his. He said, "Every time some sucker stirs his martini, it's Capone's gin he's pouring, Capone's olives he's dipping, and Capone's napkins he's wiping his mouth in."

Capone secured businesses for the combine through his own form of public relations. He first offered what he believed to be a fair price for the operation. If his money was turned down, he negotiated with the owners, talking, meeting, trying to win them over with gifts and persuasion. Then, if all else failed, he killed them. Capone convinced himself all murders at his hand were of the victim's own choosing, and he rarely felt remorse.

Through his businesses Capone became one of the wealthiest, most enterprising, and notorious gangsters in Chicago, and he quickly became a target for Young Turks hoping to claw their way to the top by bumping off the Great Goombah. He proved he was no sitting duck by quickly surrounding himself with killers who swore allegiance on the barrel of a tommy gun, among them a jewelry fence/barber named Frank Nitto (later changed to Nitti through a typesetting error at the *Chicago Tribune*), who would surface as Capone's closest ally, and eventually rule the Capone mob.

By 1924, Chicago was completely dominated by the underworld. The gangs had gotten too powerful, the politicans and police too corrupt. Chicago's working class was growing tired of seeing the bad guys win and demanded reform. Mayor Big Bill Thompson, a Republican who coined the phrase "Vote early and vote often," and put it to good use, was on the outs, given a run by "reform mayor" William Dever, a Democrat who promised to put the city back in the hands of the "people." Which people he meant soon became all too obvious; gangs grew even more powerful under his regime.

To make sure the election came in according to plan, the Chicago election judges, on Dever's payroll, hired goons to patrol the polling places, to keep the elections "honest." In many Chicago wards that meant voters cast their ballots (an intentional plural here) for the favored politican, in this case Dever, or they did not vote. Anyone with an opposing view was escorted outside and systematically and nonchalantly beaten up or run off at gunpoint.

O'Banion's gang was hired by Thompson's cronies to swing the Republican vote in the Loop and North Shore area, which was already under O'Banion's control. Deannie O'Banion's goon squad routinely burst into saloons, armed with that he called his "friendly persuaders," better known as machine guns. He announced, "We're gonna have a Republican victory celebration tonight. Anybody who votes Democrat ain't going to be here . . . or anywhere else. You vote Republican or ya ain't votin'!" Those who insisted on voting Democrat disappeared or "committed suicide." Their votes, though cast after their deaths and oddly enough for the Republican ticket, still counted.

The Democrats won that election in spite of O'Banion's force, which showed the end of the reign of Republicans in Chicago and the slipping away of power for O'Banion. The Democrats and Capone were clearly in control.

It was during their shotgun campaigning that the two gangs had their first blood feud. Frank Capone, getting carried away with his election-education program, crossed into O'Banion territory, and ran smack against Deannie's payroll police. Frankie took the losing end of the shootout and wound up on the coroner's marble slab. Al claimed retaliation in a berserk shooting rampage, taking three cops to their graves. Capone held O'Banion personally responsible for killing his brother and for igniting the retaliatory shootings of the officers. As Capone calmly explained it, the cops would not have died if Deannie had not started the fight.

O'Banion already had a gutful of the Italians; he was at odds with Torrio and other gangs he blatantly labeled "thievin' wops." He believed he was smarter, but the Italians proved deadlier. The fuse was lit, and an undercurrent of hatred now seeped to the surface. The day of reckoning between the Italian and the Irish mobs was imminent.

The Unione Siciliana and its Chicago chapter president, Mike Merlo, had been keeping close watch and putting out brush fires between the gangs. Differences had amounted to nothing more than minor spats since the factions usually stayed in their own territories. But when Merlo died of cancer on November 9, 1924, the lid blew, and the streets of Chicago erupted in violence. The first victim, Deannie O'Banion, was gunned down in his flower shop the following day by two Sicilians and a third man, Pete Gusenberg (who later died as a member of Bugs Moran's gang in the St. Valentine's Day massacre). O'Banion's face was literally blown off. The Italians finally had their revenge; their nemesis was history. The gang wars were on.

Two months later Torrio was caught off guard by Hymie Weiss and Bugs Moran, heirs to the O'Banion gang, who blind-sided him, and drilled him with four shots. Capone did not initially retaliate against Weiss and Moran because they inadvertently gave him what he wanted—control of Chicago's largest and most powerful mob.

Torrio, who managed to survive the gunning, had graciously sold his interest in the "businesses" to Capone for $5 million—cash, which Capone now had no trouble paying.

Capone, sole ruler of the combine, quickly aligned back-alley plug-uglies into his army; thieves, murderers, pimps, and street-smart toughs who knew how to juggle books and keep the wheels of corruption well greased and would obey commands without question. Nitti rose as Capone's right-hand hood; Jake Guzik, a pimp who had half the city on his payroll, became his accountant. Through Nitti's powers of knife-point persuasion, and Guzik's penchant for payoffs, the Scarface syndicate emerged not only as one of the largest but as one of the richest as well.

By 1926, Capone and his lieutenants owned more than 700 businesses, most relating to bootlegging, food, and services. The syndicate's income soared past $300 million a year; Capone boasted a personal income of nearly $60 million. He was now Chicago's richest vice lord. Scarface Al had everything he desired—power, fame, and wealth—and he even had the respect of politicians and judges from Springfield, Illinois, to Washington, D.C., though this "respect" was clearly tied to the umbilical cord of bribes and kickbacks. Even Supreme Court justices were within Capone's reach. He viewed them as "nothing more than lawyers in black robes."

But politicians were Big Al's specialty. "A pol can turn down my first offer. He can turn down my second offer. But eventually I'll find his price. Everyone says how I corrupted the poor bastard. The way I see it is the bastard just shook me down for more money."

Capone was more than happy to be "shaken down" by big shots from all areas of influence, many of whom came to him hat in hand to ask for favors ranging from contract influence-peddling to outright murder for hire. Those who asked were often socially and politically well-connected men who secretly scorned the fat Italian. Capone viewed the situation as rather comical; he enjoyed seeing them crawl to him on their knees.

With his new, upper-crust social status, Capone needed a

new image. Exit the slovenly, sinister "Scarface Al," the immigrant who wore ill-fitting suits and had food-stained ties and blood-stained hands. For Capone, "snorky" meant "elegant," so he gave himself a new name. Enter "Snorky Capone," Chicago's most famous citizen, a silk-suited dandy with diamond stickpins and imported cigars.

He also became the darling of the press. Always affable and glib, Capone never refused an interview and was more than eager to spout his views on life, corruption, business, and the general public's eagerness to buy anything wrapped in a shiny new package. When asked to explain his obvious success while others starved, he attributed it to his hard work.

"A loser's always looking for that pot of gold, that buried treasure to come to him. He thinks he can sit back and let someone else do the dirty work. But a guy of power, he's always in there digging."

To further enhance his rancid image he left huge food baskets on the doorsteps of less-fortunate but hardworking families who were either employed by the Capone empire or closely aligned with the ward aldermen who were Snorky's political puppets. As the owner of one of Chicagoland's largest and most profitable dairies, he railroaded legislation through to get code dating on milk and other dairy products so housewives would know when the items had been left in the dairy case too long. He also made sure everyone knew about his big heart and ostentatious generosity. No newspaper ever went to press in the late twenties without some quote, or story, or "act of kindness" by Big Al.

In another gesture, Snorky Capone also saw to it that the hungry received a square meal and a place to rest off the streets. He gutted old stores, which had usually been seized against the previous owner's wishes, or empty warehouses, which his troupe had bombed to "clear out the rats," as he put it, and opened up a chain of soup kitchens. The kitchens were usually oddly convenient to his chain of brothels, run by another Capone alias, "Al Brown," who advertised the houses as furniture stores selling "any old thing to lay on."

Chicago ran like clockwork, and Capone was the master at winding the clock. No law was passed, no ordinance approved without the consent of Capone. And no dignitary, no vaudeville or movie star passed cross-country without paying respects to the Windy City's number-one resident. On any given day one could find such top stars and celebrities as Al Jolson, Ed Wynn, Fanny Brice, George Jessel, Joe E. Lewis, and Eddie Cantor walking into one of Al's soup kitchens, passing along words of encouragement for the down-and-out.

But the stars were not there for charitable acts to street scum; they were there to visit in the back rooms, which were usually crowded with senators, judges, police captains, along with Big Al's boys Jake Guzik or Frank Nitti, and usually even Al himself, all very chummy. They did not dine on gruel and watered-down coffee, either. Through the back doors of the midnight missions passed some of the city's finest delicacies. Laws were agreed upon, favors granted, and decisions made over gourmet feasts, the tab all laundered through the expenses of the kitchen.

Most likely Al's fascination with movie stars began during the early days of running Colosimo's. Celebrities were almost commonplace at Big Jim's, and Al became accustomed to hobnobbing with silver-screen idols. In a vicarious way, the association made Capone a star, and he loved the adoration that came attached to stardom. Stars had instant recognition. Hotel clerks and maître d's knocked themselves out to give them immediate seating, bowing and "yes siring" and "no siring" everywhere they went. They also attracted a large crowd of sightseers, and that meant a guaranteed draw, in other words, money, wherever the stars appeared.

When Capone achieved his wealth and power, he tried his best to become a celebrity in his own right, to have the same subservient respect from the minions. Dining with, boasting to, and parading alongside stars made Snorky Al believe he too was a someone of stature.

The attraction was mutual. The famous could not get enough of the flamboyant flimflam man either. The power, the money, the absolute control over other people even to the point of murder excited them. Here was a dangerous side of life they only acted out on the screen or dreamed about in private. Stars always asked Capone to give lurid accounts of murders, details of how he outscammed other mobsters and how he ran bootleg breweries under the nose of the law. He was good for shock value. Capone never turned down an offer to take center stage, especially from a star. They were odd bedfellows trapped in a symbiotic relationship, one feeding off the other.

Capone was no fool. He knew few liked him for himself. He knew he would always be Scarface Al the gangster, never Mr. Capone the multimillionaire businessman. He knew he could never rise above his dirt-poor beginnings despite all the trappings of success, at least not as long as there were still gang wars in Chicago and innocent people getting blown to pieces and drilled full of shotgun lead on the streets. He had given Chicago a black eye. Capone thought himself respectable. Now Chicago had to become respectable to match his new image.

On October 21, 1926, Capone called his first Underworld Peace Conference. He invited the leaders of the remaining area gangs to divide up the Midwest and lay down their guns. Everyone attended except for two men, Hymie Weiss and Bugs Moran; Weiss offered the more vocal of the rebuffs, sending back the invitation with crude remarks and a vow to break into the meeting with machine guns and hand grenades.

Capone blew a gasket and put out an immediate contract on the arrogant Pole. "When a dog's got rabies, ya gotta kill it." With those words, Earl Wajciechowski, better known as Hymie Weiss, met his maker, blown to bits on the steps of Holy Name Cathedral. Capone's only major opponent now was Bugs Moran, who cheated death three years later, on February 14, 1929, in a Clark Street garage. Though Moran escaped, the St. Valentine's Day Massacre virtually wiped out his gang. He no longer posed a threat to Capone, who now reigned supreme.

But this was not enough. There was one aspect of big business that Capone had yet to own: the unions. His pursuit of union dominance would soon put him on the verge of a collision course with his old adversary Lucky Luciano. The point of impact—Hollywood, California.

Chapter Eight

He had snake's eyes: cold, piercing, dead; the kind that looked right through a victim, making him instantly aware that he was marked for death. He had neither heart nor soul, and he had no friends, only those who were afraid not to go along with him. He was the most feared and hated of all the underworld bosses. His name was Charles Luciano. Behind his back, those who knew him whispered another, more fitting name: They called him Charley Lucifer, the devil.

His time with the Brooklyn Five Pointers served him well. He earned a reputation as a ruthless murderer, a thief and a madman. By the time he was twenty years old, he had at least thirty-five murders attributed to him. He expanded his following to seize control of sections of Manhattan, the Bronx, and Brooklyn, carved up in an edgy adversarial partnership with other mobsters.

During his twenty-five-year reign of terror in New York, Luciano survived at least seven attempts on his life. He was riddled with bullets, knifed in the chest and neck, jumped and strangled from behind. But each time he recovered from his wounds and lived to pay deadly retribution, earning him the nickname "Lucky." He outlived both Dutch Schultz and

Leo Lepke, his two closest competitors in New York. Luciano had few enemies alive at any one time. He saw to that.

Unlike Capone, Luciano rarely had an entourage around him. He trusted no one. When he needed to have a murder or fire-bombing or takeover carried out, he always had plenty of people who would grant the favor, not out of loyalty but out of terror. He never spoke with newspaper reporters and was always in motion, which made it impossible for any reporter to pin him down long enough for an interview. He was completely unapproachable, cold and distant. Even the press never tried to cross him. Except once.

An overeager writer from *The New York Times* foolishly ventured too close to the heart of the gang lord, asked too many questions around town about Luciano's businesses, and naïvely believed he could use the power of the press to show up Lucky for what he was. He could not understand why his editor killed the story of a series of murders attributed to Luciano. The reporter lost his job soon after. Even that did not shut him up. Neither did three death threats. A bullet in the head finally convinced the young man that he was wrong about Charley Lucifer.

Luciano's rise to power was much like Capone's. He left a trail of bodies and a web of political corruption in his wake. He was one of a rare breed who entered a place unnoticed but left behind chaos, agony, and blood. He owned scores of businesses and had immense wealth and influence. But there were several significant differences between the two. Luciano had a distaste for bootlegging and veered away from that business as soon as he had a solid power base of wealth. He had no desire to be "popular" like Capone; in fact he went out of his way to avoid attracting attention. He never bragged to anyone, let alone offered opinions on his holdings and bank accounts, which was a Capone trait that eventually invited Treasury scrutiny and put Capone behind bars. Few people knew anything at all about Luciano, and what little they knew was only fragmented pieces of information. No one got too close or ever asked too many questions. Luciano liked it that way.

No one ever questioned Luciano's power. A great deal of it was granted to him by unspoken agreement—people assumed he was mean, cold-blooded, and fearless, and they got out of his way. He had as many politicians and police on his payroll as Capone; he controlled and manipulated as many businesses and was as ruthless as any man alive. But Luciano was far more sneaky and far more slippery. It was impossible to point to a crime, a takeover, a bribe and know for a fact that it could be attributed to Luciano.

Charley Lucifer worked silently but effectively. Among his holdings were scores of businesses, gambling and numbers rackets, whorehouses, and at least fifty East Coast unions, from bricklayers to bartenders, factory workers to window washers. Each turned over a slice of its take to Luciano and his "collection agents" who kept the unions running smoothly.

Though it was only one of his operations, the East Coast projectionists' union was a small but thriving organization. Movie houses drew steady New York crowds, giving Broadway and the legitimate stage some tough competition. Slowly movie houses sprang up across the city; by the late twenties, each neighborhood had its own theater. And each theater employed at least one man to run the highly volatile nitrate film. This film would occasionally ignite or explode because of its unstable chemical content, often burning down movie houses or injuring and maiming the man upstairs who loaded the film into the projector.

The union started initially out of a need to protect projectionists from management's carelessness or unsafe storage of the volatile film. The union also stopped management from working the projectionists excessively long hours as they responded to the demand for four-hour matinees and all-night show times. But this union, like so many others, quickly became a target for greedy men preying on its members. When the union became corrupted, it offered fertile ground on which Luciano could plant his own men.

As Luciano closed in on the East Side projectionists, Lepke gouged out the West Side, both putting their own men in as business agents of this and other unions. The attraction of unions was not power so much as a steady, accessible income from pension funds and dues. Luciano drew an estimated $50,000 a year from the projectionists' union alone. Still he saw it not for its singular potential but as only one of many holdings. This shortsightedness cost him dearly when he came up against Al Capone.

Capone had yet to seize control of the projectionists' union in Chicago. Although he enjoyed a fascination with movie stars, he did not regard movies and movie theaters as worth controlling. His businesses were more in the bootlegging and brothel line and he tended to stick with what he knew.

When he realized the fortune to be made in "owning" unions, Capone instinctively turned to bartenders, factory workers, truck drivers, service and building-related organizations. He put Frank Nitti in charge of organizing unions where there were none and infiltrating those already in existence.

Nitti's goon squads burst into factories, at gunpoint, and persuaded groups to sign union petitions. Those who did were ordered to recruit the holdouts. Those who steadfastly refused to align with the mob were at first spoken to, then beaten up, and finally killed. Nitti always had 100 percent union membership.

He had a much easier time in factories and businesses where unions already existed. He laid it on the line that he was taking over on Capone's behalf. If the name of Capone was not enough to terrorize the leaders into submission, they were systematically killed. At the next union meeting, Nitti and his pals lined the hall, machine guns in hand in an obvious show of force. There were few questions from the floor. The dues went up, and the ranks swelled. Few protested because most felt fortunate even to have a job. Union dues were understood as part of the fee for employment.

The Chicago projectionists' union, Theatre Operators Local 110, was run by one man, a short little Irish thug named Tommy Maloy. Maloy inherited control of the union from another crook, Jack Miller, who carried the formal title of business agent until his untimely shotgun death in 1920. As business agent, Miller, then Maloy, had carte blanche to dip into the union till whenever and wherever he saw fit, usually for his personal gain. The union was thriving, and pretty well self-sustaining through Maloy's skill with pistols and tommy guns, blackjacks and brass knuckles. He had no qualms about cracking the skull of any projectionist who refused to join his union or an owner who balked at hiring his men. He built his tiny empire on blood. His business formula was simple: A projectionist who complained was thrown out of work or permanently put out of commission; a theater that refused to hire union operators would find its film destroyed in a mysterious fire, or the theater would burn down, or the establishment would suddenly have a new owner.

Maloy was never a direct threat to Capone because he was a one-man organization, small potatoes, a back-alley thief who ran a nickel and dime operation—but that was before movies became big business with the advent of sound.

When sound came in, despite hundreds of new theaters opening every day around the country, membership in Maloy's union did not increase. So Maloy developed a two-part scheme. When sound was initially synchronized on records to go along with the film, Maloy insisted the theater owners hire technicians known as "faders" to operate the newfangled sound equipment. And when Hollywood found a way of putting both sound and picture on film stock, Maloy persuaded owners to pay $1,100 to the local for each fader dismissed, rather than insisting the men be rehired as projectionists. This was cheaper than keeping the faders on the payroll, so the owners anted up. That was the first half of Maloy's plan.

Maloy then revealed his second scam for keeping membership low but all the while increasing the funds in the union coffers. Maloy issued work permits to nonunion projectionists, with both union and nonunion workers earning the same weekly wages. He slammed the lid shut on new membership, an act that met with a quick outcry from the rank and file, who envisioned their union diminishing out of existance.

Union members stormed Maloy's first business meeting of 1924 spewing death threats, anarchy, chaos, and outright strikes against their own local. But Maloy's machine-gun maniacs defused the hostility with several rounds of gunfire, drilling the ceiling of the union hall. The members quietly took their seats and let the little fellow lay out his plan, which centered around hiring men by the day, with work permits.

Those who joined the union were asked to kick back only $3 each week to the local, another buck to the international, while work-permit projectionists were forced to pony up 10 percent of their weekly wages. With some projectionists hauling in as much as $175 per week (when the average worker was making only $5 to $7 weekly), few complained. The union projectionists were happy. Down-and-out men had the hope of at least some employment. Maloy was happy and wealthy and smug over his brilliant inspiration. His idea would soon blow up in his face.

Both Luciano and Capone thought they had everything under control. Gang wars were a thing of the past. Both were among the wealthiest men in the country. They "owned" lucrative businesses and controlled profitable unions that funneled millions of dollars each year into the underworld treasury. The money was pouring in and being laundered, untraceable and tax free, right under the nose of the government. Now it was only a matter of sitting back and raking it in. Or so they thought. But Hollywood and the Treasury Department had other ideas.

In spite of his grandiose Good Samaritan tactics, an increasing number of Chicagoans were growing tired of Capone. The Big Fellow had gotten too rich, too powerful, and it was no secret to anyone how he was getting his money. For years, federal agents had hoped to get at Capone. Fortunately, there were some honest men in the government, men who could not be bought at any price. They decided to target Capone. His own big mouth threatened to be his ultimate undoing.

An enterprising Treasury agent named Frank Wilson found a way to get Big Al. Wilson and his T-men started investigating the man who flagrantly earned millions of dollars but had no accountable income, no report of earnings, and therefore no record of income-tax payment.

Capone tried to bribe the men, then threatened them and their families with death; he even tried to coerce those higher up in the government to put the squeeze on the T-men to get them off his back. Nothing worked. Wilson and his men were indeed untouchable. As the 1920s wound to a close, Capone found himself up against an enemy that he could not fight, could not bribe, and could not kill. So Al, Frank Nitti, and their cronies finally were forced to look upon what they assumed would be half-year sentences as part of the consequence of being in their line of work; a short-term slap on the wrist for a long-term gain that would get the Feds off their backs. Nitti was right. Capone could not have been more wrong.

Frank Nitti was the first member of the Capone Syndicate indicted for income-tax evasion in 1930. He was sentenced to six months in jail. But now another agent, Eliot Ness, raided Capone brothels, breweries, and bookmaking operations. Ax in hand and a corps of press photographers bringing up the rear, Ness made an obvious point—Al Capone was a marked man. Once they got him, the other gang bosses were vulnerable.

Capone, though, still considered Ness and his troupe little more than annoyances. He believed his new and stronger base of income, the unions, was not as easily accessible or as easily traced. He felt that busting beer kegs, axing back-room roulette wheels, and ripping out bookie phone lines kept Ness busy and freed Al to go about his business. He only laughed as Ness tap-danced around the mob's new and more profitable racket—union control.

Luciano, already one jump ahead of Capone in his control of unions, gambling, and other ventures, sought new fields. There were millions to be made peddling drugs, something Capone detested and steadfastly refused to do. Whereas Capone saw drugs as the ultimate decay of society, Luciano saw dealing as only another source of income, no different from any other, and no worse than Capone's peddling of rotgut, brain-damaging homemade alcohol.

Luciano took control of the East Coast drug operations much as he had his other ventures—he killed those who stood in his way. He organized smugglers who had South American drug connections, and they in turn slashed the throats of those who were already drug running for other hoods. He seized back-room refineries that cut the heroin and cocaine down to fifty parts to one, strong enough to cut even further yet diluted enough to bring in a hefty price on the streets.

From this beginning, Luciano ignited a new series of gang wars, his henchmen declaring open season on small-time dope peddlers, most of whom were found dead from an overdose or shot through the brain. He cleaned house of helter-skelter dealers and fine-tuned the business into a smooth-running operation.

But New York was only the beginning. The city was filled with small-time punks looking for a quick and cheap fix, juvenile delinquents who stole dope money, and well-worn whores whom Luciano and other vice lords got on the junk only as a means of keeping them submissive. The riffraff would always be around, always easy marks; what he needed was a steady stream of well-monied dupes looking for kicks and thrills.

Hollywood was already notorious for its high life, and drugs played a major part in the story. Tales of movie-star junkies echoed from coast to coast. Sennett studios had "The Count," who always gave the first fix free. Fox had "Mr. Fix It," Paramount "The Man." They were always within reach, and would miraculously appear out of nowhere with just the right thing. They were also making a fortune off the strung-out stars.

Luciano's fascination with movie stars and Hollywood was obviously quite different from that of his overweight adversary. Unlike Capone, Luciano did not give a damn about prestige, about publicity, or about the razzle-dazzle of movies. He first came to Hollywood in 1929 with just one purpose, to move in on and take over the drug racket. Once he got there, he found a town wide open, just itching for someone like him to take control. He also found ample opportunity to plunge into areas that he hardly imagined existed in the desert town. Luciano's world of gambling, unions, and drug peddling was headed west and was about to add new business ventures to its inventory.

Luciano knew the big and steady drug money was with the movie stars. He also knew he needed an in, an introduction to the right customers, who would not only buy from his gang but send others his way. Getting that in proved easier than Luciano had imagined.

Though Luciano shunned the limelight, he was already notorious. Few pictures were ever taken of the gang lord, but when they were, they were circulated from coast to coast. Whether he liked it or not, his face was his Hollywood calling card. His name never needed to be announced twice. When anyone heard "Lucky Luciano," they opened doors in awe; especially stars who already fantasized about such men, who already knew Capone and the lore of gangsters.

Luciano also knew he could not simply walk onto a movie lot and announce his intentions. He needed a front man. He found such a man in Pasquale "Pat" DiCicco, a rich, handsome playboy with a violent temper and a charming personality.

DiCicco was bankrolled as an heir to the New York Broccoli fortune, a man-about-town who enjoyed a fast-paced reputation on both the East and West coasts. In New York, the darling of Manhattan was frequently seen with gangsters, more for the thrill of playing with the Big Boys than because of any actual involvement in criminal activity. DiCicco loved living on the edge.

He came to Los Angeles as a self-proclaimed actors' agent and manager. He had style, polish, and millions of dollars to throw around to buy the best clothes and to impress very impressionable stars. He invited himself to the poshest parties, talked his way into producers' offices, and approached the most elite tables in exclusive restaurants without rebuff. His charm and good looks were unnerving. He had complete command of every situation.

Though he had no major clients, he had an entrée to every movie studio lot in town. He gained that open door through cunning and nerve. He made a point of dining in the best restaurants—the Brown Derby, Montmartre, Musso and Frank's—places to be seen, where he knew producers would be accessible. Dressed in his most expensive suit, he approached them at their tables, presented his business card, and worked his way into a conversation aimed at further pumping up overinflated egos. He always left the conversation "up in the air," to be finished the following day in the producer's office. It never failed.

The next morning he arrived at the studio in an expensive car and announced his name. He flattered the guards with tips or gifts. They remembered him and were more than eager to let him back on the lot for future payoffs. Once inside the lot, he worked like a sideshow entertainer, moving from set to set, introducing himself, kissing ladies' hands, acting as if he belonged—which eventually he did. Leading ladies were immediately drawn to him, and smitten with his disarming charm and devastating smile. He used that edge whenever he had a chance.

It was only a short time before he met the people who had the real power over the stars: The Count, Mr. Fix It, and others who had no real names and dealt powder and pills. DiCicco himself never peddled, nor was he known to use, but through his association with the dealers, he knew firsthand which stars were hooked and how much they spent weekly on their habits. He carried the list in his head, believing that one day it might come in handy. His hunch paid off when Lucky Luciano rolled into town.

Both DiCicco and Luciano were well-known names in New York; since both were Italian they traveled in some of the same circles and had met on several occasions, so it seemed natural they would meet again in Hollywood. The pair became steady companions, Luciano quietly studying his partner, absorbing bits of information about the Hollywood hierarchy. No name ever escaped Luciano's memory, especially when it came to the drug business.

DiCicco provided a wealth of information on who bought from whom, how much drug money exchanged hands, who was being paid to look the other way, and who pulled the strings in the studios and in city hall. DiCicco gave Luciano the entrée he needed to infiltrate. Now near the top of the elite party "A" lists, DiCicco often brought Luciano along as his surprise guest. Movie moguls were flattered by the prestige such a famous man as Luciano gave their gatherings, stars clamored to brush up against the ice-cold killer, drug peddlers were eager to hitch on with his powerful organization.

The violence that was so much a part of Chicago and New York had now spread to Los Angeles. Penny-ante peddlers were gunned down, left to bleed to death in flophouses and on remote dirt roads. Dark-suited, fedora-hatted thugs armed with machine guns burst into back rooms and warehouses used to store and cut heroin and cocaine. The drilling of bullets drowned out screams and moans, and scores of bodies crumpled in pools of blood. Once-powerful drug kingpins were run out of town or threatened into submission at the point of a knife. Soon The Count and his colleagues vanished from the scene, replaced by tough-talking men with Brooklyn accents. Luciano's men moved in and quickly seized the Los Angeles drug operation. The death toll mounted and the price of drugs soared. There were no complaints. There was no one to complain to.

Los Angeles became a wide-open town, corrupt as any, from the chief of police to the district attorney. It was no secret that L.A. was controlled by bribes, payoffs, and kickbacks to city officials. Luciano knew full well that he could run free as long as he kept the wheels greased at city hall. He sent several of his men as messengers and delivered a five-word personal message to Buron Fitts: "Stay out of the way." Fitts did as he was told. To ensure cooperation, Luciano planted two of his men in the D.A.'s office. Fitts could not make a move without Lucky knowing about it.

Lucky assumed he had the town sewn up, with no competition in the drug racket. He believed he was supremely powerful and unstoppable, that he was the ringmaster of a circus filled with clowns. Lucky had just made another, serious miscalculation.

Chapter Nine

"Dear Mac," Thelma wrote her friend, "it's really wild out here. The men are something, wolves. A girl's gotta watch her britches. A lot of hard work, but fun. Hollywood's something to see . . . stars galore. Had fun making "Zane Grey's Nevada" with Gary Cooper. Nice guy. He taught me how to fence. Went up in the mountains to a cabin. Didn't think much of the hairdresser, not much of a man if ya know what I mean. Hope to get back to Lawrence soon. But until then, just remember I'll always be . . . Your Thel."

It did not take Thelma long to blend in with the Hollywood crowd. By late 1928, she had more than a dozen films—mostly comedies and a few dramatic roles—to her credit. She wrapped up her stint at Paramount and had just signed a one-year contract with Warner Bros., the up-and-coming studio since its splash with *The Jazz Singer*. She was beginning to be recognized on the street and had a reputation among the movie crowd as sweet and a bit naïve, but carefree and fun, in spite of Alice, who was usually lurking somewhere at her side. She dated frequently but had no serious romances. She drank a bit, flirted perhaps too much, and developed a sassy line of patter. She was a guest at some of the big parties thrown by Gary Cooper, Adolph Zukor, Adolphe Menjou,

Richard Dix and even at a get-together for the elite only, hosted by Lionel Barrymore.

Thelma had arrived! She was the All-American kid let loose in a fan-magazine fantasy. When Hal Roach spotted her in a First National/Warner Bros. comedy called *Vamping Venus*, he was captivated by her blond hair and dimples, and impressed that she had a natural ability to show an edge of toughness and independence yet remain feminine under those innocent looks. It was a rare combination and she was just the type he needed to put opposite his stable of comedians.

In January of 1929, Thelma received a telegram from the Roach Studios, summoning her to Roach's office. He had the best reputation for comedy since the early days of the silents. Starting as the Rolin Film Company with Harold Lloyd and the "Lonesome Luke" series back in 1917, the studio roster grew by leaps and bounds, with Roach emerging as the ace of all comedy producers. He had the "Our Gang" series, Laurel and Hardy, Charley Chase; the studio had a reputation for working like a well-oiled machine, everyone helping everyone, no stars, just one close-knit family all pitching in. The lot had a nickname: "A Lot of Fun," and those who were fortunate enough to be there were guaranteed steady employment and a chance to work with some of the best funny men and women in the business.

Thelma had mixed emotions about the Roach lot. She knew her association with it would be a career bonanza, make her noticed by other, bigger producers, and probably solidify her career as an actress. The hitch was the type of actress she would become—a comedienne. She had envisioned herself a dramatic actress, a leading lady, and fancied her roles more along the lines of her first mentor, Gloria Swanson, or even the coy, cute Clara Bow. Though she had only a few dramatic roles, she always believed that the pseudo-serious dramas at Warners would lead to heavier roles. But somehow, her bread and butter always came from comedy; comedy roles seemed to stick to her like gum on a shoe. They came easier for Thelma than anything else. A loan-out for comedy was one thing; she always had safe refuge in dramas at Warners. But she was afraid a contract with a comedy producer would abruptly ruin her chances at serious roles.

Meanwhile, Alice was ecstatic, blinded by visions of vicarious stardom as the mother of a Roach comedienne. She would have none of this vacillating attitude. Alice led the charge into Roach's office and took control.

"Mr. Roach", she announced, "I'm Alice Todd. Anything you say to my daughter you can say to me. I am, in effect, representing her as her manager."

Roach, a pleasant, dark-haired, round-faced, heavyset man in his thirties, invited the women to sit down in upholstered chairs angled slightly in front of his varnished-wood desk. The office was small but efficient, with a tasteful beige carpet, pictures of hunting scenes on the walls, two phones on the desk, and a Dictaphone wedged between a stack of papers and some scripts. The Culver City office was a stone's throw from MGM, a proximity that greatly impressed Alice.

"We understand you are interested in hiring Thelma."

"Yes. Ladies, here is my proposal. The Roach Studios is in the process of converting to sound. I need someone with a good speaking voice . . . maybe a singing voice, too. I've been looking for a comedienne who could carry rough-and-tumble, pie-in-the-face, pratfall comedy yet still come out looking like a lady. I've seen you work. I like your looks; you've got a good voice. You'd make a good foil for Laurel and Hardy and a good match for Charley Chase."

Chase was the lot's "handsome leading man," if a comic could ever be considered a leading man. He was more than six feet tall, thin as a rail, with dark hair, a boyish grin, and a pleasant manner. He had been a central player at the Roach Studios since his time as a director. He then appeared in front of the cameras, replacing Harold Lloyd and assuming the character of a lovable stumblebum. He had had an array of co-stars, but never one permanent leading lady. Roach thought a boyfriend/girlfriend comedy team would be unusual and successful. Chase and Todd were both extremely good-looking and would make a striking couple.

"I'm not really the pratfall type. I don't do my best work on my butt, especially in front of the camera. Anyway, I hoped to head toward more serious roles. Somehow I don't think Gloria Swanson would waltz around a studio with cream pie in her hair."

Thelma was quite glib and confident. She was in demand

around town, getting in with the right people, and had a steady income of $75 a week from her contract at Paramount and her one-year deal at Warner Bros.—far more money than she knew what to do with. Though her Warners deal was about to end, she was positive she would either be renewed or get picked up somewhere else. She fired her best shots at Roach, who seemed unruffled.

"Well, it's your life. But I'll tell you this much. You have no guarantee from Warner. You could be out of work three months from now. I also know how to size someone up. You are a comedienne, a natural, no matter how you see your-self."

"Mr. Roach, you may see me as a comedienne, but I don't. I think you're a little nearsighted."

Alice remained silent but was showing obvious signs of panic; she was sweating, chewing her lip, and tapping her foot nervously, hoping her daughter would not talk herself out of a job. When Roach stood up in a gesture to usher the women out, Alice spoke up.

"Uh, Mr. Roach. Before we make any decisions, just what is your offer? You know my daughter already has received other offers and we'd like to accept the best."

There were no other offers, and Alice, Thelma, and even Roach knew it. He always walked into a negotiating session knowing exactly where he stood. But he wanted Thelma or someone like her and was not about to let her go. He was also not about to let Thelma and Alice know how badly he wanted her.

Still standing he extended his hand. "It seems clear to me that Miss Todd is not the least bit interested in working for my studio." Roach knew he had them in the perfect position to make them feel lucky to get an offer. "I have several other ladies I'd like to interview."

"I understand." Alice was not a bit humbled. "But if you don't mind, we would still like to hear your proposal."

"I'm offering seventy-five dollars per week to start on a five-year contract. That sum will gradually rise to five hundred dollars a week."

"I was earning that with Zukor. That was ten films ago."

"Yes, then you should be used to it. The sum will increase according to the contract if you remain as a bit player or co-star. If your status at the studio changes, your contract will be renegotiated. If you think you can make more money somewhere else, take it."

"You know how I feel about comedy. Can I work anywhere else, just in case I'm offered a juicy role?"

"We'll work a free-lance clause into your contract. When you work for another studio while you're under contract with Roach Studios, you will be obligated to turn over part of your fee to us. What you negotiate at another studio for your work is up to you. I will insist, though, that any part is cleared through me. I will not allow you to take any role that could hamper your image as a Roach player."

Alice was ready to sign the contract, but Thelma was still dragging her feet. She had a hunch that the last part, the part about clearing roles with Roach, might mean trouble later on.

"Let me take this home and mull it over. I want to know all the ifs, ands, and buts of this thing. I also want to know exactly what I'm getting into. Something starts out smelling sweet but you find out later you've been skunked."

Alice chimed in. "Mr. Roach, pardon my daughter's bluntness. She's young, and . . ."

"I will want an answer first thing tomorrow morning. I also suggest you bleach your hair . . . platinum blond, as light as you can get it. It shows up better on film."

Thelma was stunned. She had never had any complaints about her hair. In fact, her hair was one of her better features. She thought to herself, ". . . that big gasbag tells me to bleach my hair! Some nerve . . . some fantasy with blondes, I guess."

Still in shock, the two women rose to meet Roach as he walked them to the door. When he opened the door, he stopped and turned to the women.

"Just one more thing. There's a clause in there, something I like to call the potato clause. It's a weight restriction. I like our women thin—they look better on camera. Simply stated, it says that I'm hiring you as you are now, at a certain weight, with a certain look. You get fat and you'll find yourself out of work. I have the option to release you from your contract if your weight goes up more than five pounds from what you weigh when you sign the contract. Any questions?"

Fat. The one problem that had plagued Thelma her entire

life was haunting her yet again. She had had enough of Mr. Roach's helpful suggestions. "No. I'll just suck in my gut." Thelma poked her finger in Roach's overly soft belly. "You could stand to shed a few, too. You got a potato clause in your deal?"

Roach was angered by Thelma's frankness. His face grew red and he glowered at her. She smiled at him, flashed her dimples, and winked. It worked every time.

Roach called back to Thelma, who was headed down the hall. "Swanson would take a pie in the face if the price was right."

Once home, Alice scolded Thelma for her rude behavior toward one of the most important producers in the business. Thelma was indifferent to authority, especially when it came to producers who were callous enough to demand an actress weigh a certain amount. Roach, she thought, was certainly no gentleman, and the money was not all that great. But Alice insisted she accept the deal. Thelma reluctantly agreed. She also bleached her hair to a white-platinum.

It was Alice's idea to put Thelma on another of her strenuous crash diets. She thought that if Thelma got thin at the start, as a sort of safety net, a few pounds put on during the course of the contract would not matter. For one month, Thelma ate nothing but chicken soup and salad, no dressing. She starved herself and it showed. She looked thin and drawn.

She began her first film for Hal Roach in late March. Her assignment was as a pretty housewife in the first Laurel and Hardy talkie, *Unaccustomed As We Are.* Her first week on the lot, she fainted from hunger, nerves, and exhaustion. Alice insisted on treating her daughter at home, giving the studio an abrupt explanation that her daughter was overcome with excitement and would be just fine after a day or two of complete rest.

When Thelma recovered, she gorged herself to gain back her strength—and probably as a rebellion against her mother. She put on all the weight she had lost, and then some. Fortunately, the weight gain was gradual enough that it did not show up on the film, and her participation in *Unaccustomed As We Are* went off without any further setbacks.

The film gained considerable attention as the first Laurel

and Hardy talkie. When audiences agreed that the boys' voices fit their characters perfectly, the studio made the quick conversion to sound. The film enhanced Thelma's career because it garnered so much acclaim for all those involved; it got her noticed as the pert, sexy, but tough blonde.

Thelma had two months off and made use of her freelance clause, returning to Warner Bros. and co-starring in several features best described as lighthearted dramas; the most noteworthy was a comedy titled *Seven Footprints to Satan*. It was Thelma's first starring role, opposite Creighton Hale. She also did *Her Private Life*, during which she developed a warm friendship with one of her co-stars, ZaSu Pitts. She not only made her first, and one of her few, Hollywood friends, but also established a bond that in just two years would help make Todd and Pitts successful as the first female screen-comedy team.

That July, she returned to Roach, looking puffy, about ten pounds overweight and scared stiff "The Boss" would see her and use the potato option to release her. She was scheduled to appear opposite Charley Chase in a comedy called *The Snappy Sneezer*, the first of a string of Chase/Todd comedies to be filmed on a two-month production/release schedule. Chase's extreme thinness made Toddy, as her Roach friends called her, look especially puffy.

The contract players and crew on the Roach lot were in many ways a family. Word spread quickly among the Chase group that Toddy was headed for yet another crash diet. Chase, who took an immediate liking to Thelma, was worried about her health, especially with an exhaustive production schedule already laid out for the remainder of the year and beginning of the next. His brother, Laurel and Hardy's director James Parrott, also had a constant battle against weight and had been taking prescription diet pills. Charley suggested Thelma talk with Parrott.

Parrott, a very kind and gentle man who went out of his way to help friends, gave Thelma a handful of diet pills believing they would help control her appetite. Unfortunately, they contained amphetamines, quite a common ingredient in early diet pills and not considered anything out of the ordinary at that time. The pills killed Thelma's appetite but gave her a tremendous energy boost. It was the first time she had ever taken pills or drugs of any sort, and she quickly became hooked, though most of her dependence was psychological. She not only relied on the pills for energy, she was also morbidly afraid of a repeat fainting spell like the one she had had during the Laurel and Hardy filming. She convinced herself that if The Boss saw her faint, he would fire her. The pills became a crutch to keep her on her feet, keep her from fainting from hunger; and they acted as a psychological buffer between herself and Roach's potato clause.

When Roach viewed the dailies from *Snappy Sneezer*, he liked what he saw. Todd was the perfect foil for Chase; they looked great together and played well off one another. Roach increased Todd's pay, raising her salary to the contract maximum of $500. But instead of celebrating, Thelma crumpled in tears when she heard the news. She had herself convinced that the pills had helped her in the role and that Roach would expect to see the same performance in her next films. She believed she was helpless without the drugs. Alice did nothing to convince her otherwise.

With a secure contract and a hefty raise, Thelma found herself surrounded by a crush of new friends and Hollywood hangers-on. She hated to disappoint anyone who invited her out, so she made a point of accepting every social invitation, no matter how late or how tired she was. If the social/work schedule dragged her down too much, she popped a handful of pills and washed them down with a swig of Scotch; her energy soared and she was set for the night. She quickly became known as Toddy or Hot Toddy around the movie crowd. Her social high was mainly chemical, and it was her downfall. Sometimes she was so wired and jittery from the pills that she could not sleep at all, and often she remained awake for several days before finally passing out.

Still, Alice could see only the whirlwind, glamorous movie-star life, and convinced herself that exhaustion was the price of popularity. She drilled into her daughter the fickleness of Hollywood, encouraged her to enjoy success while she had it and to live it up while she was in demand. Alice, of course, was also enjoying her share of the limelight, sliding in on her daughter's coattails. Thelma became good at burning the candle at both ends, thanks to a supply of pills and Scotch; Alice became adept at rubbing elbows with celebrities.

Sadly, Toddy felt she was never truly liked by many of her newfound friends, that they only welcomed her because of her fun, sexy, "hot" image, which she poured on wherever she found an audience. She was afraid to let go.

Thelma's health was slowly deteriorating. One December morning she crashed. She was supposed to be at work, but Alice found her sitting alone in a bedroom chair, shaking violently, perspiring heavily, and white as a sheet, with dark circles under her eyes. Alice was frantic; she grabbed Thelma by the shoulders and tried to shake her to her senses. Thelma stared vacantly, as if she did not even know her mother was in the room. Alice slapped Thelma, screamed at her, and dragged her off the chair. Thelma collapsed to the floor, still shaking.

"Thelma! Thelma darling, wake up. What's wrong! Thelma!"

Alice started to call the studio to offer some excuse for her daughter's absence, but thought better of the move and tapped the phone for another dial tone. She called Thelma's doctor, J. P. Sampson.

"Doctor, my daughter's taken ill. I don't know what is wrong. Please come to the house as soon as possible."

Sampson arrived half an hour later and diagnosed Thelma's condition as shock due to poisoning, most likely some sort of toxic reaction, mixed with exhaustion. He never took a blood sample, only routinely examined his patient. He attributed the poisoning to a poor diet. Either he never suspected diet pills or Alice steadfastly denied them. He put Thelma on a diet of fresh vegetables, grains, and meat and ordered bed rest for two weeks.

Thelma returned to the Roach Studios, bright, chipper, and looking very healthy in January of the following year. Her first film since her illness was again with Chase, *The Real Mc-Coy* in which she and Charley played hillbillies, a cute, silly comedy that added a delightful song, which was soon to become the trademark of the Chase series.

The comedies were upped to one a month, which was considered a fast but not impossible pace for such crank-'em-out two-reel comedies. Scenes were written while they were being shot, ad-libbing was standard, and the stars were encouraged to improvise within the confines of a loose plot.

Thelma and Charley hit their stride, both willing to do anything for a laugh and having the keen instinct to know what
would and would not work. Thelma began winning a reputation as a skilled comedienne who knew how to play to a camera and, yes, even take a pratfall. They were a delightful
couple, and it soon became apparent that the spark between
them was not entirely dependent on the lens.

Charley and his wife, BeBe, had an amiable but somewhat free-spirited marriage. BeBe spent long weeks away
from Charley at the couple's San Jacinto ranch; Charley spent
many lonely nights at home with a brandy bottle or writing
alone at his studio office. Charley was extremely well-liked by
both men and women at the studio; always a gentleman, always charming, and very much a ladies' man. Charley was
known to venture in and out of affairs with his leading ladies
and had an eye for blondes, especially solidly built blondes
like Thelma.

Thelma was lonely, homesick, and looking for a way to
escape from Alice, who now flew between Lawrence and Hollywood, arriving back home every few months to regale her
hometown friends with her exciting Hollywood life, dropping
names for effect and to enhance her social status. Thelma
made good use of her mother's absence to spread her wings
and fly on her own. It was not long before Charley and
Thelma's on-screen flirting sparked an off-screen dalliance.

They were ideally suited, both compassionate, caring in-
dividuals who enjoyed a good laugh, felt strong family bonds,
yet completely and wholly adored one another. In many
ways, their romance was more a puppy love than a mature
affair. For Charley, it was the thrill of romance without the
entanglements of a relationship. Thelma was not looking to
get serious with any man; she only wanted to have fun and
Charley provided her with the companionship she needed.
They were careful to give the impression of nothing more
than a close friendship to outsiders; they never went to parties
together yet always wound up talking and laughing together
most of the night. Thelma was even a frequent guest in the
Chase home and got to know BeBe very well. If BeBe knew
the truth, that the relationship was physical, she never let on.
She too was won over by Thelma's sweet, bubbly personality.

The Chase-Todd comedies reached the same level of popularity as the other Roach comedy coupling, Laurel and Hardy. Instead of being merely an enhancement to a feature film, the Chase comedy shorts were a draw in themselves. Thelma's name was mentioned in the trade papers and newspapers, and her picture was splashed in fashion and gossip columns. She was a star.

It was only a matter of time before Thelma went back to the diet pills. She drank to relax after work, drank at social functions, and drank out of loneliness. Drinking was quite common at the studios, and Thelma found no lack of drinking partners, male or female, including Chase. Alcoholism was still an affliction only of skid-row bums. The more elite "tippled," and no one took the problem seriously. Within months she started puffing up again from the booze, and fear of the dread potato clause pushed her back to the pills. She was hooked once again, but this time her addiction came in the one-two punch of drug/drink combination.

In April of 1931, Thelma again collapsed on the set. Production of *All Teed Up* was delayed several days while Todd recovered from what was termed "chronic exhaustion." After several days in bed, Thelma returned to finish the picture, then took a three months' vacation. On her agenda was a September cruise to Catalina Island and a week's rest and relaxation.

United Artists had been searching for someone to play the part of Helen in the film version of *Hell's Angels,* a Howard Hughes epic. The film had been in production for an unheard-of 104 weeks, bogged down with snags and delays since it started in 1928 as a silent movie starring Greta Nissen, Ben Lyon, and James Hall. But when sound came in, Nissen went out; her Swedish accent was too strong and unintelligible for the early crude sound equipment. U.A. was desperate to find another blonde to play the part, in order to salvage some of the silent footage in which Nissen was not easily recognizable. Toddy seemed the obvious choice, though she did not yet know it.

On the Catalina cruise she met a United Artists director, a man who would play a major role in the few remaining years of her life. His name was Roland West.

The attraction was immediate and mutual, though West was far from handsome and several years older than Thelma.

He was short, had dark hair, a tired, lined face, and soulful eyes. He was fairly successful as a director, with a handful of films to his credit, crime stories with thriller titles including *The Bat* (which West bought the rights to, produced, directed, and adapted for the screen in 1926, and in which he co-starred his wife, Jewel Carmen), *The Bat Whispers* (its talkie sequel of 1930), a Norma Talmadge melodrama called *The Dove*, and a tough-gangster bloodcurdler titled *Alibi*. He bankrolled many of his own films, pooling his money and his wife's, with additional backing by U.A. chief Joe Schenck. It was West who approached Thelma on board the ship, recognizing her from her films and the splash of press churned out by the Roach publicity mill.

The week's respite from Hollywood turned into another romance for Thelma, one of a series that seemed typical of Toddy's love affairs. She enjoyed the good times and the company; the men usually fell head over heels. West fell and fell hard. He pursued Thelma across the island and back to Hollywood. Thelma never ran very fast.

The romance centered around long talks, Thelma finally believing she had found someone who understood her loneliness, her need to escape Alice's domination, and her pent-up desire to be a serious actress, a flame that had never quite been extinguished in spite of her tremendous success as a comedienne. West understood and offered to help. Going beyond his authority, he promised her the role of the *Hell's Angels* blonde and told her to sit back and let him work on it.

Thelma returned to Roach and the Chase series in October, renewed in health and obviously preoccupied with another man and the promise of a new chapter in her career. The leading role in a drama like *Hell's Angels* was the break she had always anticipated, and she was certain the part was hers. She was as tall and blond as Nissen and just a tiny bit heavier, something she could easily deal with when she had signed the contract. Thelma recognized the serious health problems resulting from her dieting, and made up her mind to put off any weight-loss program unless it was necessary. She still looked cute and bubbly, and there were no complaints yet from The Boss.

Three weeks went by without any word from West; then, one afternoon in November, she received a call.

"Thel? Roland. Meet me at six at the Brown Derby. I might have good news."

Toddy knew the news was that she had the part. Excited, she put on her best, a white beaded gown and diamond earrings, and raced to the restaurant in her Packard convertible.

At the Derby, a maître d' escorted her to West's table. Sitting with West were two men, Joe Schenck and Howard Hughes. Thelma turned beet red and smiled. For the first time in her life she was speechless. She sat down and West did most of the talking.

"Mr. Schenck and Mr. Hughes agree you are perfect for the part. They've seen your work. There are several problems, though."

Thelma was positive it was her weight, which obsessed her.

Schenck spoke. "We're already deep into production. You will have to start immediately. Details of the contract will be worked out later. You know you'll have to be released from your obligation at Roach. Any problem with that?"

"I don't think so. I have a free-lance clause, so I think it should be all right." She paused, and looked down. "I really want the part. You know that, don't you?" She turned to West who was beaming at his "discovery." "Thank you."

The quartet celebrated with several rounds of drinks, Hughes doing more sipping than drinking, spending his silent time studying Thelma, who grew increasingly uninhibited with each drink. The party broke up shortly before midnight. Thelma went home with West, both giddy and giggly, in love with what they thought was a bright future.

The next morning snuffed out their excitement. What was supposed to be the triumphant beginning of a new life turned out to be the downslide into an abyss of torment for both West and Todd. Hal Roach earned his place in line with the other men who inched Thelma toward her ultimate destruction.

Thelma was in the midst of a full-blown Chase production, a three-reel musical called *High C's*. During a break, she asked to see Roach, who was in his office. He agreed to the meeting. He already had inside information on the *Hell's Angels* deal and was visibly angry because Thelma had not confided in him earlier.

"Before you say anything, I already know what's going on. The answer is no. I will not let you appear in *Hell's Angels*. I find it unbecoming to your character here. I spent a great deal of time and money promoting you as a Roach comedienne, not as some flier's tramp. I am exercising the contract option to either approve or reject your outside roles. This one I reject. Any questions?"

"Yes, just one. If it does not interfere with my schedule here, how can you stop me from working outside? You can't stop me from earning a living. What if I do it under another name?"

"Then wear a wig, change your height, and put a mask on your face."

"I might just do that."

"I am not going to release you from your contract. And no studio will hire you if you're under dispute here. It won't do you any good to walk out. I don't see that you have a choice."

"I've never walked away from a fight yet. I hope you're willing to go a few rounds."

"I used to be a boxer."

"And I used to be a lady."

Todd slammed the door, finished her day's work without saying anything to anyone. When she went home, she went straight to a bottle of Scotch and eventually fell asleep. The next morning she was jolted awake by a phone call from a very hot-tempered West.

"What in the hell did you do? Roach flatly refuses to let you appear in the film. Schenck's madder than a hornet. He says I wasted his time by pushing you when you weren't even available. Hughes is looking through his glossies for another girl. I thought Roach had given you the go-ahead."

"I figured he would. He had never stopped me before. He'll cool down and let me go. I know he will. Can you put Schenck and Hughes off a couple of days?"

"I can't promise, but I'll try."

While they battled it out, Thelma went on a wild drinking and shopping spree, drowning her frustration in expensive clothes and expensive alcohol. Three days later, she received the final word from West.

While he and Roach had been battling it out, the film's

co-stars, Ben Lyon and James Hall, brought a friend of theirs to United Artist and introduced her to the producers. She was perfect—blond, spunky, sassy, and available. She was hired on the spot and began work the following day. She was a bit-part comedienne who had appeared as an extra in several films, including, oddly enough, a Laurel and Hardy comedy for Roach called *Double Whoopie*. Her name was Jean Harlow. When she uttered the line "Excuse me while I slip into something more comfortable," she became a nationwide sensation. Thelma had just lost the biggest role of her life.

In the depths of despair, Toddy needed to get away, to escape. She went to the only place she had ever felt safe, to Lawrence. She met Mac, and they laughed and partied like old times. They flew to New York, saw all the sights, went to the best restaurants, and acted like two schoolgirls on holiday. Her first real trip home was the best medicine. She was relaxed and having fun, but the bottle was never very far away. Thelma acted so independent and sure of herself that the drinking never seemed to be of any significance, just part of the good times. When Toddy talked about her chauffeur, Mac assumed it was part of the wealthy Hollywood high life. Mac did not know that Thelma had already received several tickets in Los Angeles for drunk driving and had been ordered not to drive.

Her last night in Lawrence, Thelma cried. She desperately did not want to go back to California. She knew it was destroying her, body and soul. Mac was in no position to help Thelma fight Alice, who adamantly insisted her daughter fulfill her contractual obligations with Roach. Thelma returned, with Alice at her side, to the town that was slowly eating her alive.

Thelma assumed the debacle over *Hell's Angels* was all her fault. She chastised herself for not telling Roach sooner, for assuming she would be given the nod to appear in the film before she even asked Roach, for stringing West along when he was nothing more than a friend. She was ripped apart emotionally, taking every problem to heart, but she buried her feelings deep. Few of her co-workers on the Roach lot ever suspected Thelma was anything but happy-go-lucky and care-free, with the world at her feet.

When the others were a bit patronizing that one of their

own had been so unlucky, Thelma told friends that the *Hell's Angels* role was "no big deal. A blonde is a blonde and a part is a part." Thelma was a better actress than she suspected.

West, too, felt remorse over the mess that had started strictly from good intentions. He promised to make good on his vow to give Thelma's dramatic career a boost. He braced himself and mustered up his courage for another go-round against Hal Roach. This time, he was determined to win and made sure every legal obstacle had been knocked down before the fight.

The film that proved to be the final battleground for West (for a number of reasons) was *Corsair*, a melodrama in which a college football hero turns to crime to prove to the father of his wealthy, socialite girlfriend that he can support his ladylove in the style to which she has become accustomed. In the end, of course, the hero comes to his senses and stays on the straight and narrow, winning the girl's love and dad's respect. Chester "Boston Blackie" Morris was already cast in the lead, along with Frank McHugh. Toddy, West thought, was the perfect society girl.

Roach was consulted from the first, no behind-the-back negotiations. But still he refused to let Thelma depart from her bubbly-blonde image. West offered a tidy sum of money for Thelma's services, which would more than cover any loss to the studio or expenses incurred in hiring someone to fill in for Thelma on the Charley Chase series. Roach was intractable, but offered no explanation.

West stormed Roach's office with his attorneys, waved Thelma's contract under The Boss's nose and pointed out the free-lance clause. Roach coolly pointed out that he had a say in any outside dealings and he did not find this role suitable for Thelma's "Roach" screen image. He still offered no reason for his belief.

West then gave Roach an ultimatum—either Todd would be given the freedom to exercise the clause, or West would sue Roach for interfering with Todd's right to work. Right-to-work laws had not yet been tested, so both were treading on virgin ground. Roach laughed at West and played with the director much as a young boy plays with a yo-yo; he gave him a little slack, then jerked the string.

Roach gave West the green light to start production on

Corsair with Todd, but also he promised to counter the film's promotion with ads showing Thelma as a pratfall comedienne, in effect ruining any seriousness *Corsair* might achieve. West reposted, telling Roach he would change Thelma's name to completely dissociate Thelma Todd the comedienne from Thelma Todd the actress. The name he chose was one he had always favored, one he thought smacked of grace and elegance. The name was Alison Lloyd.

West immediately put Thelma to work posing for an endless series of publicity stills and newspaper interviews announcing the emergence of Alison Lloyd, the screen's most sensuous star. West told the press he had decided upon the name change so that "no taint of comedy might cling to Miss Todd's skirt." That statement sounded the first shot in a publicity war between West and Roach.

When Roach was asked for a response to the battle over his comedienne, he had an answer ready.

"When Miss Todd returns to the Hal Roach Studios, I shall change her name to Susie Dinkleberry, so that no taint of drama will cling to her pajamas."

The verbal battle nearly destroyed Thelma emotionally. Not once had she been consulted in the fight with Roach, not once had she been asked about her name change. Both Roach and West used her. For Thelma the entire affair recalled shades of her childhood, when she was manipulated by her father. She was three thousand miles away and fifteen years older, but she realized she had neither grown nor moved. She was right back in Lawrence, age ten.

Alice found the tug-of-war exhilarating; she saw the fight only for its publicity value and found it exciting that two powerful men would fight over her daughter. She could not understand her daughter's depression over the affair.

Corsair did go into production, but halfway through, Alison Lloyd was changed back to Thelma Todd. When the filming was completed, Toddy threw herself into her work, hopping from studio to studio (Roach surprisingly had no objections to other offers), appearing in such comedies as the Marx Brothers' *Monkey Business*, films for Warners, RKO, Pathé and Paramount, finally returning to Roach comedies with Charley Chase and Laurel and Hardy. It was absolutely impossible to see a comedy without Thelma Todd appearing somewhere in the film. Though Thelma was once again drinking heavily, not one word was ever mentioned about the battle on the Roach lot. Thelma was her vibrant self, sweet and charming. She kept her opinions to herself, and from all outward appearances the problem had long since been resolved. Thelma hid her wounds from everyone but her friend Mac.

"Dear Mac," she wrote one afternoon, "I am miserable. I'm so lonely. I'm looking forward to getting back home. Maybe next time I'll have a few weeks. Save a cup of cocoa for me! Till then, Thel."

While the furor over *Corsair* seemed to have little lasting effect on Thelma, it had a disastrous effect on West's career. Apparently he became fed up over U.A.'s lack of support in his battle against Roach—Schenck and U.A. took a neutral stand in the affair—and he lost his desire to produce and direct any other properties. He went into what would become permanent retirement from motion pictures and settled back into a quiet life with his on-again, off-again marriage to Jewel Carmen.

The ups and downs over *Corsair* brought West and Todd even closer as friends, though the romance had long since lost its bloom, at least on Thelma's part. They still dined together, spent some afternoons together, and chatted frequently by phone.

Though West was out of the movie business, he had his eye on other ventures; again he wanted Thelma to be a part of those plans. He talked of their buying a racehorse together, chartering a yacht, maybe even opening their own small studio when Thelma's contract with Roach ran out. He also tossed around another idea, something he had always dreamed about doing but he never had the time when he had the money. Now that he had both, it seemed the ideal business. West talked about opening a restaurant, a place where their movie friends would want to relax and dine, a place within driving distance but not too close in.

Toddy listened, more out of politeness than out of any belief something definite would ever come of West's schemes. The restaurant was the vehicle that would throw Thelma into the path of Lucky Luciano.

Chapter Ten

She was desperate to be loved, to have someone understand her longing for a romance that would be free and tender, who would not pull her into yet another confrontation and another battle. She had always been dominated by men—her father, the boy who sent her picture to the beauty contest, the talent scout, Zukor, Roach, and even West, who took it upon himself to change her name and use her as a wedge against The Boss. Thelma never knew how to fight back; she carried the hurt and frustration inside. Just once she would have liked to tell them all off and lash out against them. But she had never learned how to do that; she was taught from infancy to smile, to be sweet, and not to make a spectacle.

She was constantly surrounded by outwardly strong people who spoke up and left others to pay the price. Alice never held anything back, and if she ever really took the time to notice how completely she had suffocated her only daughter, she never let on. Alice was for Alice, and she believed the rest of the world damn well better be for Alice, too.

But inwardly, Thelma's closest associates were cowards; they had little compassion, little fortitude, they rarely showed restraint, no matter who wound up hurt at their expense. Thelma sought out these people, and they drew to her. To a certain degree, she possessed an inner strength that helped her carry on. The anger, frustration, hurt, and emotional abuse would have quickly destroyed a lesser woman; with Thelma it just took more time. Somehow, she managed to brace up, keep smiling, and carry on. Her sense of humor and quick-witted snappy comebacks were a kind of knee-jerk reaction, a defense and a release. She could make her remarks under the veil of comedy, and tell people off without reprimand. For this reason, it seemed natural that Thelma would end up a comedienne; comedy was a catharsis.

But if people had taken a good look at her, they would have seen the psychological battering taking its toll in many ways. Thelma was losing touch with her emotions; there was an emptiness at the core of her being.

Drinking was one way to fill that void; Thelma usually had champagne or Scotch within reach the second she stepped off the set. Her nights were usually spent drinking—with friends, at parties, or sitting home alone. Alice reprimanded her for drinking too much, especially after her series of drunk-driving tickets, but never took any real action. Instead, she hired Ernest Peters, a chauffeur, to drive Thelma to and from work and on shopping sprees. This luxury was also enjoyed by Alice, who was quite impressed at having a driver at her disposal. Her Hot Toddy was the life of the party, the fun-time girl who always was on the best invitation lists. Alice's name was often listed under hers and not always by the hosts' choice.

The drugs, first meant as a means of controlling her weight, were now a routine part of Toddy's life. She gulped handfuls of diet pills, convinced that if she stopped taking them, she would balloon up. Often they were her main food source, washed down with the booze.

What outward strength and courage she did not find in the bottle and in the pills, she sought through men. She had a compulsion to chase after men in authority or in a position of power. In itself, there was nothing wrong or unusual about a movie star's reaching for that next rung up the ladder. The attraction to power and the knowledge of how to achieve it were second nature to many stars. But in Thelma's case, it was different.

Her need to latch on to someone more powerful was not

so much a means of promoting herself as it was a way of attaining a strength she perceived as elusive, something dangled in front of her, yet always held just out of reach, first by her father, later by other men. The chase was a way of life for her. But when the chase ended, when the man obviously wanted to be caught, she froze. Winning was not part of the plan; she had never figured out how to end this type of game and she could not handle the affection. When the man she pursued became interested, she cooled. He then became the pursuer and she skirted emotional attachment.

It was natural that she would fall for Pat DiCicco. He was everything she had been raised to believe a man should be: strikingly handsome, powerful, rich, and aloof. Women openly chased after him and he responded to their affection with indifference if not outright hostility. He had a reputation as a slugger, a man who thought little of slapping or outright beating up a woman who crossed him. His association with gangsters was no secret. In fact, he liked to perpetuate such gossip as a means of keeping strangers both in fear and in awe. It helped when negotiating for a client.

In less than two years, DiCicco had worked his way into the studios to become one of the top managers in the business. He no longer needed to crash exclusive dinners and bribe security guards. He was now a key player, sitting alongside the men who held the power, Louis B. Mayer, Adolph Zukor, Joe Schenck. Behind his back, these men despised him; to them he was an outsider, a hoodlum, a punk kid who'd got lucky. But he moved in charmed circles, especially when the names attached to those circles included Lucky Luciano's.

Luciano flew to California every few months to check on business, to make sure his men were keeping the drug dealers in line and the stars well supplied. It was on a trip to Los Angeles, in mid-1931, that Luciano got a glimpse of something that sent chills up his back and put a knot in his stomach. While dining in the posh Brown Derby restaurant on Wilshire Boulevard, he thought he recognized the face of someone he imagined he had seen the last of long ago. He thought he saw the big, chubby face of Al Capone. This man Capone was sitting near the dance floor, close to the band, ordering the bandleader to play swing numbers, which Luciano detested.

"Impossible!" He grabbed DiCicco by the collar and pointed to a well-dressed Italian in the corner. "What the hell is that slime Capone doing here? The Feds got him. He's in court. Who the hell did he pay off, the president?"

The veins in Luciano's neck bulged. Capone was supposed to be in Chicago, on trial for income-tax evasion. The trial had begun in May and had already dragged on for five months. Though Capone bragged he would get a six-month term at most, no one doubted he would have to serve. Capone was the last man Luciano thought he would run into in Los Angeles, a town he considered his personal property.

"I pay you good money to watch things. I pay good money to people all over town. Why did no one tell me this pig was here?"

Luciano's temper got the better of him and he began shouting, which brought Capone over to Luciano and DiCicco's table. On closer inspection, Luciano saw this man was not Alphonse, but he was definitely a Capone.

Ralph Capone ran the outfit's bottling and brewery operations in Chicago; that job earned him the nickname "Bottles." By 1931, Bottles had been spending a significant amount of time in Los Angeles; it was part of Big Al's idea to swallow up service unions all over the country. Since the Capone organization already owned the bartenders' and related restaurant-industry unions in Chicago, and Capone was intriguing to the movie crowd, the move west to where the stars were was a natural progression.

The stars bragged about the new, opulent restaurants that were springing up all over the Hollywood and Los Angeles area, how they loved dropping hundreds of dollars on expensive dinners, especially now that the Depression made waiters, bartenders, anyone with a job, eager to provide the best of service.

Ralph Capone had been operating in Los Angeles, right under the nose of Luciano's men, for months. One by one, he had been taking over restaurants, bringing the owners in line much as his brother had when taking over breweries and businesses back in Chicago years ago. Restaurant owners who refused to go along were out of business.

Capone liked to hit the restaurants operated by people who could draw movie stars but who themselves were not professional businessmen. A prime example was a restaurant in the Sunset Strip area owned by Hal Roach comedienne Anita Garvin and her bandleader husband, Red Stanley.

They pooled their money and sank everything into the restaurant they called Red's. It was upstairs and quite elegant, with a band, a maître d', linens, and the best cuts of meat. Often both Anita and her husband greeted customers, the bulk of whom were the couple's movie friends.

They hired the maître d' from another restaurant, a successful operation down the street. They assumed he would organize the books, order the food, and keep things running smoothly. Oddly, though the restaurant was packed, they were losing money. Neither Anita nor Red knew enough about restaurants to immediately see the problem, so they kept pumping their own money into their business.

Then Anita began noticing that expensive cuts of steak were switched for cheap cuts of meat, the books were obviously being juggled, linens were coming back soiled, they had trouble keeping a regular staff, and tough-looking men frequently wandered in and out as if to "check the place out." Anita began asking questions and found out the maître d' was on the mob payroll and the substitute cuts of meat and other problems were a plot to drive the Stanleys out of business or force them to submit to mob control. Anita and Red refused to knuckle under.

Several weeks later, the usually crowded restaurant was empty, not one customer inside. Anita got curious and went downstairs to make sure the OPEN sign was on the door. What she found was a shock. The door was not only closed but chained as well. She removed the chain and rehung the OPEN sign, and customers eventually filtered in.

The incident was repeated several times until she found a CLOSED BY THE ORDER OF THE HEALTH DEPARTMENT sign on the door. The clientele began drifting away and eventually Anita and Red closed down. They lost the battle and their life savings. Capone's men had a new establishment.

This was an extension of business Luciano had not thought of, at least not for Los Angeles, but he eventually tried to correct the shortsightedness. When he saw Ralph Capone in the Brown Derby, acting very much as if he owned the place (which to a degree he did), Luciano put two and two together. He realized what Capone was up to and what he had been up to for some time. He quickly saw the money to be made at shaking down owners, seizing profitable restaurants, and driving competition out of business. He liked the takeover idea—a lot. Only his idea was to take things one step further, to open up gambling casinos, something not quite legal but not entirely illegal in California. Gambling laws were loose at best, and, of course, the lawmakers were easily influenced.

Luciano's sinister mind was now working at top speed. The town was still up for grabs but Capone's gang was closing in fast; he stretched his tentacles out as fast and as far as he could. Back-room betting parlors opened up, looking much like the old speakeasies, and right with them, brothels, all run by Luciano. All kept operating with payoffs and "donations" to politicians, police, the District Attorney's office, and landlords who found easy money in renting to Lucky, especially during the Depression.

But Luciano was not free to move without restraint. The obstacle was not from the law but from Ralph Capone, and in turn, Frank Nitti. Nitti, like Luciano, knew the wealth and opportunity in establishing organized drug, gambling, and prostitution rings in addition to controlling the West Coast unions. With Scarface Al headed for a fall, Nitti knew it was only a matter of months before Capone would be unable to stop him from infiltrating the Los Angeles and Chicago drug racket, something Capone had refused to do. When he saw Luciano had already made solid inroads as well as millions of dollars in Los Angeles, he knew he had to move quickly to get in on the action. In many ways, Nitti hoped Capone would get sent to the slammer—at least he would be out of the way.

It was not long before the two gangs clashed again, but this time their "war" was more covert than previous bloodlettings. The bosses argued in underworld business conferences while their underlings slugged it out in dark alley fights; they tried outbribing authorities, hoping Fitts and others would sell out to the highest bidder and run the other mobsters out of town. Instead, the greedy raked in the money and quietly laughed at the clashing titans.

Luciano had one advantage over Capone's men—he already had personal access to the stars, on their turf, through DiCicco. Of the entire Capone gang, only Al himself had a personal relationship with the famous, but it was not terribly influential when transferred 2,300 miles west through secondhand introductions. The Capone name was losing its clout with Al headed for jail. A gangster was glamorous, but a convict was a leper. Ralph Capone and his boys did not initially find a warm reception.

As Al Capone was being sent on his way to Atlanta Penitentiary, Thelma Todd was on her way up, finally achieving what few women in film had done to this point. In May of 1931, Roach called Thelma into his office for another one of the "briefings" that he often had with his players. He used them as rap sessions, letting the talent discuss problems, offer ideas, and generally clear the air. Roach gave the actors a status report on where he saw their films or careers headed. When Thelma received the summons, she assumed it was nothing more than a chance to hear The Boss tell her he was pleased with her work, and that she would continue with Chase and Laurel and Hardy. She was caught completely off guard when she saw her friend ZaSu Pitts sitting in the office.

Roach laid out his plan for the women. "Laurel and Hardy are the most successful comedy team going, perhaps the most successful team in history. It worked once, it will work again. I'm teaming you two up. It worked with Marie Dressler and Polly Moran years ago, but hasn't been tried since. I think you two will be able to pull it off."

ZaSu and Thelma stared at one another.

"Starring together, no second banana stuff?" Thelma was not yet convinced.

"That's the general idea. I have the first script already written. You two girls go on a double date to a New York nightclub. ZaSu, you're stuck with a loser. Todd, you're stuck with ZaSu. I'll direct it. It'll run three reels to give the audience a chance to get to know your characters. We start shooting next month."

"How about salaries?" ZaSu was already making top dollar as a character actress/comedienne at larger studios.

"We'll negotiate that separately, one on one. Todd, since

you're already under contract, I'll deal with you first. Pitts, we'll get back to you with a solid offer I believe you will like."

When ZaSu left, Thelma was again alone with Roach. Fortunately Alice had not been invited to this session and she had no inkling that this was going to be anything other than a chat with The Boss, so she did not try to worm her way in.

After a tough round of bargaining, Thelma signed a contract that, in her eyes, was astronomical. While the average worker was earning $20 a week, Thelma had just landed a deal that paid her $2,000 a week! It still had that awful potato clause in it, something Thelma expected but no longer feared. Her weight was no problem as long as she munched on diet pills. But the contract had something else that neither Thelma nor ZaSu expected, something that gave no hint at its manipulative intent. The two had similar contracts, but the agreements did not run concurrently. Thelma's contract expired six months after Pitts's. At first they thought it was an oversight. Later, they learned the truth.

Roach pulled the same stunt with Laurel and Hardy. He believed that allowing the contracts to expire at the same time gave the stars too much leverage, allowing them to walk out as a team. Holding one star to ransom left only one free to go, and half a team was usually no good to anyone. Roach, on the other hand, could always threaten to put the remaining star to work on his other comedies or pair the star up with another player, leaving the dissident star out in the cold.

The ploy worked with Laurel and Hardy and it worked with Thelma and ZaSu for a while.

To celebrate their newfound success, Thelma, Pitts, and the Roach gang threw a "pull out the stops" bash at the Palace Theatre, which had plenty of room for a big Hollywood studio party. Everyone who was anyone was there—Laurel and Hardy, Charley Chase, Hal Roach, Louis B. Mayer, Zukor, the Skouras brothers, who worked with the Fox theatres, Joe and Nick Schenck, Gary Cooper, Clark Gable, Jean Harlow, Alice, of course, and even Roland West, who was accompanied by his wife. The list was endless. It was also ominous. Mixing with the elite guests was a man who had seen the beautiful Thelma and had been wanting to know her for quite some time. When he saw her at the far end of the room, he pushed his way through the crowd and turned on the charm.

Thelma turned to greet the handsome stranger and a smile ignited, highlighting her dimples and enhancing her already shimmering eyes. The star was herself star-struck.

Thelma extended her hand and the stranger took it in his and kissed it.

"How very continental! I didn't catch your name. Have we met?"

"No, but that is about to change."

"I'm Thelma Todd."

"It is truly to pleasure to meet you."

The stranger stared into Thelma's blue eyes and paused for just a moment.

"I am Pat DiCicco."

Chapter Eleven

The Todd/Pitts comedies were a smashing success, propelling Thelma's career to even greater heights. She had scores of fan-magazine interviews, radio appearances, guest spots on stage shows, and cross-country tours to promote both her series and the Hal Roach Studios. She wrote beauty columns in magazines and received thousands of fan letters each week from around the country and around the world, where the Roach comedies (and other films in which she had appeared such as those for Columbia, Warners, and Paramount) played to packed houses. Thelma, not ZaSu, did most of the touring because it was Thelma the crowds wanted to see. She was put on a grueling, hectic schedule of production and tours; her energy waned.

A woman Alice had initially hired solely to clean their Hollywood home once a week was now kept on full time. Mae Whitehead did the grocery shopping, cleaning, and cooking for Thelma and Alice, Thelma being far too busy for chores, Alice being far too superior. Alice still bounced between Lawrence and Hollywood, and she felt Whitehead could also keep an eye on Thelma during Alice's absences. Whitehead basically kept to herself, did what she was hired to do, and remained loyal to Thelma, never going behind Thelma's back to Alice.

Thelma was on top of the world; she had fame, fortune, looks. She also had an avid admirer in DiCicco. Though the Roach sets were never considered "closed" (players frequently walked onto the sets of other companies, helping out in mob scenes and stunts and joining in on the fun, of which there was plenty!) there were rarely any outsiders on the lot. One of the exceptions on the Todd/Pitts set was DiCicco, who ingratiated himself with some of the cast and crew, but whom Roach kept at arm's length. He said he never trusted him. And with good reason.

DiCicco was passionately in love with Thelma, whom he called "My Lambie." They had a whirlwind romance filled with expensive dinners at the most exclusive restaurants, days at Santa Anita and Hollywood Park racetracks, afternoons cruising on private yachts (owned by friends of Pat's), long romantic drives up the coast to Santa Barbara and long weekends at the Hotel Del Coronado, a posh and popular moviestar hangout near San Diego. They sneaked off the set during breaks for paper-bag picnics and tag in the bean fields.

Thelma was slowly beginning to let down her guard, and DiCicco had the magic charm to break through her lifelong fear of getting close. Toddy was cautious and still not sure she could actually trust this man completely. Pat had power and strength and he appeared to let her into his world, daring her to open up, enticing her with bits and pieces of affection and love. It was a passionate courtship that seemed perfect—almost.

There was one area of conflict. Whenever Thelma asked about his family or friends, Pat instantly grew silent, aloof, and very cold. He refused to speak for the remainder of their date. Each time Thelma forgot and innocently made even a casual reference to Pat's personal life, he glared at her and made her feel guilty, as if she were prying. Perhaps she was; she was dying to find out if the rumors were true, if Pat knew the notorious gangster Lucky Luciano.

One afternoon at the beach, Thelma mentioned she was having a small party and told Pat he could bring a guest. The name of Charley Lucifer was never directly mentioned by

Thelma, but she and just about everyone else in Hollywood suspected the two were somewhat close. DiCicco took the invitation as another intrusion into his secret world. His violent temper finally erupted.

"Just who in the hell do you think you are pressing me? Get off my back!"

"Pat, look, I was only extending an offer. Come alone. Don't come at all. I don't care."

"You goddamn bitch. Who do you want me to bring? You want me to bring Luciano, huh? You think that would make you a big shot, a tough lady? You think you're going to use me to impress your friends? That's really all you want. Why do you push me?"

Thelma started crying hysterically. Somehow she felt, once again, that she was the cause of some problem.

"I don't care about Luciano. I know you never want to talk about him, but . . ."

"Then quit asking me about him. I know what you were getting at."

DiCicco assumed from the beginning that Thelma had a fascination with him primarily because of his connection with Luciano, something that had gnawed at him since the day he met Toddy. Though DiCicco was handsome and wealthy in his own right, he always felt submerged under Lucky's sinister shadow.

He slapped Thelma hard across the face and stormed off the beach, leaving Thelma stranded. She could not work for four days, until the swelling on her left cheek subsided. It was her first glimpse into the Jekyll and Hyde personality that was Pasquale DiCicco. It was also the first of many beatings at DiCicco's hand.

Thelma sensed she was treading in dangerous water, but it was water that was all too comfortable for her. DiCicco was exactly the type of man she expected and desired.

The romance was stormy in its good times, and the electricity between Pat and Toddy was explosive; whenever they were together they could barely keep their hands, let alone their eyes, off each other. Those who knew Thelma knew she was headed for marriage. Alice never interfered in the relationship, DiCicco was in many ways a reincarnation of John Todd.

Alice hoped for a splashy Hollywood wedding with hordes of newspaper and newsreel reporters snapping pictures and grabbing interviews. Always the stage mother, she assumed she would work her way into some of the photos to show the girls back home. Thelma disappointed her mother, and Alice made a point of rubbing Thelma's nose in her "ingratitude" every chance she had.

Thelma and Pat eloped on July 18, 1932. They ran away to Prescott, Arizona, and were wed in a quick, justice-of-the-peace ceremony. The sheriff's wife was their witness. They wired Alice from Prescott. She, in turn, started dialing wire services and newspapers to give them the scoop. Several photographers caught up with the couple in Arizona, and put a mention in the papers. Thelma had her marriage, Pat had his movie star, and Alice was left out in the cold.

Thelma phoned Mac to tell her the "good news." It was a brief phone call, but got to the point.

"Pat and I got married last week. You made the same move and look how it turned out for you! I figured if it worked for Mac, it'll work for me."

"That's wonderful, Thel, I'm so happy for you. I know you and Pat will be very happy together. I'm glad you finally found someone."

"Well, I can't stay single all my life, people start to talk."

There was a long pause on the phone. Mac knew Thelma well enough to know she was not as happy as a new bride should be, and her comment seemed somehow inappropriate.

"You okay, Thel?"

"Yeah. Yeah, sure I am. Why shouldn't I be?" Thelma was never very good at lying.

"Do you love him?"

"Pat's a great guy, Mac!"

"Do you love him?"

"I needed a friend. What's love anyway?"

"Are you happy?"

"I know of things that would have made me happier. But it's too late to start my life over again."

Mac knew something was very wrong, but she was powerless to help. She could only offer friendship and support from a distance and companionship on the rare occasions when Thelma returned to Lawrence for a visit.

Instead of pulling the relationship together, the marriage seemed to add further strain. They purchased a ranch-style home in Brentwood, something Thelma believed would entice Pat to take on the responsibilities of a family man. But Pat refused to settle down. More often than not, Thelma returned home from the studio to an empty house, with no idea where Pat was or how long he would be gone.

At times, DiCicco stayed out for hours, returning home at one or two in the morning; other times he stayed away until late the following morning. At least twice a month, Thelma would receive a long-distance call from Pat calling from New York to inform his bride that he was tied up on business and would be gone several days. He rarely explained the nature of his business.

Thelma did not know if Pat was seeing other women or if he was working some sort of shady deals with his "gangster friends" back east. She did not dare ask; any inquiry, no matter how remote, would trigger his temper and another sock in the jaw. Thelma had been married less than six months.

She had managed to wean herself from the Scotch and champagne during her courtship and the early months of her marriage. But the beatings and the fear of crossing Pat, coupled with the uncertainty and loneliness, nudged her back to the bottle. It was her only solace and the only way of hiding her misery; she found strength when the pain was dulled.

She also became more dependent on her pills, eating the speed-laced poison like candy; they gave her energy, counteracting the drowsiness caused by the alcohol. At work, she was full of fun, ready and willing to do stunts, mug for the camera, flirt, giggle, and be the sweet envy of her friends and co-stars. At home she believed her life was worse than ever and she was not sure if there was any point in going on.

Things continued to deteriorate between the couple, Thelma dividing her life between working and collapsing in bed, strung out, Pat straying farther and farther from home for longer and longer intervals. The situation reached a critical point in November.

Pat returned home from one of his frequent New York meetings and found Thelma doubled over in bed, screaming at the top of her lungs. He knew about her drinking and drug use and, at first, assumed it was some sort of drunken rampage. He shook her, yelled back at her, and threatened to leave her for good if this was the best reception she had to offer him. Then he saw her face was a scarlet-red and she was sweating.

"Pat, I'm sick. I'm really sick. Call the doctor."

For once, he did something to help her. She was operated on for appendicitis, and the operation had some positive side effects. The hospital stay provided complete bed rest for Thelma and helped get her off the pills and alcohol. It also gave DiCicco a scare and he remained at her side, a loving husband for the first time since their wedding. Thelma found some peace, and hoped things were finally getting better. But this shred of happiness was not to last long.

In February, on a cold and rainy California night, Thelma once again returned to find Pat gone—no note, no call, nothing. Bored and rebellious, Toddy called Roland West and asked him to meet her at the Brown Derby for a few laughs and a late-night dinner.

West, who had recently separated from Jewel Carmen but was still living in their Pacific Palisades home on Posetano Road, agreed and arrived shortly before Thelma. A waiter escorted him to a table near the back of the main dining room, a quiet area where he and Thelma could talk. Thelma arrived about fifteen minutes later and sat down.

"Let's do something wild, something crazy. How about another trip to Catalina? Or a cruise somewhere? Just to get away?"

West was still smitten with Toddy so it was difficult for him to remember she was a married woman. "Thel, you know I'd love to. I'd love to go anywhere with you. You're a tough lady to say no to, but Pat's even tougher. I think I would prefer to live a few more years, thank you."

"Screw Pat. I don't even know where the hell he is tonight. Probably off with some tramp somewhere. I think he's been cheating on me, but I can't prove it. I hear talk, but nothing specific."

"You still fighting with him?"

"You mean ducking him? We don't fight as much because we don't see each other as much. We're getting along okay, I guess. He's got that Italian temper. At least Mom's staying out of it now. She always used to side with Pat and she didn't even know what the hell we were fighting about. She'd just assume I started it—he's the man and all. You know how she is. Dad always kept her on the string. I stand up to Pat and she doesn't like it. She doesn't understand as much as she think she does."

"I know. I came up against it."

Toddy and West laughed out loud. They were talking about the time, right after they met in Catalina, when Thelma introduced West to Alice in the Todds' Hollywood home. Though Alice was falling all over herself to be polite to West because of his movie-director status and the promise of what he might do for her daughter, Alice was aghast that Thelma would be seen in the company of a married man—a married man who had obvious intentions toward her single—and much-younger—daughter. When West left that afternoon, Alice lashed into Thelma, calling her every foul name she could think of: Thelma was being the seductress and West the innocent victim of her daughter's charms. She refused to believe it was West who did the chasing. She never accepted their relationship when it later evolved into a friendship.

"I've broken up with Jewel, this time I think for good. We just decided we were better off apart. Since I retired from directing I'm no longer a real part of that crowd, and she still is. I'm still going to stay in the house because we'd lose so much if we divided the property up in a divorce settlement. It's big enough for two."

"As long as it works. You tried it before and ended up moving out into some small apartment."

"That was when we thought it still might work. We're friends now, and that's okay with both of us. I think Jewel might even be seeing someone, which is fine."

"What are you going to do in the meantime?"

"There's a nice piece of property at the end of the road, down the hill from the house. You've seen it."

"That row of stores?"

"Yeah. Well, it's vacant now, for sale. I was thinking of buying it, maybe opening up that restaurant I've been talking about for so long. Since Jewel and I still share our estate, we would invest in the property together, but her involvement would be in name only. It would really be my place. We've already talked about it."

"Sounds like a great idea. It's just . . ." Thelma happened to look up and see something she had never expected. Over in the corner, across the room, she saw a man in the distance, partially hidden in the crowd of diners, but she recognized him immediately. It was Pat, looking very secretive. He was talking to a dark-haired man who was impossible to see clearly from Thelma's table.

West looked at Thelma, then turned to the direction in which she was looking. He saw nothing that could have captured Thelma's attention so rapidly. Almost mechanically, Thelma rose from her chair and walked trancelike over to her husband's table, weaving past the other tables as if they were not there. When she reached the table she stopped and stared, still in a daze.

Pat, always the smooth-talking gentleman, never ruffled in public, made the introductions as if Thelma had been expected.

"I'd like you to meet my wife, Thelma Todd. Thel, this is a friend of mine, Charles Luciano."

Thelma extended her hand; she knew who Luciano was, everybody did. She had just never expected to meet him at all, let alone dining with her husband. Here was the man Pat was so determined to keep from his wife, becoming so hostile whenever she hinted at a meeting.

She had never understood whether Pat kept them apart as a means of protecting her or to have something with which to lord over her. She was never privileged to know what Luciano had said, if anything, about her, but it was assumed her name did come up in conversation with the killer. If Luciano loved anything at all, he loved blondes, especially beautiful blondes. Pat possibly sensed that and steered Luciano clear of his wife out of jealousy or fear of competition from someone he might not beat.

"It's a pleasure to meet you, Miss Todd. I've seen many of your movies. You are quite beautiful. More beautiful in person than I had imagined." Luciano kissed Toddy's hand.

Here was this monster, this killer. Yet he had a certain charm about him, instantly mesmerizing Thelma as she stared deep into those cold, dead eyes. If anyone had the ability to hypnotize, it was Charles Luciano. He was a lucky man indeed.

Prohibition was still in its last throes. Talk of repeal was everywhere, the main topic of conversation among millions of people who remembered the good old days ten years back before hip flasks were a part of fashion and imported liquor was shipped in from places farther than ten miles away. The only ones not tired of Prohibition were the gangsters who were still raking in millions of dollars a month. The idea of repeal rankled them; they had a lot to lose. Franklin Delano Roosevelt had just been sworn in as president and big-monied vice lords were lobbying hard to keep the country dry.

Getting liquor was never any problem for Luciano, and he could get the real stuff. He ordered an imported bottle of French champagne for the trio.

"I didn't want to interrupt your meeting, Mr. Luciano. I just didn't expect to see Pat, and I . . ."

"Do not worry. You are always welcome to accompany me at any time. Such beauty is something to be valued as a gift and accepted whenever it is offered." The words took on added resonance from Luciano's thick Italian/Brooklyn accent, an odd mixture that Thelma found disarmingly gallant.

DiCicco had had enough. He wanted to leave and keep his wife out of the clutches of Luciano. He knew it was just a matter of time before Luciano moved in on his Hot Toddy.

Though they were business associates, Pat knew just how evil this man really was. He had witnessed Luciano in action many times. Luciano had destroyed countless lives through drugs and prostitution, and women who became involved with him ended up in the gutter. Luciano fed off women, devouring them, then leaving them for fresh game.

DiCicco knew Thelma was powerless against powerful men and that she would easily fall under Luciano's spell. He had separated this man from his personal life, especially from Thelma. Now fate had intervened.

Luciano poured three glasses of champagne. Thelma stared at the glass; her old enemy was once again before her. She had not had a drink since her operation nearly four months ago and had stayed away from the pills, taking them only when she knew she would be invited to a big, social dinner where it would be too easy to gorge. Pat stared at Toddy, anticipating the consequences of that drink.

"Enjoy it, my dear. This is the best money can buy. Is it not good enough?"

"Yes, Mr. Luciano. I'm rather tired and I really don't care to . . ."

"In Italy it is considered an insult to refuse a drink offered by the host."

Luciano drew his brows together in more of a glare than a frown; it was this look that was more intimidating than his manner. Its meaning was clear.

Thelma looked at Pat for both approval and understanding, and in the hope that he would step in to get her out of a tense and awkward situation. He did nothing except raise his glass in a toast, making an already terrible situation even worse.

"Salute!"

Luciano raised his glass to meet DiCicco's. Thelma joined. Luciano kept pouring, kept insisting she drink and kept refilling her glass, ordering more and more champagne. Toddy gave up the fight. She knew she was back on the road she thought she had detoured from several months ago. Luciano enjoyed the company of the now-bubbly blonde. Toddy had finally met the man of ultimate power; she had reached the pinnacle. Now she was about to taste life on the other side of the mountain.

Chapter Twelve

Luciano had plenty of reasons to stay in Los Angeles. Thelma Todd was one reason, but far from his main concern. To Luciano, Toddy was a diversion, an amusement, a good-looking blonde to drape across his arm when he needed company. Her marriage to Pat was a boon; as long as she was married there was a very comfortable wall between them if and when Toddy got too close or expected anything in return.

Luciano's main concerns in Los Angeles were his businesses—gambling, drugs, prostitution, and restaurant/union infiltration. With the prospect of repeal closing in, Luciano and the other mobsters knew the only future money was in these types of dealings. The one obstacle for Luciano was Nitti, who already had shaken down most of the big restaurants and was making it clear he wanted bigger game—Luciano's turf.

By mid-1932, Frank Nitti and accountant Jake Guzik had served time for income-tax evasion and had been released, Ralph Capone was winding up his short jail term, and the mastermind, Al Capone, had just been shipped to Atlanta. In spite of its name, Atlanta Penitentiary was nothing more than Capone Headquarters, South. The same operations Capone had used in Chicago were now being carried on within the confines of steel bars and under the eye of uniformed guards.

For Capone, the pen was much safer; here there were no bomb scares, no drive-by shootings, no real attempts made on his life. For the first time in years, Big Al found a place in which he could operate freely without fear of being caught off guard by an enemy. He did not know that the real enemy was the man he trusted to run his outfit, Frank Nitti, who eventually pushed the gang into areas Capone staunchly opposed.

His "office" was a carpeted jail cell with a typewriter, ticker-tape machine, and chairs for visitors. When he needed privacy to conduct his business, the warden graciously left his office and let the Big Guy use the facilities, phone and all, for his meetings. Nitti and Guzik were Capone's most frequent visitors, and they relayed messages and orders from Big Al to the others. Jail, it seemed, was merely a minor inconvenience for the mob.

Nitti continued to transmit orders, embellishing only slightly at first, then slowly offering his own ideas to the gang. He emerged as the new, acting head of the Capone organization in spring of 1933, during Chicago's "A Century of Progress" fair, eliminating Ralph Capone from dominance. Through Nitti's manipulation, the Capone gang ran every concession booth, every restaurant, every garbage-collection service, and every laundry outfit connected with the fair. In fact, it was completely Nitti's deal on behalf of Capone. The fair was a multimillion-dollar haul, and Nitti was persona grata. Pleased with his protégé, Capone handed over his operation to Nitti, to keep it running until he got out of prison. Capone had only one message—stay out of drug peddling. Nitti heard but refused to listen.

Capone was always positive his eleven-year sentence would be whittled down to months. He had been greasing palms all the way up to the White House, and never gave up hope of freedom, right until the end. He had no idea that although his money was being pocketed, nothing was being done because his case was far too notorious and had received far too much publicity to sweep it under the rug. He was left to fend for himself. With assurances Capone would be out of the way for some time, Nitti negotiated quite nicely for the Scarface mob.

Nitti quickly sent emissaries to Los Angeles to put more pressure on restaurants and nightclubs already under its control and to infiltrate new establishments. Nitti moved faster than Luciano, had a more visible force behind him, and was therefore more effective at taking over the L.A. nightclubs. He began infiltrating long before Luciano thought of the town for anything more than drug peddling.

March 15, 1933, was the day that, for the underworld, will live in infamy. Repeal became law, bootleg booze was a thing of the past, and breweries, run by legitimate businessmen, swung open all across the country. Speakeasies once again became legal saloons and free enterprise. Fortunately for the Capone gang, the brunt of their business was already shifting from bootlegging to union organization.

Luciano had never really dealt in bootlegging, so for him, drug peddling became even more lucrative. People who had kept on the straight and narrow during Prohibition were now swilling newly legal brew with the best of them. Once they indulged in booze, many liked the high and made the easy transition to drugs. Luciano and his men were there, eager to accommodate.

Los Angeles quickly became the new center of organized crime, an open territory still being carved up by two ruthless factions. When Luciano's men closed in on an establishment for gambling or prostitution, they often found Capone's men already there organizing the unions or seizing control of the liquor, linen, or meat orders. Luciano did not like anyone to cross him, especially anyone associated with his foe Capone.

The crisis was especially acute because Luciano was battling an enemy that threatened to fight him on his own ground. Unlike Capone, who was Neapolitan, Nitti was Sicilian and therefore had developed the same gut instincts. The two Sicilians were similar in another area—they were both deceitful for their own advantage and would stop at nothing to achieve what they wanted. To them, even their own destruction or death was considered part of the price to pay for ultimate victory. To them, there was honor in death.

With Capone behind bars, Nitti felt free to cross barriers Big Al would not approach. Nitti eyed the drug operation in Los Angeles, something Luciano had locked tightly in his grip. Luciano, in turn, wanted control of the restaurants, something Nitti had pretty well sewn up. The two vultures circled one another, eyeing each other's method of operation, looking for a weakness or opening that would let them rush in and destroy the opposition. It was increasingly evident the two were headed for a bloodletting.

There was another avenue for piling up millions of dollars that was as yet untouched by organized crime—the motion-picture industry. The end of Prohibition forced the mobsters to take a good look around for new areas of corruption and control, and they finally cast their eyes upon the golden goose that was Hollywood.

The shakedown of the motion picture industry actually started in Chicago, with two loudmouthed braggarts named Willie Bioff and George Browne.

Bioff was by far the more evil, the more cruel, the sicker of the two. He started life as a shill, luring men into Southside whorehouses. He was only nine years old when he approached men on the street telling them that his "mother was gone for the afternoon and his little sister was awfully cute." Those he lured in were steered not to Willie's house, of course, but to a back-alley brothel filled with more mature, well-worn women. To Willie, it was all a game.

As he got older he realized the easy money in running a red-light inn. The only outlay was in paying off police who were often open to such extra income. The girls did all the work; he received a large percentage of their take. When he married in his early twenties, he and his wife recruited farm girls, promising them work as "household helpers," paying their expenses and telling them exciting details of the "big city." Usually these girls were uneducated, backwoods types who thought the big city meant a chance at freedom from farm chores, a chance to get out of a one-horse town and meet a man of substance. They were partially correct. They did get away from farm work and they did meet men of substance, sometimes. But there was no freedom. Bioff and his bride kept the girls locked up, literally holding them prisoner in the brothel. Those who tried to escape were punished by Bioff, who would twist their breasts with pliers and threaten to throw acid in their faces. It kept the girls in line.

Once one of his girls got the best of Willie. She escaped after suffering a severe beating at Willie's hands. She ran to the police department and somehow managed to filter through the cops on the payroll. Bioff was arrested and sentenced to a six-month term for aggravated assault and battery. Willie served only one day of the sentence. He greased the right palms and was released. But there was a slipup; the conviction was never expunged from his record and remained outstanding. Willie thought his problems were over, but this would come back to haunt him.

Eventually the enterprising Bioff expanded his holdings by shaking down the Fulton Street shopowners. There were delis, fish markets, butcher shops, all importing and buying food by the bulk for resale to bigger businesses. Bioff kept to his own side of the street, the "Jewish" side. He offered protection for the price of a few dollars a week. Some paid immediately because they recognized a shakedown from the old country. Those who balked were "spoken to," and told that the rest of the owners were footing the bill for those holdouts who were refusing to kick in.

If the guilt trip proved unsuccessful, Bioff told stories of shopowners being bombed out, their produce drenched in gasoline, their families beaten or ultimately killed. His protection was to prevent that from happening, though Willie, of course, was the man who ordered the terrorist attacks. For those who still held out, the prophecy of bombs, destruction, and death came true. Bioff also earned part-time income working for the Teamsters' Union as a slugger, collecting dues from those who were reluctant to join or holding out on their kickback to the union. Between the Teamsters, brothels, and butchers, Willie had a nice fat income.

George Browne was similar to Bioff in appearance. Both men were short, fat, wore wire-rimmed glasses, dressed in expensive suits, and wore their hair slicked back. But unlike Bioff, Browne was better educated—he had gone to school, dropping out in the fifth grade.

Browne also sold protection on Fulton Street, but he worked the "Gentile side," using terrorist tactics similar to those successfully employed by Bioff. Browne's primary source of income was as business agent of the Chicago Stagehands Local No. 2, which was affiliated with a national group called IATSE (International Alliance of Theatrical Stage Employees), the union that controlled most of the stagehands in the big theaters in New York, Chicago, and Los Angeles and a moderate percentage of the Hollywood studios' stagehands. He went through tough times during the Depression. When a great many of his men were thrown out of work, Browne generously accepted a pay cut from his $250 a week to $187.50 a week, and agreed to reduce his work with the union "to be fair."

The pair first met on Fulton Street, during one of their weekly protection shakedowns. They sized each other up and knew there would be a bloodbath before one could come out on top and control the entire market section. Instead of fighting, they worked out an agreement—each continued to shake down the shopowners on his side of the street, but the funds were pooled in a partnership they cleverly named "B&B," for Bioff and Browne—or Browne and Bioff, depending on which was asked.

From the Fulton Street shakedowns, they expanded their domain to Browne's Stagehands operation. Dues were immediately raised 1 percent, or about five dollars a week, to fund the B&B operation. Then, over dinner, the two dreamed up a plan to tap the theater owners for steady, tax-free income.

Using the threat of a stagehands' strike, Bioff and Brown approached Barney Balaban, who headed Chicago's largest and most successful movie house/theater chain, the Balaban and Katz Theatres.

When they first approached Balaban, they were summarily ejected from his office, a bit of spunk the pair had not expected. They had come hat in hand and a bit nervous, something they realized was a serious error and miscalculation with Balaban. They never even had a chance to explain what they wanted. But they were undaunted and determined not to let Balaban get the better of them. They understood that once the biggest was won over, the others would be easy pickings. Their philosophy was accurate.

Their second attempt was a bit more forceful. They were arrogant, aggressive, and prepared to pull the stagehands out of all B&K theaters if necessary. This time Balaban listened. Browne did most of the talking. He laid out the deal—Balaban was to fork over $20,000 to the B&B combine in lieu of a pay raise for the stagehands. That money, Browne explained, was to go into a fund. The fund was to be set up for union members who had emergencies and could not work, to loan to the members, and to get stagehands who were laid off back on their feet.

Balaban understood what Browne was really saying: The

money was a bribe to hold off wage hikes, pure and simple. Balaban granted Bioff and Browne power they might not have had at this point. But he was still reluctant to pay.

When Browne was hospitalized with an ulcer, Balaban visited him in his private room to "talk over the pay raises." Balaban explained that Tommy Maloy had been pocketing $150 a week from Balaban, and in turn Maloy never asked for pay hikes for his men. Balaban offered to take care of Browne in the same way.

Browne thought the deal was rather funny. He was worried about approaching Balaban when all along Balaban had been paying off in a corrupt partnership with Maloy. Browne told Balaban "no deal." He knew he had him right where he wanted him.

Balaban finally agreed to pay the twenty grand in a check made payable to the B&B soup kitchen, which was a racket similar to Capone's in that it was a good place to launder money. The check would be turned over to the pair by Leo Spitz, Balaban's attorney.

Spitz met Bioff and Browne the following day in their office, check in hand. But before turning over the money, Browne later testified, Spitz insisted he be allowed to keep $1,000 for "carrying charges." The reverse shakedown by Spitz confirmed a suspicion Browne and Bioff had all along— no man was above corruption. Bioff and Browne agreed to cut Spitz in, believing that he, too, was now ripe for further pay-offs, and pocketed the $19,000 for themselves.

When Spitz left, Bioff and Browne did a little fandango. They knew Balaban was a sucker, but they had never dreamed the scheme would be all that easy. They thought Spitz was a fool. They were still laughing when they went to Club 100, a nightclub owned and operated by a gent named Nick Cirella, aka Nicky Dean, a very close pal of Frankie Rio, who was Al Capone's cousin and enforcer/hit man for Capone gang heir Frank Nitti. As it turned out, Bioff and Browne were bigger suckers than Balaban.

It was early 1934, Prohibition was a glorious memory, and the booze was flowing above the tables. Bioff and Browne downed drink after drink, getting louder, more boisterous, and more obnoxious with each drink. They started bragging to each other about their "kill," how smart they were, reenacting their lines, what Browne said, what Bioff said, what Balaban said. Each time, the story grew more colorful and the amount of the shakedown increased. They had no idea they were being watched and their words carefully listened to by Cirella, who did not miss a trick when it came to finding new avenues of income for himself or for his cousin. Their big-mouthed bragging cost them autonomy over their racket. They would now be forced to share their wealth.

Cirella bought beer and bourbon for the two, who also helped themselves to several rounds of "26," a popular dice game, dropping hundreds of dollars at a time. Nicky Dean, always the congenial host, offered the pair his best girls, who led the boys upstairs for an evening of fun and frolic. Cirella had more than enough information and knew the boys would be busy and out of earshot for most of the night.

Cirella got on the phone and quickly reported the story to Nitti, relating details of names, places, and amount taken in. He also made it clear that the Chicago Stagehands Local No. 2 was an "owned" union, meaning it was corrupt and under the control of a specific group of men. Again Capone's motto held true: "Once corrupted, always controlled." The Stagehands Local was corrupted and controlled by men who were corrupted, therefore prime to be controlled. Such a union, already paying bribes and set up for more, was exactly the type of enterprise Nitti envisioned as the future of organized crime.

Nitti sent word to Bioff and Browne that he wanted to arrange a meeting with them, regarding union business, the following day. The two were flattered that their nickel and dime antics had caught such a powerful eye as Nitti's and arrived at the Lexington Hotel fifteen minutes early. They were held downstairs until Nitti passed the word for them to head up to his office.

Nitti laid out his plan simply and carefully so there would be no mistake. The Syndicate (composed of all major-city ruling gang bosses) wanted in; it would take over the Stagehands Local, leaving Bioff and Browne as bagmen, the men who did the collecting. The Syndicate would split fifty-fifty, and offer protection and enforcement if anyone tried to come up against B&B. In other words, their position was secure, for a price.

Nitti also sweetened the deal a bit more. He offered to back Browne in his bid for president of IATSE, a post Browne had previously sought but lost. Nitti knew that if the Syndicate controlled the entire IATSE union, it could pull off similar Balaban-style shakedowns in theaters across the country. Nitti told Browne he would arrange to make sure the East Coast and other big-city locals would also back Browne for office. He rattled off the names of vice lords in Cleveland, St. Louis, New Jersey, and New York. He named New York boss Leo Lepke, who, Nitti said, promised to deliver the entire East Coast. Nitti also tossed around the name of Lucky Luciano, someone he had not approached about his proposition, but someone he could not overlook if his scheme was to work.

Nitti knew Luciano would be trouble. The fuse between the two was short, and getting shorter by the day because of the long-standing hatred between Luciano and Capone, and the more recent rivalry in Los Angeles. Luciano wanted in on the restaurants; Nitti wanted in on the drugs. Neither seemed willing to trade pieces of his kingdom for a slice of the other's action.

Nitti called an underworld conference, drawing the Syndicate leaders from across the country to Chicago. Luciano was the real target of the meeting and he knew it. He refused to reply to Nitti's invitation until the morning of the conference. He arrived ten minutes late as a show of disrespect for Nitti. Nitti mapped out his plan.

Capone's West Coast representative, Johnny Roselli, who had been keeping an eye on several operations in and around Los Angeles, explained to the group how unions were set up in Hollywood, which studios and companies employed how many men and from what unions, covering which specific jobs. He gave an estimated total of the income skimmed from the union dues and pension funds, which amounted to in excess of half a million dollars.

Roselli also pointed out that the majority of workers in Hollywood were not members of any union, therefore ripe to be organized, especially with the Depression threatening to throw them out of work and lose them what little income they had. The Depression was also a lever to entice men with illusions of even higher pay and job protection. Roselli believed there would be little resistance from the Hollywood work force, especially if the workers were given a fair and democratic choice—join up or don't work.

Nitti explained the obvious advantages if the group

worked as a Syndicate, as one massive monster spitting out orders and gobbling up the profits, rather than as scattered groups fighting one another for control. The bosses were in agreement except for Luciano, who stood up from his chair at the table and pounded his fist.

"I don't trust you. You and that fat pig friend of yours, Capone. Why should we kick in with you? Who decided you should run this Syndicate? You own nothing in Hollywood; I control the real money and the big theaters are in New York, not Chicago. You got nothing."

Nitti steadied his temper before he replied. "Charley, you and I are both Sicilians, blood brothers. I understand you and you understand me. This is not Al's plan, this is mine. Through George Browne I have already put the wheels in motion. We will soon control the American Federation of Labor. This movie business . . . there is plenty to go around. If we fight, we gain nothing. I am only the figurehead; we are all equal partners according to the size of our territory."

"I will not throw my territory to you. You have never shown yourself to be a man of trust. You are Sicilian by birth, but not by blood. Your blood runs different than mine."

"If you do not come in with us, we will take what is rightfully ours. Leo Lepke is already prepared to move in his people [Murder Incorporated]. You do not fight only me, you fight us all."

Luciano was silent. He knew he would either have to fight a gang war he had no chance of winning or join in with the pirates.

"You need me. You have something I want. I want freedom to move in on nightclubs on the West Coast. I want your assurances you will not interfere with my drug operation there."

Nitti thought carefully before making such a promise in front of witnesses.

"I will only grant your request for nightclub operations. We will settle our other differences at another date."

Luciano stormed out of the meeting, but knew what he would have to do. He sent his answer by messenger the next week. It was a two-word telegram—MI INCLUDE, meaning "include me in."

That hour-long meeting set the wheels in motion for the most outrageous, explosive shakedown in history, never again

matched for its cunning, boldness, ruthlessness, and long-last-
ing ramifications on an entire industry. In that meeting, in the
cold, wintry months of 1934, in a conference room in a Chicago
hotel, the "Million Dollar Movie Shakedown" was born. What
those men believed they were organizing was simply a
squeeze, a tapping of income of rich, naïve movie men and the
organization of yet another union. No one in that meeting had
even guessed at its potential impact on history.

Nitti had known Tommy Maloy for several years, as all
gangsters knew or had heard of one another and their dealings, especially when there was money involved. Maloy had a
reputation around Chicago as a tough union man, and he ran
his projectionists' union with raw nerve. He was unstoppable
until 1934, when he approached Nitti for two favors.

Maloy had been under pressure from the Treasury Department for income-tax evasion, a plague that by now
haunted almost every gangster. He owed some $81,000 in
back taxes and faced federal charges that threatened to put
him behind bars for several years. He pleaded for Nitti's help
in getting the case reduced to a short six-month sentence or
fine as Nitti had done with members of the Capone gang.
Maloy also needed a second favor, one that eventually cost
him the whole operation.

He wanted Nitti to support him for first vice-president of
IATSE in the same election Nitti and the Syndicate had already groomed Browne to win as president. Nitti promised
support in exchange for the "road map" to Maloy's local—the
names and addresses of those on the payroll, the amount of
bribes being paid out, the amount of money Maloy had been
skimming, and the working of the projectionists' union itself.
Maloy assumed it was a trade for greater power and handed
over his life's work to the power-hungry Sicilian. Nitti then
went one step farther. He ordered Browne to take over
Maloy's union in a "caretaker capacity" until after the election, which Nitti promised Maloy he would orchestrate.
Maloy had handed over everything, lock, stock, and barrel,
and was now an expendable commodity. Maloy was too blind
to see the writing on the wall.

The girls from Lawrence—1925. From left: Toddy, Ann McMahon ("Mac"), Katherine McMahon (Mac's sister), and Ann Monahan, behind the Todd home   G. MULLANEY

Mother Alice and daughter Thelma. Alice never could let go of her little girl.
AUTHOR'S COLLECTION

The publicity photo that brought Alice to Hollywood. "Hot Toddy" in a test photo for "American Venus." A bit too much skin for Mom's liking   AUTHOR'S COLLECTION

Comedy's most handsome couple—Thelma and Charley
Chase in a publicity photo. If fate had only played a different
hand.   AUTHOR'S COLLECTION

ZaSu Pitts and Toddy in the Todd-Pitts comedy *Seal Skins*   AUTHOR'S COLLECTION

Thelma, Frank McHugh, and Chester Morris in *Corsair*. Roland West tried to make Toddy a dramatic actress and billed her as Alison Lloyd.   AUTHOR'S COLLECTION

A very puffy Thelma in a candid shot. The effects of drinking are starting to show . . . and it's back to the diet pills.   AUTHOR'S COLLECTION

Thelma in a publicity photo, wearing the mysterious sardonyx ring. Was it stolen from her finger when she was killed? AUTHOR'S COLLECTION

Thelma, Charley Chase, Charley's daughter June, and Patsy
Kelly on the Hal Roach lot   AUTHOR'S COLLECTION

On the set with director Gus Meins, co-star Patsy Kelly,
Thelma, and Eddie Foy, Jr., of the Todd-Kelly
series   AUTHOR'S COLLECTION

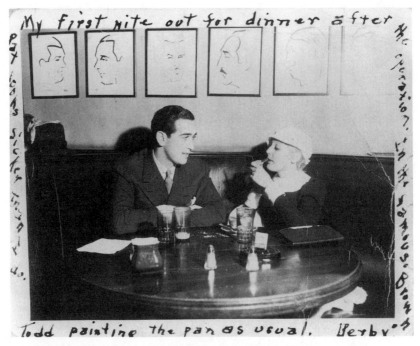

My first nite out for dinner after the operation. In the famous Brown Derby. Pat looks sicker than I do. Todd painting the pan as usual. Herb

"My first night out for dinner after the operation. In the famous Brown Derby. Todd painting the pan as usual. Pat looks sicker than I do." Toddy and Pat DiCicco shortly before their divorce.   G. MULLANEY

Charles "Lucky" Luciano. They called him Charley Lucifer behind his back.
AP/WIDE WORLD PHOTOS

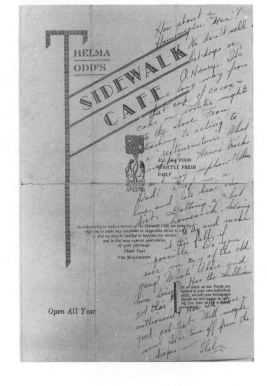

"Life isn't very exciting. People bore and distract me to death . . ." One of Toddy's last letters to Mac written on board West's yacht, the *Joyita*.
G. MULLANEY

The cover of a Sidewalk Cafe menu. The letter was written to Mac about one year before Toddy's murder.
G. MULLANEY

Toddy with White King, only a few months before Toddy's
murder.   AP/WIDE WORLD PHOTOS

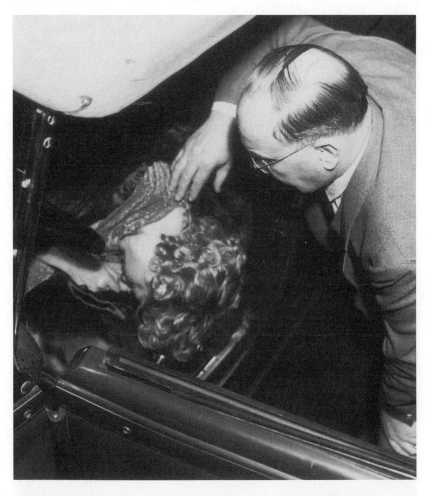

Toddy as police found her Monday morning. LAPD Bert Wallis poses for the press. Notice Thelma's clenched fists and the position of her body in relation to the steering wheel—too far to the right of the wheel to be in a position to start the car. AP/WIDE WORLD PHOTO

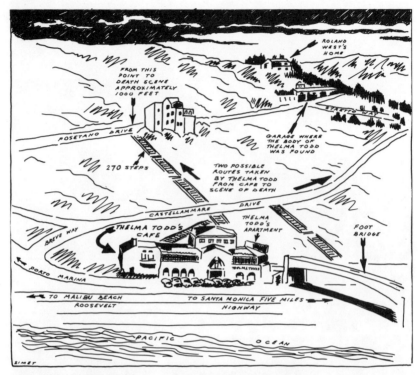

Scene of Todd's death   COPYRIGHT © 1988 BY JAYE ZIMET

Thelma Todd's Sidewalk Cafe. The arrow on the right was drawn by Thelma to indicate the location of her apartment. West's apartment was in the corner, near the overpass/bridge. The infamous double-locked door was to the rear, behind the apartments.   G. MULLANEY

The garage. Thelma
was found dead behind
the right-hand door;
West parked his car to
the left. Charles Smith's
apartment is above, the
Jewel Carmen home
up the side steps.
JAMES ROSENFIELD

The cement steps . . .
an improbable route,
an impossible climb for
Thelma.
JAMES ROSENFIELD

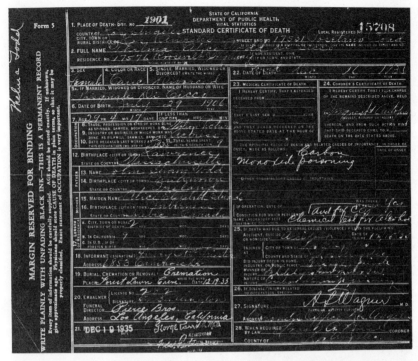

Official death certificate—after the inquest. One question remains: Why was Harvey Priester the informant and not Alice Todd or Roland West?

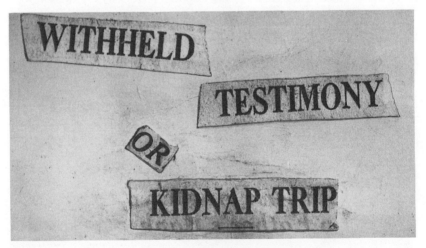

The threat to Trocadero head waiter Alex Hounie
COPYRIGHT 1935 *LOS ANGELES TIMES*

Roland West and Rudy Schaefer waiting to testify at the inquest COPYRIGHT 1935 *LOS ANGELES TIMES*

Martha (Mrs. Wallace) Ford and George Baker, witnesses, as they arrive at the Hall of Justice to testify. Mrs. Ford claimed she spoke with Thelma on the phone Sunday afternoon, fourteen hours after her supposed time of death. AP/WIDE WORLD PHOTOS

Maid Mae Whitehead.
She found Toddy's
body.
COPYRIGHT 1935
LOS ANGELES TIMES

Roland West on the stand
COPYRIGHT 1935 *LOS ANGELES TIMES*

Chapter Thirteen

Their marriage was on the rocks and both Pat and Thelma knew it was only a matter of time; they were now only going through the motions as a married couple. Pat spent more and more time in New York, almost as if Los Angeles had ebbed back into a "vacation town" for him. He always seemed to fit in better on the East Coast: His manner, polish, and style were more sophisticated than required for Hollywood and Pat always stood out as more of a dandy than he really needed to be. He let his client list wane until he became an actor's agent/manager in title only. He did not seem to care much about losing touch with Hollywood. His dealings in New York increasingly centered around the theater and he moved in and around the Broadway set.

There were rumors he had found a new love interest in New York, but he never told Toddy about that or any of his other dealings, which increasingly focused on Luciano, Lepke, and other gang lords. Though they had been married nearly two years, the gulf between Toddy and Pat only widened, mostly due to Pat's secretiveness. After a while, Thelma quit trying to include herself in his outside activities, except for one involvement—Lucky Luciano. She was now very much a part of Luciano's life.

While the wheels of what would become the Million Dollar Movie Shakedown were slowly beginning to turn in Chicago, Luciano was gearing up his drug and gambling operation in Los Angeles. With assurances from Nitti that Luciano's boys would be free to move in on nightclubs and restaurants, they became increasingly visible in many of the exclusive night spots. Prices for dinners and drinks went up considerably across town, even more in clubs that offered live music. The establishments needed the extra income to make a profit after Luciano took his share, which was sizable.

But Luciano began to realize why Nitti had left the discussion about drugs "for a later date." He now saw that Nitti was determined to get a stranglehold on the Los Angeles/West Coast drug racket. Nitti's men were undercutting Luciano's on the streets and hijacking shipments purchased by Luciano. Luciano often found his peddlers beaten up, drugged, or killed. He was combating the tactics he himself had used just a few short years ago to infiltrate the drug scene—with one difference. Nitti usually left his enemies with a deep, fatal gash in their throats.

It was an odd relationship. On the one hand, the Luciano/Nitti combine was working together, though not exactly by choice, to move in on theatrically oriented unions on one coast, yet on the other hand, the same men were slugging it out, knocking off each other's men one by one, waiting for the one chance to run the other out of town for ultimate victory. Something had to give.

Thelma was seeing Lucky approximately every other week, and by 1934, she was becoming sexually intimate with the gang lord. She began to notice a gradual change. Luciano had always been rather sullen and prone to violent outbursts, but now she sensed a new tension about him; he was more withdrawn and was increasingly on edge, lashing out at the slightest provocation, and more often than not, taking his temper out on Toddy. In that respect he was much like DiCicco, only in Luciano, the outbursts had a much harder edge; they were more explosive and more deadly.

For Lucky, Thelma had at first been a prop. But one night while they were dining at their usual nightclub, the Brown Derby, their relationship altered course. This was one of the last nights for the trio of Lucky, Pat, and Thelma. This was also to be a major turning point in Thelma's life, the beginning of her rapid descent into hard drugs.

Thelma had returned to drinking since the night she met Luciano. Lack of willpower had little to do with her return to the bottle. No will could match the awesome and terrifying power Luciano exerted with just one look from those sinister eyes. To say no to Lucky for any reason could be a death sentence. Toddy knew this; she had understood this long before she met Luciano, but she had an uncontrollable passion for such men. Meeting him was the culmination of a lifetime of being taught to seek them out, and to succumb to their wishes. She was drawn to Luciano by an irresistible force, walking almost zombielike toward her destruction. Drinking would be only half the means to that end.

Luciano despised women whom he could not completely control, and he wanted to completely control Thelma. He needed to get DiCicco out of the way and kept sending him on errands back home to New York, leaving Thelma increasingly alone. Thelma still had no idea Luciano was behind the wanderlust of her spouse. As it turned out, Luciano had had an eye on Toddy long before he met her, but Pat proved a roadblock, going out of his way to keep his wife and his friend separated.

To control Toddy, Luciano needed to get her hooked on something more substantial than diet pills. The only time he ever trusted a woman was when she was completely subservient, yet he knew a junkie could never be trusted. This was a paradox Luciano could never get around. With her dependence on the pills, and her lack of resistance to his influence, Toddy looked like easy prey.

At dinner, Lucky pointed out how tired Thelma had been looking and inquired how she maintained her hectic work schedule. Not thinking Luciano was up to anything more than pleasantries, Toddy told him how she pushed herself as hard as she could, then unwound at home with Scotch, which promptly put her to sleep until the next morning, when she reported back to work. Pat remained silent.

"Thank God for makeup men and hairdressers. A good sock in the jaw with pancake hides a multitude of sins!"

"Pat tells me you have been taking diet pills. Do they

really help you maintain your weight, if you don't mind my asking such a personal question?"

"They help. They keep the weight down and the energy up. It seems to work. I've been doing it for years. They're prescription, but harmless . . . I think."

"Do you take many?" It was now obvious even to Thelma that Luciano was asking an unusual number of personal questions. He was never one to pry into anyone's business and expected the same treatment in return. Thelma knew Luciano was one of the main drug suppliers on both coasts; it was one of the many stories that preceded Lucky's arrival in Los Angeles. People in the studios, many of whom were regular customers of Luciano's dealers, also talked. Thelma suspected Lucky was trying to get at something, but she was afraid to jump the gun and ask a direct question. No one ever asked Lucky a direct question about anything.

"I don't really know how many I take. It varies, depending on where I'm going and who I'm going to be with."

"Pat tells me you take many of the pills, too many for your own good. He worries about you."

Pat is sitting right here, Thelma thought to herself. He can speak for himself. I've never known Pat to worry about anyone but himself. "I take care of myself, Mr. Luciano."

"You can call me either Charley or Lucky. If you would rather, I can give you something that will do the same as your diet pills, without taking as many. One, maybe two at the most all day instead of the handfuls you now take."

Thelma was afraid to refuse the offer. Pat was obviously angry, because his face became flushed and he tapped his fingers. He, too, knew what Luciano was doing and finally told Lucky he would deal with him later, in private, when they could be more discreet. Pat seethed inside. He finally threw down his dinner napkin and rose from the table.

"I think it's time we leave. Thel, I'll take you home. This was supposed to be a social dinner, but you can't seem to separate your work. We did not come here to discuss drugs. And, Lucky, my wife does not have a drug habit as you imply."

Several months before, Luciano had mentioned Thelma's drug problem, hinting she might be susceptible. Pat had stood up against Lucky then too, threatening to kill him if he ever got near Toddy. Luciano had laughed, knowing DiCicco had little power over him. The threat was a gesture at best.

"Thelma, I will pick you up tomorrow, Saturday, and we will go for a drive. I enjoy driving up the coast; it relaxes me. I will arrive promptly at noon, if your husband has no objections."

If Pat did object, he never voiced his opinion. He was leaving for yet another New York business trip the following morning, Luciano had seen to that. Pat and Thelma had also begun going their separate ways several months ago. Thelma was in no position to refuse Luciano's offer.

Luciano pulled up to the house in a chocolate-brown Phaeton, a car similar to the new Phaeton Thelma had just bought. Luciano was in the backseat. A tall, heavyset man emerged from the driver's position and rang the doorbell. Though he was not wearing a uniform, he was Luciano's Los Angeles chauffeur, also Luciano's Los Angeles bodyguard.

Thelma locked the front door and was escorted into the backseat of the car, next to Luciano. She deliberately wore a white cotton dress and scarf as a contrast to Luciano who always wore dark clothes.

After an initial hello and a friendly kiss, there were no words exchanged. With Luciano, one did not begin a conversation, one waited until he spoke. Thelma stared out the window thinking it was going to be a very long afternoon.

As they headed north, past Ventura and into remote areas along the oceanside, Luciano opened up. He always seemed more comfortable when there were few others around.

"Yesterday I told you that you seemed tired. Is everything okay between you and Pasquale? I know the marriage is no more between you two."

Thelma was not sure how much Pat had told Lucky about their marriage, which had crumbled long ago.

"We get along. We don't fight anymore."

"Pasquale has a violent temper. I despise men who abuse beautiful women as he does."

Thelma looked at Lucky and smiled an obligatory smile. She wanted to know why Lucky had invited her out and was growing more uncomfortable and nervous as the conversation pressed on.

"I know you have been taking too many pills to stay awake. They are bad for you. The men who sell them do not care who buys them, as long as they make money. If you are interested, I have other things that are better for you. You can take far less and achieve the same results. So many pills are not good for such a beautiful lady."

"Please don't think me rude, but I'm fine. Everything is under control."

Lucky's eyes narrowed; it was that look again, that look that presaged something evil.

"I know what I am talking about. When you feel tired and must go on, take one or two of these. But only when you feel tired." Luciano paused as if he knew his next statement belied his real intent. "It is very easy to become addicted to these."

Luciano held out his hand and opened his fist. It contained a large bottle filled with white pills. He stared at Thelma and she dared not refuse his offer. She took the pills and started to put them in her purse, thinking she would throw them out once she was alone. She knew exactly what Lucky was up to.

"Why don't you take one now, to see if you can handle them?"

"I'm not tired, I had a good night's sleep."

"Your eyes betray you, darling. I repeat my request. We have a long afternoon ahead. If you have a problem with them, I would rather know about it right now and I can suggest something else."

"No, no problem." Thelma knew she was cornered, once again, by a powerful man. She took two pills in an act of defiance against Lucky who suggested she take only one. She felt a strong rush a short time later. Her energy soared and she grew slightly dizzy.

Luciano watched the show and smiled. "They are the essence of those pills you were taking. They are what you were really desiring. They will give you the energy you need."

The pills were pure speed. By the time they reached Santa Barbara, Thelma was running with a burst of energy she had never felt before. She and Luciano had a picnic on the sand, complete with French champagne, caviar, and cold lobster. Luciano was quite smug that he had set Toddy on the track he intended. He knew that from here on, it was just a matter of time before she was completely his, to use and abuse as he wanted.

When she returned to her empty house that night, she felt the crash from the drugs. Exhausted, she collapsed in a chair and thought about her life, her troubles with Pat, and the sudden interest Lucky seemed to be taking in her personal habits. She eyed the bottle of pills and threw them toward the living-room wall. The bottle bounced but did not break. Thelma poured herself a drink and plummeted into a deep depression. She had told friends she thought life had already passed her by and there was no future.

Thelma's life was on the verge of several major changes once again. The first occurred in March, when she finally sued Pat for divorce. The grounds were mental cruelty. They had been formally separated since February 20 and the divorce was uncontested by DiCicco, who did not even appear at the court proceeding. Represented by her attorney, A. Roland Button, Thelma said very little on the stand, only nodding her head once or twice when asked if DiCicco had been cruel, had beaten her and had deserted her on several occasions. Thelma said only that Pat was surly and rude to her in public and in front of her co-workers and friends, was quarrelsome and nagged whenever she talked about a possible business partnership with another friend [Roland West], and that this partnership was the possible purchase of a restaurant. Her attorney added that DiCicco was offensive to Thelma's "delicate and refined temperament."

Thelma never mentioned any underworld involvement by DiCicco and no questions about it were ever raised. The proceeding was short, a divorce was granted. The break was clean, neither owing the other any money or other financial consideration.

Another change was in her work situation. Todd and Pitts had become very close; their comedies were extremely popular and the girls clicked as a team. But things were quite different when Pitts was more or less forced out and replaced by Patsy Kelly.

ZaSu Pitts left Roach in the spring of 1933, in a contract dispute over salary, and went on to become one of Hollywood's highest-paid character comediennes. The bone of contention was the staggered expiration dates between her contract and Thelma's. Pitts's contract had lapsed, Thelma's still had several months to run, so the girls could not negotiate as a team. Roach threatened to let Pitts go altogether rather than meet her salary demand of $3,000 a week. She also demanded a percentage of the Todd/Pitts films, something no star on the Roach lot, and very few elsewhere, had acquired. Roach offered a slight pay hike, a flat-out no to the demand to own a piece of the action (even Laurel and Hardy could not get that) and gave her a "take it or leave it" offer. She left and was replaced by Patsy Kelly, a masculine-type actress whom Thelma liked but never really considered a close friend as she had Pitts.

The comedies were still as popular as ever, but for Thelma, some of the initial spark had gone. She thought about leaving Roach when her next contract expired and getting away from movies for a while—an idea Alice abhorred and considered "running out" on the people who had made her what she was.

In many ways, Alice was right: Thelma wanted to run out on Roach, whose "potato clause" had turned her into a diet-pill drug addict, on Pat, who had destroyed her self-esteem, on West, who had used her as a pawn in his egomaniacal drive to take credit for creating a new star, and even on Alice, who had pushed and pulled her in directions she did not want to go and into contracts she did not believe were in her best interests.

The alcohol continued to offer an escape, but it was not enough. Thelma rose from the chair and walked over to the corner of the living room where the bottle of pills had settled on the floor. She sat on the floor, clutched the pills in her hand, and cried. She wallowed in her depression for several days, but came out of it with a definite plan of action, something she hoped would offer solitude and possibly a way out.

She phoned West and arranged to meet him in his Palisades home. She had made up her mind that the restaurant was a positive step and she would go in on the deal West had proposed more than a year ago. Jewel Carmen (who was estranged from West but still shared living quarters in the huge, Spanish-style home), West, and Thelma mapped out their agreement. Carmen would supply the actual money for the cafe and be the financial backer though a great deal of her wealth was funded by West's early film career. West would take care of the hiring, ordering, and general running of the business as his full-time job. Thelma would lend her name to the establishment because she was the "draw" of the three and popular enough to get a steady movie crowd to dine at the beachside cafe. In August 1934, Thelma Todd's Sidewalk Cafe was born.

Alice loved the idea. She was now not only a prima donna mama, but the mother of a restaurateur as well. She now had a formal role in Hollywood; she would often act as hostess and use the spot to throw parties for her friends. There was only one aspect she did not like—the living arrangements.

Since Toddy's divorce from Pat, she had moved back in with Alice in their Hollywood home. The couple's Brentwood house was sold, and the profit split between Pat and Thelma. Thelma felt she could no longer divide her time between living in Hollywood, working in Culver City, and helping run a restaurant at the beach. Also she did not especially want to stay with Alice, from whom she needed to reestablish her independence. So she packed her bags and headed to the Palisades.

The building West bought was two full stories with a third, half story on top. The right side of the second story was converted into two apartments, each having a separate key for privacy. Thelma lived in front, West in back. To enter, each needed a master key for the front door, then their own, personal key for their private door. They usually entered the apartment area through a double door on the second floor, a door that opened to a courtyard facing Posetano Road.

The left side of the second floor was a bar area, a cocktail lounge that West also used as his office, complete with phone and personal booth. The bottom floor had the restaurant to the left and a drugstore to the right below the apartments, with a hallway/entryway in between. The third floor, the half floor, was officially a storage room, but there were rumors that gambling (dice, cards, and numbers) was going on there "behind closed doors."

Alice said repeatedly that she would have preferred that Thelma take the second-floor living quarters for herself, and that West either move back into his house on Robelo Drive, or convert the third-floor storage area into his quarters. She saw no need for West and Todd to live that closely, especially since West was still technically a married man. Alice obviously never cared much for Roland West and his marital arrangements.

Stranger still was the living space provided for some of the restaurant staff. Charles Smith, the cafe treasurer, and his wife were put up in a small, deteriorating room above the garage below the main house. The apartment was cramped, only three rooms, and the plaster was crumbling. Todd and West parked their cars in the garage, and whenever a car was started, the rumble shook the Smiths' apartment, which also filled with exhaust fumes. West kept promising to patch and paint the apartment once the restaurant was successfully under way.

Rudy Schaefer, Jewel Carmen's brother and the cafe business manager, and his wife lived in the main house with Carmen, taking up residence near the back. Without a doubt, the restaurant was now the main preoccupation of the once-quiet West/Carmen home on Posetano Road.

The restaurant seemed the perfect diversion for Toddy. It kept her busy in between her two-weeks-on/two-weeks-off Todd/Kelly comedy shooting schedule, and it helped keep her mind off her loneliness and depression. But unknowingly, by opening the restaurant, she had opened the door to Luciano. It was exactly the type of business he devoured to feed his growing empire.

Lucky himself never entered the restaurant; he rarely operated that way. Instead he sent emissaries, men who checked a place out, took note of which workers carried union cards, which outfit sold the food and liquor, and reported back to Luciano. He especially avoided direct contact with the Sidewalk Cafe because there were already rumblings about his association with Thelma Todd, and he wanted to allay those rumors as much as possible. He had bigger plans for both Todd and her cafe, especially the third-floor storeroom, which he thought the perfect setup for a gambling operation. He now had to put his scheme into action.

Luciano waited for the perfect opportunity to strike. He knew Thelma would play a definite part in his scenario and he already assumed he knew how to force her to capitulate through drugs and emotional attachment. Roland West, though, was an obstacle he had not completely figured out. Luciano watched him for some time before making his move. He wanted to make sure he did not prematurely tip his hand and scare West off. He wanted to be certain that when the time came for him to seize the storeroom for gambling, West would be more than happy to hand over the keys.

While Luciano laid the groundwork for the infiltration of the Sidewalk Cafe, he still faced several more serious problems. One was getting Nitti out of the way in Los Angeles; it was becoming evident that the two could not operate drug operations in the same town; one had to seize control and Luciano believed it should be his by way of eminent domain. He also knew Nitti would launch a still bloodier battle to win the drug racket.

Lucky also had to make sure he was going to receive his fair share of the take from the theater—union shakedowns that were about to begin rolling back east. He knew if anyone was planning to cheat him out of his cut, it would again be Nitti, because of the long-standing gang rivalry and Lucky's initial distrust and reluctance to go in on the scam.

Luciano was right on both counts.

Chapter Fourteen

Nitti and the Syndicate were clearly behind Browne. The men trusted him because he was more than a two-bit hood, which was all they ever considered Bioff. It was evident the initial shakedown of Balaban was Browne's idea. He had ambition and had boosted himself through the ranks of his union, which was more than Bioff had ever tried. When the big IATSE international convention came around in June of 1934, Nitti and the Syndicate made sure Browne was put in as president. As promised, Lepke and Luciano brought in the East Coast votes; Nitti and the Midwest took care of the rest of the country.

The meeting looked more like a rogues' gallery or police lineup than a union meeting. Men in dark Chesterfield overcoats lined the hall with tommy guns and shotguns; some patrolled the aisles, others paraded outside the building in an obvious show of force. Every delegate inside had been told how to vote, and when the roll was called, every conventioneer came through as ordered. Browne was in by a landslide. The Syndicate then billed the union for traveling expenses of its "security force," which IATSE, that is, Browne, gratefully paid.

The message was clear—the Syndicate had got Browne

elected president; now the Syndicate was an equal partner in all IATSE union dealings. Browne drew a Depression-era salary of $25,000 a year, along with maintaining his $250 weekly as business agent of Chicago Stagehands Local No. 2. Bioff was appointed "personal representative" of Browne for a $22,000 per year take. Browne now believed he was in power to do as he pleased. He soon found out how mistaken he was.

In 1934, President Roosevelt was trying to line up the labor vote in the hopes of winning a Democratic majority in both the House and Senate. The union leaders were to serve as unofficial advisers to the president, and in turn, they were allowed to lobby for legislation that would enhance their unions. Among the labor leaders he courted was George Browne. Browne thought a move to Washington would put him in closer proximity to the White House, thus furthering his ambitions. When Nitti got word of Browne's plan, he ordered the fat union goon into his office.

"You stay put, where we can watch you." End of discussion. It was clear to Browne that he was nothing more than a puppet. Frank Nitti held tight reins on his boy.

Everything was finally in place, except for one loose end—Tommy Maloy. Maloy was already in with the mob; he had signed the pact by asking for Nitti's help when the theater owners refused to pay his high Depression Era projectionists' salaries. One by one the owners had withstood firebombings and even death threats. But Maloy knew that with the backing of Capone/Nitti, no one would dare stand up to him any longer. That was why Browne was put in to head the projectionists' union—to shake down theater owners where Maloy had failed.

On Christmas Eve, 1934, at a party attended by Nitti, Browne, Bioff, and other Chicago-based hoods, the topic of Maloy's future arose. Nitti was flatly informed that Maloy would not stand for someone taking over his union and booting him out, that he could not be intimidated into giving up control and he would die before losing his projectionists. Nitti already believed the projectionists were vital to the Syndicate's gaining complete control over the theater/motion-picture industry and that the projectionists had to be aligned under the IA banner. Maloy was now expendable.

On February 4, 1935, on a cold, windy, icy afternoon, a

speeding car drew alongside Maloy's Cadillac on Chicago's Lake Shore Drive, machine guns blazing. Maloy's bullet-riddled body was later found slumped behind the wheel of his bloodied and punctured car. The projectionists' union was now, formally, swallowed up in the IATSE, under Browne's (that is, Nitti's) rule. The Million Dollar Movie Shakedown was on. The boys were gunning for Hollywood.

With every stagehand and projectionist in IA's pocket, Nitti and the Chicago gang laid out plans for the push west. Citing Barney Balaban as an example, the outfit moved in on other Chicago theater chains, demanding similar payoffs, laundered through the B&B soup kitchens, which were now affiliated with Capone's charitable flophouses. The first Chicago chain targeted was Warner Bros. Bioff and Browne cornered James Coston, zone manager. The two used a ploy similar to the Balaban pitch, but made it sound as if they were giving Coston a deal.

Bioff explained that the pressure was on to hire two projectionists for every theater booth, but for $100,000, he would be able to keep conditions just as they were. Bioff told Coston the one hundred grand would have to be shared by all the chains, and that Warners' share was only $30,000. Coston refused. Bioff explained that the money was only a fraction of what it would cost to double the theater payroll.

Coston flew to New York to talk with his bosses. He did not fly alone. His flight companions were Bioff, Browne, and Nicky Dean [Cirella], who waited in the hall as Coston talked to his superiors. He was given the go-ahead to pay. Upon their return to Chicago, Nitti counted out $15,000 for himself; the rest went to Bioff and Browne, and to Dean, who used the funds to open a nightclub/gambling casino on Chicago's downtown Rush Street. The enormous gambling profits were shared with Nitti. He now knew why Luciano had fought so bitterly for the rights in Los Angeles. The wheels were turning in Nitti's head once again.

Several days later, John Balaban, brother of Barney, was invited to lunch with Bioff and Browne. Bioff gave John the same pitch he had given Coston about having to hire more projectionists unless money was paid. But the Balabans were already marked as dupes. Their price for such protection was much higher than the shakedown deal for Coston. John Balaban was required to pay $120,000.

Balaban protested, saying his brother had paid Tommy Maloy far less for the same purpose. Bioff explained that Maloy was long gone, that the game was starting again from square one. Balaban left the luncheon meeting, saying he would get back to Bioff after he had talked it over with his brother.

Barney filled John in on the earlier shakedown; they knew they were in no position to back down. But they thought $120,000 was excessive, especially since they had handed over $20,000 several months earlier. The brothers agreed they would pony up only half the demand, $60,000 and not a penny more. They already knew how to make out the check. There were no arguments from Bioff, Browne, or Nitti, who rubbed their hands together in delight over the windfall. One by one other Chicago theater chains fell. Only two months after Tommy Maloy's death, Nitti and his boys hauled in more than $332,000 dollars.

They were far from through. In fact, they were just beginning to go after the jugular—Hollywood. Nitti called a nationwide conference to lay out his grand scheme. Called to the table was the same gang as had attended the first conference, with one exception—Lucky Luciano was neither invited nor welcome. Lepke, Nitti claimed, represented the East Coast quite nicely. Luciano, he told the gang, was busy on the West Coast, chasing his tail in small-potatoes restaurant and gambling rackets and unable to attend.

For Nitti, the plan was so simple it was laughable. With the Chicago theaters under Syndicate control, the Hollywood studios were sitting ducks. Browne and Bioff would pull the workers out on strike and shut the exhibitors down, leaving the studios with no place to show their films. They would have to kick in or go out of business. Nitti did warn that it might take some doing, some convincing on the part of the "boys" to show the Hollywood billionaires they meant business. But, he told the group, the Syndicate had walked down that street before. The boys laughed at the clever remark and the relative ease at which one million dollars, minimum, was just waiting, ripe for the plucking. Luciano's name was never mentioned in the meeting, an oversight that meant more power and possibly more money for Lepke for his East Coast support.

There are no secrets in the mob, especially when one gang is openly going against another, when one boss is making a fool of another. Nitti was obviously making Luciano out to be a chump. He took control of Luciano's East Coast theater unions, merged them under the Capone-controlled IATSE, and aced Luciano out of the picture and out of millions of dollars in potential profits.

Nitti could not operate long without word filtering back to Luciano. At the very beginning of the takeover, Luciano had known there was little he could do against Nitti. So far, the profits seized had been in Chicago-area shakedowns. No money had been directly squeezed from New York, though the money ultimately came by way of the theater/studios corporate offices there.

When word got back to Luciano that Nitti, once again, planned to cheat him out of something he felt was rightfully his, he went berserk. He knew that eventually Nitti's boys (Bioff and Browne) would cross him, and when they did, he would be waiting for them. Luciano planned to kill the two jolly men, reacting more out of anger than out of logic. His real target should have been Nitti, but right now, Luciano was too blind with anger to set up any real strategy; he wanted to murder someone, anyone, connected with the Capone outfit. Bioff and Browne happened to be the front men. And they were headed to New York.

The B&B partners were coming after still more Balabans. The family was already primed because now two brothers had fallen without much pressure, and the Balabans had not yet seen the last of Nitti's boys. The Balabans proved to be the key to the entire shakedown.

One brother headed a chain of New York exhibitors called Publix Theatres, Incorporated, taking over the job when Sam Katz (of Balaban and Katz) resigned. Shaking him down would initially be up to Lepke's men. Another brother was already in Hollywood, heading a production arm of RKO Studios. And much to the delight of Nitti and his troupe, their old "friend" Barney was apparently slated to run Paramount Pictures in Hollywood, his term to begin in a little more than a year, in 1936. The Syndicate made a safe bet that the brothers were talking about the shakedown, the threats, the payoffs from other theaters and how much they personally had added to the B&B coffer. Nitti believed the brothers were doing the P.R. work for him, so when Bioff and Browne came to collect, they would only have to hold out their greasy little hands and say how much.

In a gesture aimed more at putting on a show of fair play than at any real conciliation, Nitti telephoned Luciano in Manhattan and told him Bioff, Browne, and Nick Cirella would be coming to New York to shake down the RKO offices, run by an Englishman named Major Leslie Thompson. He told Luciano he believed Thompson was already ripe because Browne had arranged a meeting to "discuss union matters," and he was sure the Balabans had already tipped him off as to the nature of that meeting. They were going to play a game of "bad cop/good cop."

Cirella and Bioff were to threaten Thompson with a massive strike of all stagehands and projectionists aligned with the IATSE unless pay raises were granted to all men in the union. Lepke would be at the meeting as an obvious figure of intimidation. Then Browne would enter, offering a peaceful alternative, saying that a settlement fee could be arranged. Browne would explain the fee would cost $150,000. As Nitti put it, the plan would go off without a hitch.

Luciano asked only one question throughout the entire conversation. He spoke calmly. "What is my cut?"

Nitti again hedged, telling him the profits were being laundered through the soup kitchen and eventually the money would be funneled to all parties involved, as agreed. Luciano quickly added up the damages.

"So far you have taken in nearly half a million dollars. I have not seen one penny."

"Lepke is taking care of . . ."

"Lepke is a Jew bastard. He does not speak for me, he does not represent me. You do not speak for me either, Frank Nitto. We will settle our differences soon. I am watching. I am waiting and I will win."

"Look, Lucky. We have had our differences, but . . ."

Luciano said just one word, *"Morte,"* meaning "death."

Luciano hung up the phone. Bioff and Browne must die,

then he would go after Nitti. They were, he believed, invading his territory, agreement or not. All bets had been canceled when Nitti devoured the profits, leaving little for the rest of the Syndicate. Lepke still had his fingers in the pie and had been consulted on every move; the gangs from Detroit and St. Louis usually deferred to the Capone outfit due to its strength and the proximity of Chicago. Luciano was the only one left out in the cold.

The scam against Thompson worked almost as well as planned. Thompson tried to negotiate the price, but after some convincing, Bioff got RKO's Thompson to fork over $87,000, to guarantee that a strike would be held off for "a time." Bioff, Browne, and Cirella knew Thompson had spoken to the Balabans when he offered to write a check that would be made out to the soup kitchen, ready for them to pick up the next day. Browne chuckled and told Thompson this deal would be different. He wanted cash up front, no check. Thompson made arrangements to pay Browne $50,000 on the spot. The outstanding $37,000 was paid to him through the Chicago office, which was convenient for the Nitti group.

Nitti knew there was no stopping him. By this time, Capone had been transferred to Alcatraz and was completely out of the picture. Nitti was free now to run the operation as he pleased.

The studios negotiated with the major labor unions as one, to work out a basic agreement; the monied movie moguls sat on one side of the bargaining table, the union goons on the other. The trade unions involved were concerned with production rather than with the technical end as was Browne's IATSE. The Hollywood unions were under the primary control of the American Federation of Labor, and though IA was part of the AFL, it was not privy to the basic agreement. Thus Browne was not privileged to sit at the table. That was something Nitti and Browne had to change if they were going to achieve power in Hollywood.

Nitti trusted few men, and he did not completely trust Bioff and Browne. He remembered that it was through their drunken mouthing off that he was first tipped to their initial shakedown scheme. He knew that given a few beers, the paunchy pair might talk too much. When Bioff was shipped off to Hollywood to scout out the lay of the studio land, his constant companion was Johnny Roselli. Browne had his shadow, too, Nicky Dean, who accompanied him on all trips to New York.

As president of MGM/Loew's, Nick Schenck was considered the most powerful man in the motion-picture industry. His brother, Joe, was chairman of the board of 20th Century-Fox. Nitti knew if he snagged the Schencks, he'd snagged the golden goose—Hollywood.

On April 15, 1935, Browne and Bioff entered Nick Schenck's New York office, announcing that when the basic agreement was negotiated the following year, he would be negotiating with IATSE. No firm date was set, just a vague "next year," so Schenck ushered the men out the door with three departing words, "Go to hell."

Since Schenck had his fingers in every pot connected with the industry, he already knew about the Chicago and New York exhibitor shakedowns and knew exactly with whom he was dealing. Schenck, though, still considered himself too powerful to be touched. He had the shock of his life when, in late summer, he was told that Bioff and Browne were planning a massive, industry-wide strike through all unions connected with the AFL.

It was no surprise, though, when Schenck received a phone call saying he could avert such a strike for a measly $100,000. Schenck knew Bioff and Browne meant business; he knew about earlier firebombings in theaters, about death threats, and he knew the power of the Syndicate. He approved the payoff as the lesser of two evils, but he still refused to allow Browne/IATSE to sit in on the basic agreement.

By mid-1935, the Syndicate had shaken down the Chicago exhibitors for $150,000, the New York exhibitors for the same amount, and the Hollywood film manufacturers for $100,000. Nitti and the gang found the money good, but they also wanted the power that came only with controlling all Hollywood unions. That power was tied in with negotiating the basic agreement. The Syndicate was prepared for the challenge.

Nitti pulled off one of the most clever union tactics in history, a scheme that was tried for the very first time with the shakedown, and has been copycatted successfully since that time. Instead of pulling out all IA/AFL-affiliated workers in one massive strike, allowing Schenck to hire scabs to fill the jobs, Nitti used his power to organize a wave of disruption.

He ordered theater projectionists off the job at random in Chicago, New York, and Los Angeles, for several minutes at a time when reels of film were supposed to be changed. When reels ended, new reels would be set up at a record-slow pace. He emptied theaters with stink bombs; tightly rolled, highly flammable nitrate film was ignited and tossed into the theater aisles. Pretty soon, moviegoers stayed away from MGM-owned theaters, afraid of the trouble. Browne also let it be thought that MGM was unfair to labor, and that it was making millions while keeping salaries at poverty levels—which was not true, of course. While the scheme was in motion, workers were kept on the job at union salaries while the box-office dip drained studio profits.

After more than two weeks of chaos, Schenck picked up the phone. He knew exactly whom to call and he knew the number to dial. Schenck reluctantly agreed to meet with Bioff and Browne.

But for the duo, Schenck was not enough. Now that they knew they had him crawling, they insisted other Hollywood studio big shots join the bargaining session as well. The others agreed, hat in hand, to speak with the goons.

Sitting across from Bioff, Browne, Cirella, and Roselli were Austin Keogh (vice-president of Paramount), Albert Warner (vice-president and treasurer of Warner Bros.), Hugh Strong (personnel supervisor for 20th Century-Fox), Leo Spitz (for RKO), and Schenck. Since they had the moguls on the run, the boys put their cards on the table—each of the major studios (MGM, Warners, Paramount, and 20th) was to kick back $50,000 each year to Browne and the Syndicate. The smaller studios (Columbia, RKO, Universal, and twelve other companies) were let off with a light sentence; they had to pay only $25,000. The Roach Studios was mentioned as one of the twelve companies, but there is no record of whether Roach actually paid the ransom. There is no record that any of the companies avoided paying, either. There was no argument when Browne demanded the money, and no questions asked when Browne asked that IATSE be represented at the next round of talks on the industry-wide basic union agreement. Nitti won. He "owned" Hollywood.

The money paid off to Browne was laundered in an elaborate scheme worked out by both the Syndicate and the studios so there would, technically, be no record of any money changing hands illegally. For example, the $50,000 MGM bribe was recorded as commission paid to Willie Bioff for selling raw film stock on MGM's behalf. Similar arrangements were worked out with the other studios in the form of sales commissions, "donations," and miscellaneous funds set up for union workers courtesy of the studios. In all, the first year's take was more than half a million dollars. Not bad for a scam that started out as nothing more than a routine shakedown.

Luciano had not seen one cent of this money. Bioff and Browne were scheduled to come to Hollywood to meet with the studio bosses; Luciano vowed it would be the last meeting the pair would ever attend.

He bided his time. He suspected that when they headed west sometime in September, it would be without Cirella or Roselli. It was especially important that neither of Nitti's men be around when the contract put Bioff and Browne on the road to their "untimely deaths." Luciano did not want to trigger an open war with Nitti, at least not yet. He had similar plans for Nitti, but he wanted to telegraph a message to Nitti first, by way of Bioff's and Browne's murders, to let Nitti know that he would not be played for a sucker. Sending the pair back to Chicago on a marble slab, Luciano thought, would send an appropriate warning.

Luciano stayed in Los Angeles to set his trap, and to see firsthand the ramifications of the shakedown. He also set his roving eyes on another restaurant, one that had potential— The Sidewalk Cafe.

"How about a hamburger, Mac?" Thelma shipped a menu back home to show off her new line of work. "We don't sell hotdogs or O'Henry's . . . it's a long way from that cup of cocoa and cake on winter nights to the above. From teaching to acting to a 'restauranteer.' What next? . . . I'm getting a bit homesick. Going to try and make it this fall if possible . . . how I'd love a good gab-fest. Well, maybe soon. Thel."

The restaurant was taking up an inordinate amount of time, which Thelma had not initially expected. Her understanding about the restaurant was that it was hers "in name only," but West seemed to have a difficult time keeping things under control. The Sidewalk Cafe had been open less than a year, it was usually packed with stars like Clark Gable and Spencer Tracy and with West's and Todd's studio friends, but the books never quite balanced—the cafe always ended each month in the red. Some attributed the loss to Toddy's good nature and bad business sense; for example, the cash register was always stuffed with IOUs. But Thelma knew the real problem had to be deeper than letting a few friends "float" for a few weeks. She finally confronted West when he asked her for still more money to keep the cafe going.

"I've given you a couple of thousand dollars a month. Where does the money go?"

"When a restaurant is just getting started, there are a lot of hidden expenses . . . paying off the bills for the tables, linens, decorations. It should settle down soon."

"I personally pumped enough money into this place to buy all that stuff three times over. This was supposed to be Jewel's contribution. And yours. Not mine."

West did not have an answer. He knew Thelma was not supposed to be a financial backer, but somehow she was turning out to be just that. The Sidewalk Cafe was becoming more and more Thelma's place, not just in name but in the amount of money she poured into it. It had been West's dream to open such a restaurant, but he saw his dream disintegrating before his eyes.

"This will be it. I'll go over the books at the end of the month and see where we're headed, see exactly where the money is going. All I know is [Charles] Smith tells me we need more money to cover the bills than we're taking in."

"I don't trust Smith."

"You think he's juggling the books?"

"Do you?"

West did not answer. He was suspicious of Smith, but he had known him for years and he was good with numbers. If Smith was tapping the register, West was hard-pressed to figure out why. But he soon found the answer.

Several days later, two men approached West in the bar area of the Sidewalk Cafe. It was late in the afternoon, between the lunch and dinner crowds. Thelma was still at the studio. The men spoke in very serious, hushed tones and requested that West talk with them in his private office.

After quickly glancing around to see whether they were being watched, the two followed West and closed the office door. The men said very little, but made their point. West was to increase his liquor and steak orders when two other men came around to the back of the cafe the next morning. They would take the orders and West was to accept their price without question. He was also to order linen service from a new laundry and hire bartenders through the union.

West turned white as a sheet and stared at the men. From the way they spoke, he gathered the cafe had been pressured by the mob for quite some time and he was just now finding out about it. He suspected Smith had known all along and had already agreed to the demand. This time around, the men were upping the ante.

West hedged and then told the men he refused to give in to any such demands. The men cited fires, bombings, death threats, and vandalism that had happened to other restaurateurs who refused to knuckle under.

"I'll talk your offer over with my accountant and business manager. They make all decisions in those areas." West was hoping to buy some time to get to the bottom of things with Smith.

"You don't understand. We are making the decision for you, saving you the time and trouble."

West understood, but he still needed to confront Smith.

West asked Smith point-blank if he had known about any demands to order food and liquor from certain men. Smith emphatically denied any such knowledge. West was not sure if he believed Smith.

When the salesmen came to the restaurant the next day, as expected, they told West how much he was to order. The prices were outrageously high and the food and liquor was far more than the restaurant required for the weekly fare. West complained that the restaurant did not require that much food. The men told West not to worry, that the order would be adjusted.

When the shipment arrived, it was adjusted. Though the price was not lowered, the amount of food and liquor was decreased in line with West's previous orders. West had not only been shaken down, but cheated. Worse yet, there was no one he could turn to for help. He could not go to the district attorney's office, which already had a shady and questionable reputation going back at least fifteen years, since the days of Thomas Woolwine and Asa Keyes.

With the "trade deal" set, West went back to Smith to find out about the money shortage. West believed that capitulation with the thugs was directly tied to the problem with the books. West believed money was also being kicked back. West, though, was still not sure if the mobsters were Luciano's or Nitti's people. He needed a scorecard to keep track of the underworld players.

According to Smith, the books jibed. He strongly suggested West grill Schaefer about any irregularities. West considered Schaefer on the level and honest. Besides, the fact that he was a brother-in-law seemed to put him above suspicion. Smith was too quick to blame someone else for the red ink in the books, which made West suspect him even more. West reasoned that if Smith was good enough at math to set up and handle a restaurant's complicated books, he was good enough to paper over the cracks after money slipped through.

Thelma insisted they have the books gone over by an independent auditing firm after the first of the year. She also suspected Smith, but never confronted him directly, nor did she say much about her suspicions to anyone. Thelma was not one to gossip, but she did indicate that if they found proof of anything underhanded, Smith would be fired on the spot.

West did not tell Toddy about the thugs and the orders. He did not want Thelma directly involved in that situation, and he believed he could handle it, given enough time and money. He still dearly loved Thelma; he considered her his best friend and he was already concerned about her welfare. West knew she kept company with Luciano, and he also knew Luciano had been supplying her with drugs. He just hoped he could keep the con men at bay until he found out who they were and figured out a way to deal with them. He was afraid that if he let Thelma in on the problem, she would try to intervene, go to Luciano for help or tell him off, and quite possibly get herself killed.

West assumed it was Toddy who was completely under Luciano's spell, and that Luciano had little need for Thelma.

What he failed to realize was Luciano's attraction and need for Toddy, or more accurately at this point, her restaurant. West did not know the men who approached him were Luciano's boys, and that this was Lucky's first step to take over the third floor. With West playing into his boys' hands, Luciano now had a foot in the door.

Luciano never came into the Sidewalk Cafe in person and never showed up at the apartment door. On occasion, Toddy would dine in public with him, but they were somewhat discreet and never invited friends to join them at their table.

When Lucky wanted to see Toddy, he had someone call for her at the cafe or her apartment. She would then drive or take a cab to a prearranged rendezvous point and wait for Luciano's brown Phaeton to pull up to the curb. Luciano loved to take long drives; he said it helped him unwind. The bulk of their "dates" consisted of drives along the coast, north or south, but away from the city. Sometimes Thelma would not return to the cafe until the next day. West never questioned her because any interrogation always triggered a shouting match.

Luciano was losing ground in Los Angeles in both the restaurant shakedowns and drug peddling. Nitti now reigned supreme and his men were successfully infiltrating Luciano's drug-trafficking areas. Word was that Nitti wanted to push further, into gambling. Lucky was on edge; he had to move quickly if he was to maintain his control over those areas in L.A. The strain was showing, though Luciano did his best to hide his anger and irritation.

Toddy sensed something was wrong. During one of their drives, she asked questions, and pressed perhaps too hard. Luciano slugged her in the face, exploding in a rage and threatening to kill her if she ever tried to butt into his private life again. Thelma had suffered through Luciano's temper tantrums before, but this was the worst yet. She was more in shock than upset, more frightened than angry. But this time she did not cave in. She did the only thing she knew how to do—just glared back at him, no tears, no shouting, just returning that look Luciano so often used to intimidate others. It was apparent Thelma was finally coming into her own, and was gradually pulling herself out from under Luciano's spell.

Though he had gotten Thelma addicted to hard drugs and renewed her alcohol habit, she was slipping out of his grip.

The look surprised Luciano, who calmed down and
stared back at her. It caught Lucky off guard and he opened
up—slightly. But what he said was enough to tip Toddy off
that something of monstrous proportions was brewing. Luciano mumbled the names Bioff and Browne and Nitti—they
had become an obsession, they occupied Lucky's mind
twenty-four hours a day. He could barely talk without utter-
ing those names with profanity and death threats attached to
them.

Thelma had heard of Bioff and Browne; by now everyone
in the movie industry had heard the names or knew of the
men. Many people suspected they were tied in with the mob,
but no one outside of the studio executives yet had the complete picture. But through fragmented bits and pieces of Luciano's ravings, Thelma was beginning to get a fair idea of
what had transpired in New York and Los Angeles. Her childhood background gave her an understanding of the mob. It
did not take her long to figure out that Nitti had supported
Bioff and Browne in their push for union control, and that
they had somehow used Luciano's power in New York to get
to the New York theater executives. Toddy was also able to
pick up the fact that Nitti had cheated Luciano out of some
share of money. Toddy did not yet have the complete picture,
but she had a solid outline. And she began to ask questions
around town.

As they continued to see one another, it was becoming
increasingly clear to Luciano that Thelma knew more than it
was safe for her to know. Luciano assumed it was only a matter of months, at the most, before Toddy would put the whole
story together and figure out exactly what money it was that
Nitti owed him.

Luciano sensed that Thelma was getting too close. He
also knew he had slipped up, he had underestimated Toddy,
told her too much, never realizing the disparate pieces of information were coming together and taking shape in Thelma's
mind. She accurately connected the names with the roles in
the shakedown. She took random shots, but kept scoring direct hits. He ordered several of his men to follow her at work,
hang around the Sidewalk Cafe, and try to find out what they
could about Thelma and what she might or might not know.

As the fall of 1935 approached, the Sidewalk Cafe was beginning to draw a steady clientele of shady characters who said little and ate less, just sat and stared and listened.

Luciano knew Los Angeles was proving very unlucky for him. Since he had first tried to infiltrate the town, it had brought him nothing but bad luck. New York was slipping away, he had let Nitti get the best of him, he was in danger of losing his drug operation, and now an actress could prove a serious problem. The town was caving in on him. He had to act fast.

Bioff and Browne were at the top of his list of problems that needed eliminating. They were expected in Los Angeles in several weeks and Lucky had to get his plans in motion. Though he did not entirely trust Lepke after the shakedown scam, Luciano needed to enlist two of his men from Murder, Incorporated for the hit. Luciano flew to New York for an emergency conference with the other New York boss. Lepke sided with Luciano as far as his rage over the shakedown swindle, but told him hitting Bioff and Browne would only make the problem worse.

Lepke pointed out that Browne, as the head of a major union, and Bioff, as his right-hand man, had become very visible, and were considered, by those who did not know better, respectable labor leaders. Though the two laughed at the idea, the point was well taken. A hit on a labor leader would send waves all the way to the White House, and it would not take long before it was discovered that it was Luciano who had ordered the killing.

Lepke also pointed out that Nitti would be forced to come forward and speak up for Bioff and Browne and avenge their murders. The national work force would be behind Nitti, and he would come out a hero.

Luciano knew Lepke was right.

"Why should I waste my time on two fat pigs when I can rid the streets of real trash? Nitti is the one who should die. He has been begging to die for some time. He has gotten too big for his own good."

"My people are at your disposal."

"This one I will do myself. I share the honor of slaughtering the pig with no one."

On that September afternoon, Luciano and Lepke believed they had sealed the fate of Frank Nitti. Luciano's next stop was Chicago.

Chapter Fifteen

"There will be blood flowing from every gutter in every street in America before I'm through with you, Frank Nitto." Luciano pounded his fists on Nitti's desk, screaming, swearing, threatening the gang lord with death.

"You have cheated me for the last time. I am well aware of what you are doing, trying to squeeze me out of my own territory on the West Coast, skimming my cut of the shakedown in New York. You have lived your last day on this earth."

It was apparent that Luciano was not making idle threats. He meant every word he said and had already put his assassination plot into motion. He knew how, when, and where he would do away with Nitti. All Lucky had to do was nudge Nitti in the right direction, to put him on the road to meet his fate.

Nitti knew he was up against the wall and had no choice but to come out fighting.

"You refused to go in on our deal in Hollywood. You threatened us all. You wanted power that you had no right to demand. Why do you think you deserve any cut from the take?"

"I gave you my projectionists, the theaters."

"Only because if you refused, Lepke would have given them to us anyway. You had no choice, and you have no say."

"Then we will fight it out. I already have Lepke, Schultz, and the others behind me. I also have Detroit. You can take your two-bit punks and try to stand against us. You will lose and you will die, Nitto. I will do to you what I should have done to that scum Capone years ago. I should have slit his throat back in Brooklyn. It was the only time that I showed mercy and I have been paying for it the rest of my life. You will not be so lucky. I have no mercy left in my soul."

Nitti was now pounding his fists louder than Luciano. "You can't kill me. You won't get close. You'll be dead in the gutter before you can give that order. I could kill you now."

"And you will fall the first time you leave this hotel."

There was a long silence. Both men cooled down slightly, realizing their conversation was getting nowhere.

"What do you want, Luciano? Money?"

"It is too late. I cannot be paid off, bribed like some dirty politician. I want my men to sit alongside yours in the IATSE. I want East Coast representation in the union. They will join my other men who are already sitting on boards of the Teamsters and IBEW [electricians' union]. Or I pull New York out."

"You can't do that. Lepke won't stand for it."

"Lepke is in with me. He does as I say."

"Don't bet on it. Lepke turns as the wind blows. You know that."

"And I should trust you instead?"

"Trust no one."

There was another long pause.

"I repeat my demand."

"Before I can grant anything, I must talk to Browne. He does as I say, but it would be up to him to make appointments to the board."

"I want an answer by noon tomorrow."

Nitti sat back in his chair behind his desk, the desk once used by Al Capone. Luciano turned to leave, but stopped at the door.

"One more thing. I also want you off my back in Los Angeles. You let Roselli do as he wants, as long as he stays out of my rackets."

"Why do you think they are your rackets?"

"Because I already own them. Gambling, drugs, prostitution. I do not want to come up against your men, or hear stories about your men putting the squeeze on my people."

"As I hear it, the town is still up for grabs. You only own something as long as no one takes it away from you."

"I promise you this, no one will take that away. I will rip the town apart before I let you walk in. Understand that, Nitto."

Nitti rocked back in the chair, studying Luciano. He knew Luciano was generally a man of few words, and what he did say he meant. Lucky Luciano did not make a promise he was not ready to deliver.

Luciano slammed the office door and left. He waited for Nitti's answer in a room at the Sherman Hotel, in downtown Chicago, just far enough away from the Lexington to be comfortable. He was ready for a showdown the following day, whether he received infiltration of the union or not. For Luciano, the point was already moot; he knew he would infiltrate that union in time, as he had done with all the others. He simply wanted Nitti to get the machinery rolling before his appointment with death. No matter the outcome, Luciano was ready to kill Frank Nitti.

The next morning, Luciano was prepared for a bloodletting. He dialed Nitti and asked him to meet for lunch at a Southside Italian restaurant. Luciano asked Nitti to come alone; Luciano promised he would do the same.

The two met at noon, were escorted to a small table in the back of the restaurant, and dined on a meal of spaghetti, ravioli, and Chianti. The meal was cordial, but it was apparent that both men were on edge and very suspicious of one another. Nitti informed Luciano that he had spoken with Browne, who said he was agreeable to putting two of Luciano's men on the IATSE board, the names of the men to be decided at a later date. Nitti still would not compromise on his stand about squeezing Luciano out of the drugs, gambling, and prostitution rackets in L.A., which touched off Lucky's hair-trigger temper.

"What must I do to make you understand I am ready for war? Do you think this is a joke? We draw boundaries, Nitto.

You stay on your side and live. You can have the studios. I want my operations to run without interference from you."

"Why should I hand to you what I can keep for myself? You are no threat to me."

"Then you seal your fate."

With those words, the two men rose from the table and headed out the door. As he stepped across the threshold, Luciano stopped, turned to Nitti, and asked him to wait for a moment, he had run out of cigarettes. Within seconds after Luciano's hasty retreat, a car sped around the corner and opened fire, spraying bullets across the front of the restaurant, shattering glass and concrete. Nitti dove for the pavement. He was not shot, but cut and bleeding from flying glass. Luciano calmly walked up to Nitti, who was still facedown on the sidewalk. He put his foot on Nitti's back.

"This was a warning. Stay out of my way. Next time you will not be so lucky."

With that, Luciano walked to his car and drove away. Nitti rose from the ground and stared in Luciano's direction. He said nothing.

Luciano headed back to New York for several weeks to take care of business, then returned to Los Angeles to proceed with his affairs there. He was confident he would not receive any more trouble from Nitti.

With renewed determination, Luciano ordered his men to put pressure on Roland West to lease out the third floor of the Sidewalk Cafe. West adamantly refused to cave in to their demands. Tired of the game with West, Luciano decided he had to take the problem into his own hands, and called for a private conference with West. The conference was conducted in Luciano's car, as always, where there was little chance of being seen or heard.

"We are taking over the top floor for gambling. Your restaurant has a steady stream of Hollywood stars; they have money to spend. They will also attract other people of means."

"No. I will not invite you in!"

"Mr. West, you have already invited us in. You did that when you accepted our consignment arrangement."

"As I recall, I had no choice. It was buy our liquor and food from you, or we'd be out of business."

"You always have a choice. The deal I am proposing is strictly business. The third floor is empty, used for storage. It is not making money for anyone. I will lease the room from you through a leasing corporation I will set up. The corporation will obtain the proper licenses. You will make money through the lease, I will make money through the gambling. What I offer is legal, and it will be profitable for us both."

West assumed Luciano already knew about the gambling that was going on in the third floor. Luciano had kept close tabs on the restaurant's dealings, and it was logical to assume Luciano was not only aware of the sub-rosa gambling, but knew who played there and how much was taken in "under the table." Their conversation about a business venture may have only been posturing on both sides. Luciano had already determined he would take over the gambling at the cafe.

West later related the details to Thelma, hoping she would either buy him out of the cafe altogether or approve the leasing arrangement, which needed the signatures of both of them. West was desperate for any movement that would get Luciano off his back.

The dream was turning into a nightmare, though West and Todd did enjoy both the hard work of running the restaurant and the chance to socialize with their friends while acting as the ultimate hosts. What neither had been prepared for was the intense pressure of dealing with customers, business managers, accountants, service people, and most of all, gangsters.

West began, "I've been threatened, I've been lied to, I've been pushed as far as I'm going to go. You brought that gangster into the cafe. It's up to you to either give in or get me out of the entire deal."

"Let me set you straight. I did not invite Luciano into the cafe," Thelma responded. "I have never even seen him at the cafe. I made a point to keep that part of my life separate . . . and private."

"Well, it's not private. The entire town knows you've been seeing him."

"What the hell do you want me to do? Say it's okay to go in with Luciano? You might as well just give him the restaurant then. I will not have the place run by hoodlums. It's enough someone's draining our money, the books are probably being juggled, and God only knows what else. Now you want me to just open the door and invite him in?"

"Then buy me out. I've had it. This isn't turning out the way I had hoped."

"And you think I'm thrilled with the way things are going? I've been turning down movie offers to help run this place. It's been a lot more than name only for me."

"Then buy me out."

"How am I supposed to buy you out? With what? For how much? Every dime I earn I put into this place to keep it running. God only knows where the money's going."

"Then let's sell together and split the money."

"No."

"So I'm stuck as long as you want to hold on, is that it?"

"In a way."

The discussion had escalated into an argument; Thelma was trying to get it back on track.

"Roland. Let's just sit tight. Luciano will back down. He's got other interests, I'm sure. If he knows he can't get the top floor, he'll give up."

"How can you be sure?"

"I've done some homework. I can always use leverage."

"What do you mean?"

"I can't tell you, and please don't ask."

What Thelma knew about, or at least thought she knew about, was the movie shakedown. During one of their drives, Luciano had rattled off the names Bioff, Browne, and Nitti. Thelma kept her mouth shut and listened. She also caught the names of two organizations, IATSE and the AFL. When she pressed Luciano about their connection, he exploded and went into a wild rage, slapping her, swearing, threatening to kill anyone and everyone. Thelma knew there was a connection between Bioff and Browne and Nitti, and she noted the rapid rise in power of Bioff and Browne. There was also talk in the studios about Bioff's strong-arm tactics in recruiting men into IATSE. Thelma, working in many studios and knowing people from all walks of life, heard stories and kept a running account in the back of her mind. Still, she had only vague assumptions and ideas. She was not positive of anything until October 1935.

She still was not sure how, or even if, Lucky fit into the picture, outside of the fact that one of the last times she had seen him, he was threatening to kill Bioff and Browne. In October, Luciano's attitude changed almost entirely; he seemed more arrogant, somewhat calm, smug and calculating, as if a well-timed practical joke was about to come off. When Thelma casually dropped Bioff's and Browne's names, Lucky brushed them aside, with nowhere near the malevolence he had shown only a short time ago. The odd turnabout puzzled Toddy.

Luciano would say only, "They've been taken care of," then abruptly change the subject, making it apparent there was to be no more discussion, ever, on the topic of Bioff and Browne. Still, Thelma was not satisfied. There were too many "tough-looking men" hanging around the studios. The unions, in particular IATSE, had gotten too much power almost overnight, and there was too much speculation that the union officials were part of "the mob."

Thelma found the answers to some of her questions at a Hollywood party given by one of the Schencks.

It is no secret that management and labor are strange bedfellows; one cannot work without the other, yet the two have always been, and always will be, adversaries. But while they must work together, management and labor-union leaders rarely party together, let alone consider one another friends. It struck many people as odd that Willie Bioff was present at Schenck's party. Odder still was the fact that Schenck and other studio bigwigs were paying homage to the fat man, slapping him on the back, laughing at jokes that were not funny, pouring him drinks, and flattering his already inflated ego. The dance of courtship was noted by everyone in the room, including Thelma.

There was something even stranger going on at the party. Among the movie stars, movie moguls, and maids were men who looked rather uncomfortable, as if they did not fit in and they knew it. They never made eye contact yet seemed to be watching everyone in the room. These were some of the same men who had turned up at the Sidewalk Cafe and at the studios. She did not know yet if they were Luciano's men or Nitti's (because of Bioff's presence), but she was positive they were gangsters.

Thelma phoned for her chauffeur, Ernie Peters, to come and get her, and left the party. When she returned to her apartment above the cafe, she turned on the radio to muffle her phone call. She was frightened and did not want West to hear.

"Mom? I really need to talk to you. Something's going on. I'm not sure what yet, but I just have a feeling. I need to talk. Will you wait up?"

With that call, Thelma gulped down a handful of pills she hoped would steady her nerves, and chugged down a glass of Scotch. She then quietly left her apartment and hiked up the 270 cement steps that eventually led to the path toward the garage of Jewel Carmen's house, the garage where she kept her chocolate-brown Phaeton convertible. She started the engine, which echoed through the garage in a loud "varoom," filling the room with exhaust. The engine settled down to a muffled roar, and she backed out of the garage, leaving the doors open. She was positive she saw someone peering out of the room above the garage, and assumed it was Charles Smith, who had probably been awakened by the roar of the engine.

By the time she reached her mother's Hollywood home, the drugs and booze had already taken effect. Thelma was somewhat incoherent, her speech was slurred, yet she was still jumpy and far from settled down. Alice was disturbed by the state and condition of her daughter. She grabbed her by the arms and shook her.

"What's this all about? What's the matter with you?"

Thelma tried her best to speak. "Mom, Mom, listen to me for one minute. This is important. There's something going on and I'm not sure what to do about it."

Alice would not let Thelma talk. "I thought I told you to stop taking those drugs. Look at you. And you've been drinking again. You're going to bloat right back up."

"Listen to me!" This was one of the rare times Thelma spoke up to Alice. "Don't you care what's happening? I need to talk to you! Why don't you let me talk?"

Toddy started crying and Alice finally realized the seriousness of the situation. She sat alongside Toddy on the sofa.

"Things have gotten out of control. I don't know what to do about it."

"How? You mean with Roland?"

"Sort of. We've been offered a deal to lease out the storage room as a gambling casino."

"You're not going to do that, are you? Who made the offer?"

"Luciano, to Roland. Nothing directly to me, yet. Roland said no, but he also wants me to buy him out, or he'll just sell out altogether somehow."

"You're not selling out!"

"No, don't worry. I like the cafe. Something's wrong, though. We're losing money; I can't figure it out. Smith may be juggling the books, but I don't know for sure. I don't know enough about those things and neither does Roland. The first of the year I'm going to check it out."

"That can be fixed easily enough if that is the problem. I don't think it's anything to get this upset about."

"That's not the whole story. It's the gambling thing and Roland. I think Roland would hand the room over to Lucky if he had a chance. I know he's scared. I am, too."

Thelma stopped talking for a moment and stood up from the sofa.

"Do you have anything to drink?"

"In the cabinet."

Thelma walked over to a small cabinet against the back wall, where Alice kept liquor and cocktail glasses. Thelma poured herself a drink, then headed back to the sofa. She sipped while she talked.

"There's something big going on. I think it has to do with the studios and one of the unions. I saw Willie Bioff at a party tonight."

"So?"

"Mom, he's on the board of one of the unions. He's also in with Frank Nitti in Chicago. I know the mob is in with the unions. Everyone knows that."

"Thel, they've always been. Even back in the old days. Your father used to talk about that, remember?"

"There's more. The party was at Mr. Schenck's. He was friendly as can be with him. That's not normal. Then Lucky was going on and on about killing Bioff and Browne and Nitti and how they cheated him. Since he's come back from Chicago, he no longer talks about that, but some of his men . . . I think they were his men . . . were at the party tonight, too."

"I don't understand what you're getting at."

"It all adds up. Don't you see? Somehow Lucky must be involved with Bioff and Browne and Nitti, and somehow they must all be involved with some sort of deal with the studios. There's either some payoff or intimidation or something going on. Why the hell would those bastards be at the party? Everyone was whispering all sorts of thing. Someone said some guys in the union were talking about strike threats. They thought they were going out, but then nothing happened . . . except Nitti's guys and Lucky's guys are now in with the union and the studios."

"Thel. I think you should stay out of it. You should know better. Just forget about what's going on. You of all people should know what these men can do. I would also stay away from Luciano."

"And how do you suppose I do that?"

"Let him know you're seeing other men. Tell him about Harvey [Priester] or your beau in San Francisco. He'll move on, they always do."

"It's too late for that. I think someone should know what's going on."

"Then go to the authorities."

"I don't know if anyone in the police department could help. I'd have to go to the district attorney or someone like that."

"Then do it, but be careful."

Thelma did not reply. If she did go to the authorities, she wanted to be sure she had all her facts straight and that meant more checking. Thelma believed she could not ignore what she knew; she was already in too deep with Luciano to pretend she did not know anything about his connection with Bioff and Browne.

What she really needed most of all was just to get away for a week, away from everyone and everything to think things through. She had had enough of Hollywood parties; they were no longer fun and they devoured what little free time Thelma had. For her, parties were now something she did only when necessary, or only if the invitation came from a close friend.

She wrote another letter to Mac, from the yacht *Joyita*, owned by West and Carmen. (*Joyita* was an inside pet name between the couple, carried over from the name included on the Sidewalk Cafe sign, "Joya's").

". . . I wouldn't mind tripping back myself, but what with my work and restaurant I'm pretty busy. Snuck away for a week however on the above yacht and feel fine. But will be back in the straight-jacket any day now. Life isn't very exciting as I keep away from all parties etc, with the exception of very intimate ones. People bore and distract me to death. Getting smart or 'old maidish'. I don't know which. . . . Well here's to seeing you, if not hearing from you. With love always, Thel."

Thelma returned to work refreshed and with a more positive outlook. She made up her mind that she would try to ignore what she knew or suspected about the dealings between the unions and the studios. She was lively and perky around the restaurant and at the studio, a return to her old bubbly self.

West heard nothing from Luciano's men for about a month. Toddy had not seen Lucky since their October drive. Both West and Toddy assumed the gambling idea had blown over. Business was picking up with the upcoming Thanksgiving holiday, and money problems with the cafe were settling down. The cafe was now breaking even and staying in the black. Thelma assumed either Smith had been warned about the upcoming audit and straightened up his books, or it was just a fluke of the season with the crush of business bringing in more money than was being siphoned off. Either way, she thought she could finally start paying back some of the debts she had run up with the friends who loaned her money when the cafe seemed to be in trouble.

The peace turned out to be the lull before the storm. Four days before Thanksgiving, Luciano blew back into town and insisted on seeing Thelma; he also warned her to keep their meeting confidential, which she did not do. He picked her up, as he usually did, and they drove for a while before heading to the Brown Derby for dinner.

By the time Thelma arrived at the restaurant, she was visibly shaken and irritated. Luciano was also angry. The two were not speaking. Toddy later told friends Luciano had wrangled with her all night about giving him the storage room for gambling. He was insistent and vowed he would not walk away without the papers. They had argued violently in the car, Thelma refusing to give Luciano what he wanted.

Toddy also said she had brought up another subject—the union tie with the studios. Luciano kept pressing to find out what she knew; Thelma told him (bluffing, of course) that she knew plenty, hoping she could use it as a bargaining chip. She told Luciano she would keep silent if he backed off on the cafe gambling. The discussion was at a stalemate until the couple got halfway through dinner.

Luciano spoke quietly but definitely. "I am not a man to beg. I am not a man to repeat my demands. I am offering you a fair deal. If you do not go along with my offer, I am now prepared to take your restaurant over. I will bleed you dry."

"And I will fight."

"I have already cost you thousands of dollars. How far are you willing to go before you have had enough?"

"You can push Roland around, but not me. I'll fight if I have to. And if you push, I'll go to the D.A. about your dealings out here. I'm sure he'd love to get an earful."

Thelma had no idea the D.A.'s office had already been infiltrated and that Fitts was already under the very strong thumbs of some of the most powerful men in the country. The city as a whole was corrupt in the thirties; the government, the law were just pawns in the game.

Luciano smiled at Toddy's hollow threat.

"You do what you have to do. But I will open the gambling casino by the first of the year."

Thelma was angry and threw down her white linen dinner napkin. She had enough of this evil man they called Charley Lucifer. The game was over. She now had the courage and strength to walk away.

Thelma stood up and yelled at Lucky, turning heads across the room.

"You'll open a gambling casino in my restaurant over my dead body!"

She stormed across the room toward the door.

While she was still within earshot, Luciano calmly stood up and spoke in a very gentlemanlike tone. "That can be arranged."

Chapter Sixteen

By 1935, Thelma Todd was one of the screen's most popular and most beautiful comediennes. She received nearly five hundred fan letters a week; her salary with Hal Roach was reportedly going to be upped to more than $3,500 a week. She also had a contract offer from Nick Schenck at Loew's/MGM if she decided not to sign again with Roach. She had looks, she had charm, and she had scores of friends. Though she avoided the limelight and tried to divide her time between the restaurant and work at the studio, she was very much the center of attention. Men of all means and social status vied for her affections. She had suitors across the country and was continually receiving flowers and gifts from admirers, something that greatly distressed Roland West, who could not resign himself to the basic fact that he and Toddy would never be more than just good friends.

West was openly jealous of Toddy's suitors, made wild accusations about her "sleeping around," and continually threatened to lock her out of her apartment if she ever came home late from a date or party. Toddy respected West, but she did not love him. The few times she did go out, she stayed out till all hours of the night, often to deliberately rile West. West had double-locked the main door on at least two occasions, leaving her knocking, pounding and shouting, and finally waiting all night outside. Neighbors in the Palisades community repeated stories of the bitter quarrels West and Toddy had through the front door; quarrels that echoed through the hills on very quiet nights.

Though the relationship between West and Todd was beginning to fray around the edges, they still put up a good front in public. They kept their business to themselves, and rarely discussed their problems with friends out of fear that rumors about a "breakup" would damage the fragile cafe business, which was finally operating under its own steam.

But friends did know about Toddy's "delicious affair with that San Francisco businessman," as she put it, and that she was also reportedly the fiancée of a man named Harvey Priester, an insurance counselor for movie stars, who spent a great amount of time at the Sidewalk Cafe. Most considered the affairs only the latest in a long string of broken hearts Toddy seemed to leave behind. But West viewed them as personal humiliations that made him out to be a fool. Though he said little, those who knew both Toddy and West knew he was seething and about to explode.

Along with scores of suitors and party invitations, there was another result of Toddy's immense popularity, a darker side. Mixed in with the hundreds of fan letters were vile, threatening missives—threats against the cafe and death threats against Thelma herself.

She called the bomb squad at least once in response to a telegram she received at the cafe, a telegram stating that a bomb was planted in the bar area, set to go off at noon. The cafe was closed for the day and searched, but no bomb was found.

Toddy's maid, Mae Whitehead, told police that Thelma received so many death threats, especially in 1935, that she routinely bundled them up in paper and took them down to the police station as part of her chores as maid. But there were threats from two separate sources that gave Toddy a real enough scare that for protection, she bought a white bull terrier, which she named White King, and she began carrying a small handgun in her purse at all times.

The most sinister of the threats came from someone who signed himself "The Ace" and had a drawing of the ace of hearts in the lower right-hand corner. The first of six notes arrived February 2, 1935, and they continued through November. What made the notes so frightening was that they named specific men Thelma had either known as friends or had been linked with romantically. The first note stated she should "pay $10,000 to Abe Lyman in New York by March 5 and live, if not our San Francisco boys will lay you out. This is no joke." The note went on to list men she had known, including Priester, Rudy Schaefer, Roland West, and Lyman. At the same time, she was receiving long-distance phone calls from a mumbling voice identifying itself as "The Ace of Hearts."

It was apparent that "The Ace" had done his homework. Whoever wrote the note was well aware of Thelma's friends and the extent of her involvements. She had been romantically linked to Abe Lyman at one point. He was a popular bandleader; in fact he had been playing at the party where Toddy initially met Pat DiCicco.

The note was turned over to the Los Angeles Police Department, who examined it, filed it, but did nothing else.

Two weeks later, Abe Lyman received a handwritten note, similar to the one mailed to Toddy. His was also from "The Ace" and warned, ". . . if you are a friend of Thelma Todd warn her to pay $20,000 or she dies . . . she must pay the money to Major Bowes at the Capitol." The letter was mailed from San Francisco. Bowes, like Lyman, knew nothing about "The Ace" or any reason for such a letter. Lyman immediately phoned Thelma to report the note; they shared the information and Lyman handed his letter to the LAPD.

Thelma's second extortion note arrived two months later, also signed "The Ace" but demanding $15,000. Again it was turned over to the LAPD. The first two notes were mailed from San Francisco and did not particularly bother Thelma. But when the third note, and then the fourth, arrived postmarked from New York, Thelma got scared. She immediately thought of Luciano and turned the subsequent notes over to the Los Angeles bureau of the FBI. If the threats were in any way connected to Luciano, she wanted protection, especially in light of Luciano's demanding the third floor for gambling.

The FBI examined the note, but could not trace its author. It assigned bodyguards who followed Thelma everywhere she went. Nothing turned up. When the fifth note arrived, demanding she drop $20,000 at a destination on Hollywood Boulevard, Thelma had had enough of the "constant companions," as she called the bodyguards, and decided to take action herself.

Instead of dropping off the money, she dropped off a note, saying she would deliver the money in person the following day. She wanted to see this "Ace" face to face.

The following day, Thelma drove her convertible down Hollywood Boulevard toward the Warner's Theatre, which was the spot "The Ace" had determined as the rendezvous point. She had blank pieces of paper in an envelope in her purse, along with her .22 revolver. She was half a block away when she saw a man standing near the curb, very nervous and, judging from his erratic demeanor, obviously not a tourist. She assumed he was "The Ace." When he saw Toddy's car, he shielded his face, so she never had a good look at him.

As she pulled up alongside the man, he hunched over the passenger side of the car, still looking down, covering his face. He told her to meet him at a remote spot near the beach and he would collect his "present" there. Thelma answered, "Not on your life, pal," and sped off, returning home frightened. She related the full story to police, who reprimanded her for venturing out alone. They told her that next time, if she insisted on pulling such a stunt, she should have an unmarked police car following in the distance. Thelma agreed.

As expected, "The Ace" sent another note, demanding $20,000 and demanding Thelma deliver it in person. Again, the spot was on Hollywood Boulevard, near a hosiery shop. Again, Thelma agreed, and arrived with the stack of fake money in an envelope in her purse. As the man leaned over and reached out, Thelma opened her purse. The man quickly withdrew his hand and fled on foot through an alley, eluding police.

Thelma believed the man either saw her gun in the purse or suspected she had a police escort. In any event, several weeks later, on August 19, the FBI in New York arrested thirty-four-year-old Harry Schimanski, superintendent of an Astoria, Long Island, apartment house, on charges of attempted extortion. How they tracked him down is unclear, but in his small New York apartment they found scores of pictures of Thelma Todd glued to his mirror, his walls, his dresser. He also had piles of press clippings with almost the complete history of Toddy, detailing all of her involvements. Next to the pile of clippings was a list of names of men with whom Thelma had been involved. Schimanski was obsessed with Thelma. He initially pleaded not guilty on October 31, and was held under indictment by a grand jury.

In the fall of 1935, Thelma received another set of extortion letters, similar to those from "The Ace" but signed "A Friend." They demanded Toddy pay sums up to $50,000 or she would be killed or her restaurant burned down. Twenty-eight-year-old Edward Schieffert was arrested in New York eight days after Schimanski's arraignment and charged with attempted extortion. Schieffert, a drugstore handyman, freely admitted to sending the letters to Todd. He told authorities that Miss Todd was his dream girl and he thought the publicity would help her career. Police tracked him down after he phoned a New York newspaper, declaring Schimanski was innocent and "The Ace" was still at large. He was found mentally unstable and committed to Bellevue State Mental Hospital. Police believe he may have been responsible for both sets of letters.

Though Toddy was not physically harmed by the letters, she was put under a great deal of extra stress, which came on top of her problems with West and the cafe. Her nerves were frazzled; she was continually fidgeting, unable to sleep. Once again she reached for the bottle of pills. By November, she was an addict, hooked on tranquilizers to sleep and amphetamines for energy, all downed with Scotch. It was another return to a safe refuge. Only this time she was there to stay.

She received little comfort from Alice, who was still pressing on the issue of Luciano and the Bioff/Schenck party. She nagged Thelma to go to the authorities to tell what she knew about Luciano's operations on the West Coast. Toddy steadfastly refused to listen to her mother's advice, but each time the subject came up, Thelma's resistance grew slightly weaker. By the end of November, Toddy indicated she was considering making an appointment to speak with Buron Fitts about Luciano's infiltration of many Hollywood nightclubs, the attempted infiltration of the Sidewalk Cafe, and his ties with drug peddling in the studios, including his part in her own addiction.

Luciano had been moving freely around Hollywood since his confrontation in Chicago with Nitti. Nitti's men stayed mainly within the bounds of the studios and unions; Luciano's centered on drugs, prostitution, and gambling in and around L.A. It was later learned that Nitti more or less "gave" Luciano free rein in those operations as a concession for Nitti's double-dealing on the Million Dollar Movie Shakedown, and as a token to thwart another assassination attempt and prevent the full-scale gang war Luciano had promised.

The Sidewalk Cafe meant nothing more to Luciano than another notch on his belt, albeit a large notch because of its potential draw as an upstairs casino. West was knuckling under to the scare tactics Luciano used in the cafe; he had his men wander in and out, sit at tables and order very little, and in general check the business out and follow West. West knew who the men were and he knew he was being watched. Luciano believed West was sufficiently worn down and would be a pushover. He now had to work on Thelma.

Thelma was also being watched, though just a little more carefully due to the bodyguards surrounding her during the extortion incidents. Luciano's men made their point, though. They pulled up alongside her car while she was stopped at traffic lights, brushed by her in stores, walked past her on the street, dined at the same restaurants. There was nothing she could do about it because the men were doing nothing illegal.

Toddy had a premonition that something terrible was about to happen. In early December, she told her dressmaker, Helen Ainsworth, who owned an exclusive dress shop on Sunset Boulevard, that she had to make some serious decisions, that she was not sure of the future. She said, "I'll probably be broke, so I'm paying my dressmaking bills now, while I have the money. I don't know why I'm living the way I am, the way things are. There's going to be a change in my life, and it's going to happen before the first of the year." Ainsworth assumed Toddy meant she was leaving the restaurant, selling out, maybe quitting her acting career and leaving town. Thelma never elaborated.

Then she wrote back home. "I've fallen in with a tough bunch of characters. I'm not sure what I'm going to do about it. I'm really frightened for the first time in my life." She also said she hoped to get back home later in the month, for Christmas. She would never keep that date.

Thelma probably suspected she would never make it to Lawrence. She did the bulk of her Christmas shopping early that year; she had everything bought, wrapped, and shipped back home by the first week of December. The rest of the presents were stored in the trunk of her convertible, wrapped and ready to go. She told her mother to make sure to hand the gifts out "just in case I'm not around to play Santa myself."

Alice asked where Thelma thought she would be going during the holidays. Thelma refused to say; she just smiled and told Alice "not to worry." Alice brushed the comment aside as her daughter's paranoia, or just idle chatter. She believed the men who had been sending threatening letters had been caught. She also believed Thelma had been taking the notes too personally and had been under too much strain to think rationally. She had no idea that her daughter suspected Luciano was about to close in.

Though his men were evident, Thelma had not seen Luciano himself in two weeks, since just before Thanksgiving, when they had had the argument at the Brown Derby. Lucky's last words had been a death threat, which lit the fuse, and Toddy knew something had to explode somewhere. Luciano's temper had been simmering, and was now boiling. She fully expected to hear from Luciano and was very concerned that he had not approached her since the fight. She knew that with such men, silence was worse than a threat.

On December 11, Toddy finally gave in to pressure from her mother about going to the authorities. She phoned the District Attorney's office and asked to speak to Buron Fitts. Fitts was in a meeting and unable to come to the phone. The voice on the line asked who was calling. When Thelma gave her name, there was a long pause; then the voice on the line asked for a number where she could be reached, where Mr. Fitts could call her back. Thelma gave the number at her apartment at the Sidewalk Cafe.

A "representative" from Fitts's office called Toddy back about one hour later and asked the nature of her business. Thelma said it was personal and refused to offer any further details over the phone. The "representative" said he would call her again momentarily to set up an appointment. The "representative" then phoned five minutes later, again inquiring about the nature of her business. Todd maintained it was personal. There was another long pause. Then an appointment was set up for Tuesday, December 17, 1935, at 11:30 A.M. Thelma jotted down the time, but no reference to whom she was to meet. That appointment was the catalyst that set off a rapid-fire chain of events that would lead to her macabre death just one week later.

West reportedly saw the note jotted on the cafe calendar and questioned Toddy about the appointment. West assumed it was some sort of doctor's appointment since he was concerned about Thelma's health. She looked thin and drawn, and was tired and nervous; the drug/alcohol combination was taking its toll on her appearance. West had been pressuring Toddy to get help, and he assumed she had finally taken his advice. She offered no information on the appointment.

Then, with a sudden sense of urgency, Thelma decided to convert the third-floor storeroom into a steakhouse as an addition to the Sidewalk Cafe. Toddy laid out the details of her idea to West and Rudy Schaefer, but made an obvious point of snubbing Smith, whom she said she still did not trust. She also asked West and Schaefer to leave Smith out of the plans until it was time for construction to begin. As she explained it, the steakhouse would be a nice alternative to the downstairs restaurant, which focused primarily on seafood.

West was concerned about the cost of building and opening the addition, especially since Thelma wanted to rush it through by January 1 (the deadline Luciano had set for his takeover). Thelma promised, initially, to back the addition with her own money and not tap into the cafe's account. Once the steakhouse was running under its own steam, the money from the steakhouse and cafe would be pooled into one account. She reasoned that if she used her own money, there would be no need for her to tell Smith because the cafe finances would be separate at first.

She quickly convinced West that the steakhouse was the key to end their troubles.

"Roland, it's a wonderful idea. There's no place like it at the beach, or anywhere around here, for miles. It would also put the storage room to good use, leaving no space available for 'other purposes.'"

West got her meaning loud and clear. If they beat Luciano to the punch, he would have to look elsewhere for a gambling site. They spoke in vague references, never mentioning Luciano's name aloud.

"You're playing with fire, double-crossing someone like that."

"It will be my deal, and I'll take the heat. I know I can handle this one. If you beat them at their own game, they'll find someplace else to go. It won't be worth the hassle for them. Believe me, I know about this type of thing." Thelma paused and spoke almost as an afterthought. "Anyway, by next week our problem should be solved completely. I'm going to a higher authority."

"The appointment?"

"Forget you saw that and forget I said anything."

With that, Thelma rolled up her sleeves and got to work. West never pushed to find out any details of the appointment and pretty much stayed out of her way during the initial phase of construction. He was relieved that Toddy seemed to be regaining that spark and zest that had slipped away. He was pleased that she had something to occupy her time, which, he hoped, would end some of their bickering.

Todd poured all her energy into the third-floor steakhouse. She put every dime she had and every cent she could beg, borrow, or steal into a quick remodeling (which may have explained the sudden decision to pay off her dressmaker). The steakhouse was to open January 1 for a New Year's celebration.

Thelma had an elaborate Art Deco sign painted and posted it on the main cafe door. The remodeling would finish sometime during the week between Christmas and New Year's.

The sign was splashy and an attention getter. THELMA TODD ANNOUNCES THE OPENING UPSTAIRS JANUARY ONE . . . THE FINEST RESTAURANT IN CALIFORNIA . . . SERVING AND SPECIALIZING IN STEAKS OF JOYA'S . . . UNEQUALLED $2.00 . . . PRIVATE DINING ROOM AVAILABLE. There was no turning back.

The upcoming steakhouse was the talk of the studio and the Hollywood community. Thelma gave details of the construction and the menu to anyone who would listen. The steakhouse would have more of a posh New York atmosphere to it than a Western motif, with peach and white tablecloths, silver cutlery, white china edged in silver, flowers on the tables, and a maître d' at the door. It would serve nothing but steak and fresh vegetables, offering every cut of steak imaginable. It would seat about one hundred guests, and the room itself could also be rented out to private parties, something that could not be done downstairs.

She hoped her news would come to the attention of Lucky Luciano, who always managed to have a set of eyes and a pair of ears around every corner. Her news scored a bull's-eye, but she was not to find that out for another week.

With the upcoming holidays, the rush to open the steakhouse, and Thelma's work schedule, there was little time left for her to devote to the downstairs cafe, which she left completely in West's hands. What little free time she had, she spent with Alice or in flying up to San Francisco to see her "businessman," whose identity she kept hidden from everyone, including West. What had begun as a change of pace had escalated into an all-consuming passion and in a matter of days further deteriorated the relationship between West and Todd. West's fuse was short and now he openly resented the fact that Toddy had in effect abandoned her duties at the cafe, leaving him to order supplies, serve as maître d', and supervise the daily routine of the restaurant during the busy holiday season.

To make matters worse, Thelma had been getting a crush of invitations to holiday parties, and West was left alone to answer the phone and take messages. He was rarely invited to social functions as Thelma's escort and rarely even invited to the parties for which he was taking information for Toddy. Even worse, Thelma had left a list of names and asked West to either accept invitations or reject them according to her list. Most of them she asked West to turn down. That put West in an awkward position, making excuses for Thelma. She did not leave West holding the bag out of malice; she simply was not thinking about him. Her mind was dealing with five different problems, and she loved the excitement.

The tension between West and Toddy was growing. They started by sniping at one another; then those taunts escalated to all-out quarrels. As the second week in December approached, the arguments were no longer kept behind closed doors, in the privacy of the restaurant office or West's or Todd's apartment; cutting remarks were being exchanged in front of cafe guests and friends, and over the telephone that West used at the second-floor bar. It was apparent to anyone within earshot that there was serious trouble between West and Todd. West told Thelma that he was tired of being her personal secretary and that after the holidays they had better come to some serious decisions about the cafe and their relationship.

West had hoped that Toddy's enthusiasm for the steakhouse would eventually lead to one of two outcomes. Either Toddy would run the third floor and he would run the cafe— allowing a separate but equal coexistence and keeping them out of one another's way until tempers cooled enough for them to work together again—or Thelma would get tired of taking on so much responsibility; running the steakhouse single-handedly would exhaust her and she would finally agree to sell out altogether. Either way, West believed, given enough time, the problems would resolve themselves and their friendship would be saved. But things only got worse.

To avoid confronting West, Todd began staying out later and later, returning home well after 2:00 A.M. at times. Sometimes she would be with Alice, sometimes at parties, other times just sitting alone at a nightclub or staying late with friends on the Roach lot. Toddy told friends she was doing it deliberately to "get Roland's goat" so that he would either be awakened by the racket she made returning home or have to get up to unlock the double-bolted door between the apartments.

Todd and West started bolting that door in October. There had been a rash of burglaries in the area, and West and Smith had seen prowlers around the cafe on three occasions, hours after it was closed. One morning, West found gouges in the main door, as if someone had tried to break in, chipping away at the lock. Either the would-be robber was scared away by the barking of White King (which woke both West and Thelma), or he had given up because he was unable to break the lock.

Then, during the first week in December, there was another series of break-ins at the beach. Three homes down the road from the cafe were robbed. Police believed the robberies happened during the afternoons, when the women were shopping and the men were at work. Police also believed the robber had been casing the area to find out exactly when certain homes would be vacant. Unfortunately, during one of those burglaries, the owner happened to be home. A woman in her mid-forties was beaten and tied up while the robber looted the house. The woman recovered, but she either refused or was unable to identify the intruder. He was never captured.

If Thelma took the problems with West, with Luciano, with the cafe, and with the outbreak of robberies seriously, she never let on. She remained bubbly and sweet to her friends and always accommodated strangers and tourists who stopped her to ask for an autograph or picture. She was still as good at burying her emotions as she had been as a child coping with Alice's dominating personality.

Those who knew Thelma during the last month of her life said she was in better spirits than she had been in weeks. She was optimistic about the future and excited about the third-floor addition, and she brushed away any problems with West as "just one of those things that will blow over," not to be taken seriously. She actually believed Lucky Luciano was out of the picture, though his men still loitered in the cafe, watching the progress of construction on the steakhouse. She confided to one Hollywood friend that if Luciano was going to do something about the steakhouse, he would have done it the instant word got out about the remodeling. Toddy assumed that since nothing had been said or done, she had gotten Luciano out of her life. But nothing could have been further from the truth. She was to see Luciano one last time.

Chapter Seventeen

Someone else was also about to reenter Thelma's life—Pat DiCicco. DiCicco had spent a great deal of time in New York since their divorce more than a year and a half ago and subsequently had seen little of Thelma and stayed out of her affairs. But word of the opening of the steakhouse apparently attracted DiCicco back to the Palisades, and those who knew him speculated that the reason for his sudden and renewed interest was that he smelled money and was probably scheming to get his hands on the pot of gold. Others suspected his plot went much deeper.

Toddy was shocked to find DiCicco sitting in the Sidewalk Cafe on Wednesday, December 11. It was late afternoon and Thelma had just returned from the Roach Studios, tired from an early-morning call on her comedy titled, appropriately enough, *Hot Money*. She usually had food sent up to her apartment from the cafe kitchen, but on this day, she just happened to walk through the downstairs section; she never revealed the exact reason for her detour. When she saw Pat dining alone, eating a salad, she hesitated for a moment, then approached his table.

"Hi, stranger. What brings you out to this neck of the woods?"

"I want to see you. It's been a long time."

"You here on business?"

"Just the usual."

The conversation was cordial, but strained on both sides. Though they put up a front of nonchalance, it was apparent that they were uncomfortable. DiCicco pressed on, gradually making what is believed to be his primary reason for the visit clear.

"I see you're opening up the top floor. Looks like it should be a success."

"I hope so. I sunk everything into it."

"West a part of it, too? I thought he was supposed to be the financial backer for this place."

"Not the upstairs, that's mine . . . at least at first. I was pouring a lot of money into the cafe and thought if I was going to throw money away and go broke, it was better to do it on a place that would be mine, more or less."

"You need a manager." Pat was not asking, but rather informing Thelma of a fact.

"That's my department, for now."

"You're going to do it all yourself? You'll go under. You and West are having a difficult enough time keeping this place together. I don't think you'll be able to do it."

"Thanks for the vote of confidence."

"It's not just that. I didn't mean it that way. You know I still care about you. You know how I always worried about you . . ."

". . . Yes, I remember. I still have the bruises."

Realizing his line was not working, Pat tried a different tack. "Look, I'm a business manager. I'll be up front. I think you can make a fortune with this place with the right management. I'd like in."

Thelma did not answer; she only stared at Pat. It was now beginning to add up. Thelma remembered how she had first met Lucky Luciano—at dinner with Pat. She had always suspected Pat had some dealings with Luciano or other gangsters, but she could never be certain; he was always very cautious. What so-called underworld connections he did have he wrote off to being in the limelight, being an actor's manager and heir to a fortune. He always told Thelma those things seemed to follow.

Now there was something more to Pat's story. The timing of his visit, his bluntness at wanting "in"—and using that word, a word Luciano threw around many times. He was making an obvious play for the steakhouse, the same room Lucky had been itching to get. Thelma had never been positive that her association with Pat, and subsequently Luciano, was tied in to the cafe's financial problems, but she could never find evidence that it was not.

Toddy suspected that Pat was probably working as a front man for Luciano in one last attempt to infiltrate the third floor before construction was finished. She knew that if she let Pat get a foot in the door, Luciano would sneak in through the crack. She sensed a setup and laughed.

"I'm sure you would like 'in,' as you put it. Please tell Mr. Luciano no dice. It's over."

"Thel, I don't know what you're talking about. What in God's name does Lucky have to do with any of this?"

"Pat, I'm not stupid. Quit playing games."

"I really don't know what you're talking about. I haven't seen Luciano in a few months. I don't know where he's been and frankly I don't care. I thought that a partnership of sorts would be good for us both."

"If not Luciano, then what's your angle?"

"Cards on the table? I've been out of circulation for some time. The steakhouse would be a good way for me to get back in touch . . . meet some people and get my management business back on its feet here in L.A."

DiCicco was always smooth, and Thelma couldn't always tell when he was telling the truth. This was one of those times when she suspected he was covering something, but she was not certain. She was always a soft touch and considered Pat a friend; she also hated to say no to anyone. But this was one hunch she believed she had to follow. She smelled trouble, a setup, and knew Luciano had to be lurking in the shadows somewhere.

"Sorry. It's still premature. I'm not even thinking about that yet, it's too far ahead. I just want to get the place going and I'll find the time to do it."

"How? You work all day . . ."

"I'm sticking to the series right now, no outside films. The contract with Roach is up next year, and I don't know yet if I'm going to renew. I have another offer that could be a better deal, get me away from the grind of a series. I have to say no for now, Pat."

With that, Thelma kissed Pat on the cheek and headed back to her apartment. She had a feeling Pat was not finished and the tension over the steakhouse would soon reach a crisis point. She felt an obvious pressure, and she felt it was coming from a dark storm brewing just in the distance, a storm named Luciano.

Thelma took a short nap, and was roused from sleep about 5:30 that evening by the phone. It was a call from one of the Skouras brothers, who was one of the executives of the Fox Film chain. They chatted briefly and Thelma goaded him into bringing a Christmas party to the cafe on Sunday.

"If you're going to have a Christmas party, why not hold it at the cafe? I'll set it up for you."

"But it's for eleven people."

"I'll reserve a table, it will be no problem."

"Okay, okay. Sunday. For dinner. What time is good for you?"

"How about seven o'clock?"

"Fine."

"I'll bet you won't come. You're going to stand me up, aren't you?"

"No! No! I promise I'll be there with eleven people. We'll make you work!"

"I'll bet you one hundred dollars you won't show."

"You got it."

"Okay, the bet is on. If you don't show, I'll collect one hundred bucks. I'll be around the studio Monday morning to collect my bet!"

"Don't count on the money! I'll be there!"

Toddy made a note on her calendar and rang downstairs for West, who was chatting at the bar with some friends. He picked up the phone and made a quick note of the Skouras party for Sunday night.

Several hours later, Thelma received another call, this one from Stanley Lupino, English stage comedian, father of Ida and Rea Lupino, then budding starlets. Lupino and his wife, Constance, had just arrived in Los Angeles and quickly put together a private party for Saturday night at the Café Trocadero on Sunset Boulevard. The party was in Thelma's honor, as a thank-you for her appearance on behalf of a comedy film they had done together three years ago called *You Made Me Love You*. This was Lupino's first trip to California since the film. Among the invited guests were theater mogul Sid Grauman (who owned several Hollywood area theaters including Grauman's Chinese), movie choreographer Arthur Prince and his wife, Harvey Priester, theatrical agent Al Kaufman, and other movie friends.

When Thelma accepted the invitation, she told Lupino about the brush with DiCicco. Lupino offered his opinion that possibly Pat was on the level and that he perhaps did want to get back together with Thelma. Thelma laughed and maintained her suspicion that she could not trust Pat, that he always seemed to have some ulterior motive. Lupino offered to extend the invitation to the party to Pat if Thelma was interested in bringing him. Thelma said she would mention it if she ran into DiCicco again. She also told Lupino that she did not know where DiCicco was staying, so he should not count on his being at the Trocadero on Saturday night.

Thelma phoned West again downstairs, and told him she would not be at the cafe on Saturday night, that she had decided to accept a party invitation.

"Think you can handle things alone?"

"Again?"

"The party doesn't start until seven-thirty or eight. Anyway, Lupino's throwing it in my honor as a thank-you. I can't very well turn it down, can I?"

"I'm coming up."

West slammed down the phone and headed up to the twin apartments. He knocked on Thelma's door and she invited him in. West was angry and looking for a fight.

"You did this last Saturday night. Now you're going out again this weekend? I understand it's important. I understand you have to go out with certain people. I also know you haven't been partying as much as before. But you've got to decide what you want. You can't just come and go as you please anymore."

"How many of us does it take to run one room? We do have other people working here, you know. I can't imagine what catastrophe could possibly come up in one evening that can't be fixed the next day!"

"I just hate having to mix with all those people all the

time, especially during the holidays. Everyone always asks for you, and I never know what to tell them."

"Tell them what you want. Those who know me well enough to really care probably know where I am, those who don't . . . well, the hell with them. I have to live my life, too."

"Just take it easy during the holidays, okay? You come back from those parties late at night, drunk, then you're useless the next day."

"Getting awfully basic aren't we, Roland?"

"You know what I mean. With Jewel sick and all, it's always falling on my shoulders. I'm not as young as you, I can't do everything at once like you."

"I promise this will be the end of it. Next Saturday I'll stay at the cafe like a good little girl. Okay?"

"I've got things I've got to do on Sunday. I'm buying a new car for Jewel, for Christmas. I've also got places I've got to be. I want your word you'll be able to take care of things on Sunday."

"What's so important?"

"I just have a lot of personal business, that's all. You've got to stay put on Sunday."

"If it means that much, okay. I'll stick around. Anyway, I've got guests; Skouras is coming to dinner Sunday night, remember?"

"Then it's settled."

West headed toward the door, to go back into the bar area, when Thelma called out after him.

"Oh, I forgot. I've got to stop by Martha Ford's Sunday afternoon. The party's not until four or so, so I'll be here all morning."

"Cancel it! Enough is enough!"

West slammed the door, and Thelma followed after him. They continued the argument into the bar area of the cafe, in a rear room. Their voices were loud and carried through much of the area.

"I can't cancel the party. This is only the third one I've accepted this month. Don't you start laying down the law to me, mister."

"And don't think you can come and go as you please!"

"Remember this, it's my name up there above the door. You asked me into the place because my name was a draw.

The only way it's going to remain a draw is if I attend some social functions once in a while, especially during the holidays. People remember who does and doesn't come to parties, you know. Martha's a close friend."

"Then she of all people should understand."

"It's a casual affair. A lot of people from the studio are going to be there. Her brother-in-law works at Roach. I can't say no, and I'm not going to. I'll only stay an hour or so."

"Do as you please."

When they walked back into the room, the few people who were in the lounge looked down, rather embarrassed at overhearing a quarrel, all but one man, who stared at both Toddy and West. Thelma stared back.

"Maybe you should help. You're here all the time anyway."

The man quietly rose from his table and left. He was one of Luciano's men.

Thelma returned to her apartment, locked the door, and took a good long drink. She thought about the weekend ahead, the parties, the fight with West. She wished she could run away, and seriously thought about doing just that after the holidays. Toddy phoned her mother, had a long talk about the weekend. They planned a Saturday evening shopping spree. Thelma finished her drink and slept the rest of the evening.

Luciano was in New York this second week of December, but he was still very much aware of what was going on some three thousand miles west. His men sent continual updates on the progress of his drug, gambling, and prostitution rackets and of the union/movie studio situation.

But Luciano was particularly interested in Todd and the affairs at her cafe. When he was told about Todd's meeting with DiCicco, Luciano acted surprised that the two had talked as long as they had, but he did not inquire as to the details of their conversation. He knew the scenario by heart and he knew the only important information he needed was the final upshot of the meeting—whether DiCicco would get back with Todd and stake a claim in the upstairs eatery.

There was something else that concerned Luciano, and that was Toddy's call to the D.A.'s office. Lucky had several men in the building, one planted as a "mole" right inside the office, where he could obtain any information Luciano might need to enhance his dealings. Such infiltration was not standard practice, but it was not uncommon, especially in towns as openly decadent and corrupt as Los Angeles in the mid-thirties. There were good, honest cops and prosecutors—in fact, the bulk of the LAPD and the prosecutors in the District Attorney's office were clean and aboveboard. But if the man with the power, the man in charge, could be influenced, if not all-out corrupted, then those underneath him would have little chance of getting to the real truth in controversial cases. Once corrupted, always controlled.

Luciano had been informed of Todd's phone call immediately after she had dialed Fitts's office the first time. The return call by a "representative" was a formality. When she made the initial call, Luciano knew instantly that she was going to talk. Chances were that someone other than Buron Fitts would hear what she had to say. What Luciano did not know was exactly what information Toddy planned to pass along to the D.A. Even information about his muscling in on the cafe and a look at the books could prove damaging.

Luciano knew the problem could be serious, even with the tremendous amount of money he was spreading around the district attorney's and police departments. He knew Todd could be trouble. She was a big-enough name to get something into the newspapers, or possibly take her complaint higher than the D.A. or LAPD, especially since she already had contact with the FBI from the Schimanski/Schieffert extortion letters. The FBI was one organization Luciano could not fight, at least not at this time. He had to take action on his own. He had to get to Toddy before she talked to Fitts's people.

Charles "Lucky" Luciano flew in to Los Angeles late Friday night, December 13. He arrived quietly and told very few people that he was in town. He stayed at the home of a friend in Beverly Hills. He had a busy weekend ahead.

The key players in the Thelma Todd murder were now in place.

Roland West was in a highly emotional state, exhausted from the burden of running the cafe almost single-handedly and frustrated from the recent series of arguments with Toddy. Both were draining him and he was struggling to maintain his composure in public. He believed he was on the verge of a nervous breakdown. Though many of the problems were his own doing, he blamed his recent distress on Thelma. As the holidays approached, he wanted out of the cafe entirely. He knew Thelma would never sell out, especially with the third-floor steakhouse ready to open. He was also jealous of her friends and her invitations to what sounded like swank Christmas parties while he was stuck working.

The second key player was Pat DiCicco. After his lunch with Toddy, DiCicco stayed in Los Angeles. Thursday night, he went to the Trocadero, where he found Ida Lupino making the final arrangements for the Saturday night bash. He tapped Ida on the shoulder, catching her off guard.

"I hear you're giving a party. Why am I not invited?" DiCicco was quite serious.

"Why, you're invited if you want to come. But the party's for Thelma."

"Oh, Thelma and I are pals. Of course I'll come."

How DiCicco found out about the party has never been revealed. One thing is certain; Thelma neither invited him nor expected him to be there. When Ida called Thelma on Friday and told her about the previous night's exchange with Pat, she was shocked.

"I guess he's going to be my escort then?"

"I think he intends to meet you here, from the way he talked. I told him it's a party for you. It would be rather gauche, don't you think, for him to invite himself, then bring a date?"

"With Pat, nothing surprises me. I guess you'll be setting a place for two then."

The third player in the drama was treasurer Charles Smith, who sent his wife away for the weekend, from Friday through Monday. He said she had gone to visit relatives, but was vague about which relatives they were and where they lived. He was now alone in his room above the Posetano Road garage where Thelma parked her car.

The final player was Luciano, who was calculating his next move in the refuge of a posh Beverly Hills home.

Friday the thirteenth was a bad omen for Thelma Todd.

Chapter Eighteen

Saturday, December 14, began as most days did at the Side-walk Cafe—West woke up first, then opened the restaurant and bar areas for the staff, who usually began arriving shortly before 10:00 A.M. The cafe catered to the lunch and dinner crowds and was open every day of the year until 2:00 A.M. Though the cafe served breakfast-type dishes, the earliest any-one could eat was 11:30, when the kitchen opened. That in-cluded West and Todd, who ventured up three roads to the main house on Robelo Road if they were hungry in the early morning.

Saturdays were the busiest days of the week. Because the cafe was not located near any business districts, it drew mainly the beach crowd during the day, and Saturday was considered "the" day to head to the beach. For many, a stop at Thelma Todd's for lunch was considered part of the rou-tine. The cafe was usually packed on Saturday night, espe-cially during the holidays; reservations were often required to get seating in a reasonable time.

Thelma slept until well past noon, as she usually did, ex-hausted from a long week at the Roach Studios and burning the midnight oil making plans for the upstairs steakhouse. On this day, she felt no need to hurry to get out of bed. West had finally agreed to give her the entire day to herself on condition she would make her best effort to cut the Ford party short on Sunday afternoon and spend most of the day taking care of cafe business. After some discussion, Toddy agreed and peace was made.

While West was downstairs chatting with lunch guests and taking reservations from dinner patrons, Toddy spent the early part of the afternoon calling friends, writing letters, paying bills, and listening to the radio. Sipping on a watered-down glass of Scotch, she took a long, hot bath, set her hair, and phoned Alice.

"We still on for shopping?"

"Yes. I have a list of presents I need to buy. I don't think I'll be able to get it all done before you have to go out, though."

"I'm pretty much done with my shopping, so wherever you need to go is fine with me. What we don't get done, you can wrap up by yourself. I'll have Ernie drive you where you need to go after he drops me off. I've got to come back here and change, anyway. How does that sound?"

"Fine, dear."

"Okay. I'll swing by in about an hour and we'll take it from there."

Thelma and Alice spent the bulk of the afternoon Christmas shopping. Thelma appeared to be in one of the best moods she had been in for months; she chatted about the studio and the steakhouse and made girl talk with Alice.

They returned to the cafe just before 6:00 P.M. Peters raced around to the right rear car door to open it for Thelma. As Thelma stepped out of the car, she turned back to Alice.

"You going to head back home? I was hoping you'd stay for a while. I want you to see what I'm going to wear tonight. It'll knock your socks off!"

"I still have a few things to buy. I might as well take advantage of the stores' late Christmas hours. I'll have Ernie drive me back when he comes to get you; then I can see this outfit of yours. He can take me back to Hollywood after that."

"Fine with me, just as long as you see my dress."

"Do you really think Pat will show up as he promised?"

"I hope so. Why do you think I'm going to all this trouble?"

"Are you thinking of getting back together, or just trying to whet his appetite a bit?"

"Who knows? Pat's a little boy. If the package is pretty enough, he'll take a swipe at it. Maybe I just want to make him jealous, dangle the carrot a bit."

"Just be careful. Don't get in too deep before you know exactly what he's up to. It's like Pat to invite himself to a party just to meet other people. Don't let him use you, Thelma."

"Don't worry."

Thelma blew a kiss to her mom. Peters closed the car door and escorted Toddy to her apartment as he always did after he dropped her off at the cafe. She waved a cheerful good-bye and shouted after him to be back by 7:30. He nodded in agreement and drove off with Alice, who was in the backseat.

Toddy showered, smothered herself in expensive perfume, spent close to an hour putting on her makeup and fixing her hair in the fashion Pat liked best—pulled back off her face, then piled in curls on top of her head. It was the look of the scoops of curls that had earned her another nickname, "The Ice Cream Blonde." The name was picked up by newspapers and perpetuated by the Roach publicity department, which thought it presented a better image than the nickname Hot Toddy. Then she carefully put on the dress she hoped would score a bull's-eye with DiCicco.

It was a shimmering blue-satin, lace, and sequined evening gown. With it, she wore new satin evening slippers, sheer stockings, and a gorgeous mink coat to ward off the evening chill. She also bathed herself in diamonds—$20,000 worth of diamonds and gold jewelry in the form of earrings, a necklace, a bracelet, and the diamond ring that she wore on her right hand. On her left hand, Toddy still wore the sardonyx ring Pat had given her shortly after their wedding; it was a ring that she really liked, in spite of the fact it represented a love/hate relationship and had bitter memories attached to it.

Peters returned to the apartment promptly at 7:30, according to Toddy's instructions. He stopped the car, opened the rear door for Alice, and escorted her to Thelma's apartment. He knocked on the door and Thelma told him she would be out in a minute. Peters returned to the car and

waited by the right rear door—the door through which
Thelma usually entered the car.

As Thelma was about to leave for the party, West
emerged from his apartment, tired and mildly irritated that
Thelma was dressed to kill.

"That's overdoing it a bit, isn't it?"

"You like it?"

"You look like a million bucks. You also look like you
spent a million bucks."

"Thanks, I think."

"What time are you planning on getting back?"

"I don't know. Whenever the party's over, I guess. You
going to wait by the door with a clock again?"

"No. I'm not going to wait up at all for you the way I did
the other weekend. When the cafe locks its doors at two, I
lock my doors, too."

"You going to lock me out or something?"

"Not if you're back by two o'clock." West smiled but he
was only mildly joking.

"I'll be back by two-oh-five."

"Two, and not one minute later. I'm double-locking the
outside door, so remember to bring your key." (West was obviously forgetting that Thelma rarely used the outside doors
after dark.)

"I'll wake you up instead."

West was now visibly irritated by what he perceived as
childish behavior on Thelma's part. He had put in a tough day
and was clearly not in the mood for games. He was also not in
the mood to wait up until all hours of the night to see if
Thelma had her key or not.

For the first time in her life, Alice did not interfere in the
discussion. Instead, she walked back down to the car and
climbed in, possibly because she was tired from the afternoon's shopping. She heard a muffled exchange of words between Thelma and West. The conversation had now escalated
into an argument.

The last words Alice heard were from West, who shouted
down the stairs after Thelma, "Be sure and be home by two
o'clock . . . and don't drink too much."

Thelma did not respond to his remark about her drinking.
She climbed into the car. Peters slammed the door after her,

entered on the driver's side, and drove off, first dropping Alice off at her Hollywood home, then dropping Thelma off at the Café Trocadero. The time was 8:15 P.M.

Ernie Peters returned the car to the livery, where he spent most of the night waiting for Thelma's call to drive her back home. The livery was in Hollywood, about a thirty-five-minute drive from the Café Trocadero. He arrived at the garage around 8:55.

At the Trocadero, most of the Lupino party was downstairs in the cocktail room, drinking, laughing, and enjoying the evening, when Toddy entered. Stanley and Ida greeted Toddy, along with Harvey Priester, who had arrived at the party alone, expecting to spend the dinner with Thelma.

"I'm supposed to meet Pat. Have you seen him?"

Priester was surprised because he thought the two were not even on speaking terms. "No. How did this all come about?"

"Long story. He's supposed to be here, my escort, I guess."

"Is there something going on?"

"No. I have no interest in Pat. Call it more a curiosity."

When Ida kissed Thelma on the cheek, she told her she had not seen Pat nor had he ever sent his regrets saying he would not attend. Ida and Thelma talked about whether or not to keep a place at the table for him anyway. Ida was angry at DiCicco's rudeness and embarrassed for Thelma, who appeared to have been stood up at her own party. Thelma was hurt, but kept smiling and laughing as if she did not care.

What Toddy did not know was that Pat DiCicco was already at the Café Trocadero. He was upstairs in the second-floor dining room, at a table near the dance floor, on the opposite side of the room from the table set up for the Lupino party. DiCicco was not there as Toddy's escort. He had brought his own date, dark-haired actress Margaret Lindsay, and he had no intention of joining the party.

Slowly, around 10:00 P.M., the guests of the Lupino party started finding their way from the downstairs cocktail area to the upstairs dining room. DiCicco saw the crowd, which he recognized as part of the Lupino party, and he mentioned to Lindsay that Thelma must be in the restaurant and was probably downstairs. Though they had just arrived, Pat acted edgy, as if he wanted to leave.

"I'd love to go down and meet her." Lindsay had no idea that Pat was one of the expected guests and that a place had been reserved for him at the Lupino table, next to Toddy's spot.

"I don't think we'd better. I think we'd better stay here, upstairs. I really don't want to run into Thelma tonight."

"Something wrong?"

"No. I'd just rather not see her. I had lunch with her the other day. That was enough for one week."

"You seem nervous."

DiCicco decided to tell Margaret his version of the truth about the evening.

"I was invited to dine as a guest of the Lupinos. I explained to Ida that I had a previous engagement with you and wouldn't be able to sit with them tonight. But I don't think she told anyone. I have a funny feeling there's still a place for me there. I'd just rather not run into them." He, of course, had lied about his canceling out for the Lupino party.

"Then why did you insist we come here tonight?"

Pat did not answer the question. "Let's say we just leave." Pat spoke the words, but made no physical attempt to move. He nervously looked around the room and studied the guests who were finding their seats at the Lupino table. Pat and his date had not yet been discovered by the Lupino gathering, or if they had, no one had yet mentioned it to Thelma, who was among the last to head upstairs.

Those who either were at the party or knew of the evening believe DiCicco deliberately invited himself with the intention of standing Thelma up, then adding insult to injury by showing up with another woman. DiCicco had that type of mean streak in him. He was angry at Thelma for not jumping at the chance to hire him to manage the third-floor steakhouse. This evening was a well-thought-out, carefully calculated attempt to get even with Toddy for the rebuff.

At 10:15, Thelma entered the upstairs dining room. Ida met her at the stairs and pulled her aside. The two slipped away from the party, whispering and giggling together. Thelma acted coy, as if she had a juicy secret she wanted to share, but wanted someone to pull it out of her.

"How's your love life?" she asked Ida.

"Oh, I haven't any just now. I'm too busy at the studios to find time to date."

Ida was trying to establish her acting career in America and considered that her main priority for the moment. But she turned the question on Toddy.

"So, how's *your* love life? You've always got something going on."

"Ida, you wouldn't believe it! I have something going on—and how! I'm smack in the middle of the most marvelous romance I've ever had with a man from San Francisco who is just too grand for words! He's a businessman . . . a rich businessman. And he's a nice guy. You know what gentlemen those San Franciscans are."

"What's his name?"

"That's my big secret. I'm not telling a soul."

"Come on, just his first name."

"I really can't. I've got so much going on right now that I really want to keep that part of my life separate from the details down here."

"Does Roland know?"

"I think so. He's taken a few calls. But he's never said anything about it. With Roland sometimes it's hard to tell exactly what he's thinking. He hides his feelings."

"Things okay between you two?"

"You know how that goes. We're still dear friends."

"You in love with this man from San Francisco?"

"You'd better believe it!"

Ida later testified that Thelma seemed very happy and that she "lit up" when she talked about her "mystery man." She said Thelma was very much in love; therefore it was highly improbable that she would have taken her own life, as some people suspected.

The two walked over to the table, arm in arm, still laughing. When Thelma was helped into her chair by Stanley Lupino, she commented on the empty place next to hers. Lupino explained it was meant for Pat, who was obviously not planning on attending the gathering. He angrily ordered the waiters to remove the extra setting from the table.

Thelma asked one of the waiters to pour a glass of champagne for her, which he did. Thelma sipped it, which was unusual behavior; she usually downed drinks in rapid succession at parties. The "tea-totaling," as he later put it, was noted by Harvey Priester, who made a private joke to Thelma. The two laughed and she told him, "Roland warned me not to drink too much. For once I'm taking his advice!"

The band started playing, and the dance floor quickly filled with couples. Stanley Lupino asked Thelma for the first dance, inasmuch as she was the guest of honor. Toddy was all smiles and happily accepted the dance with the Englishman. As they twirled around the dance floor, they saw a startling sight—DiCicco and his date sitting together, dining, drinking, and laughing. Neither had expected to see Pat there, let alone with another woman. The shock froze Toddy, who stared blankly.

Suddenly, in a mixture of anger and courage, Toddy walked Stanley over to DiCicco's table. Neither Lupino, DiCicco, nor Lindsay knew if Thelma was going to pick a fight and they braced for the worst.

Toddy spoke coolly but politely. "Fancy meeting you here."

Pat and Thelma exchanged introductions and the usual round of Hollywood chatter—"Nice to meet you," "What do you do for a living?" "Maybe we'll work together sometime." Then Thelma got to the point.

"You know the Lupinos were expecting you. You did invite yourself." Toddy made no mention of the fact that she, too, had been expecting him. She would not give him the satisfaction.

"I phoned Ida earlier today and sent my regrets. I had an engagement with Margaret that I did not want to break."

"Why did you come here, then?"

It was the same question Lindsay had asked, and it received the same lack of reply from Pat.

"I hope you weren't waiting for me, too, Thel. Did you come alone?"

"Harvey is my escort." She had not really lied. Priester had served as her escort in Pat's place.

"You'd better square things with Ida," she added.

"I'll call her tomorrow and explain all over again why I couldn't be at the party tonight." Pat emphasized the words "all over again" to make the point that he had called before.

Pat and Toddy stared at one another for what seemed an eternity. The looks were later described as a mixture of longing, regret, and a plea for understanding. Both Lindsay and Lupino had wondered if the two intended to get back together.

Thelma finally broke the silence. "I have to get back to my party. Nice meeting you, Margaret."

"I'll see you very soon, Thel," DiCicco called after Thelma as she headed back toward her table.

The time . . . 10:30.

The party got into full swing. Thelma was as giddy, fun-loving and bubbly as ever, dancing with all the men, laughing, flirting, and telling risqué stories about actors and men she had known as a starlet. She kept everyone captivated, laughing, eager to hear all the dirt. Hot Toddy knew how to spice a story.

Oddly enough, DiCicco and Lindsay stayed at their table, too, though they did not dance. Pat kept glancing across the room to Thelma's table, almost as if he were there strictly to keep an eye on her. Lindsay got the feeling that Pat had made the date at the Troc in an effort to make Thelma jealous. He seemed disturbed that his scheme had not worked.

At 12:15 A.M., DiCicco abruptly excused himself and made a phone call; the call was placed to an unknown party. DiCicco appeared very nervous and edgy upon his return to the table. He stared at Thelma and glanced down at his watch, almost completely ignoring Margaret Lindsay. One hour later, DiCicco and Lindsay left the Café Trocadero without saying good-bye to anyone from the Lupino party.

Thelma watched Pat leave, took note of the time, then leaned over to theater mogul Sid Grauman, with whom she had shared many dances that evening.

"Hey, Sid. Could you do me a favor? Could you call Roland and tell him I'll be leaving here shortly? Roland wanted me back home by two. I'm obviously not going to make it and I don't want to hear him yell and scream at me over the phone. Do you mind?"

"No, not at all."

Toddy requested one of the waiters to call for her chauffeur, who would arrive in about half an hour. Thelma lost track of time waiting for Ernie Peters.

West was just ushering out the last of the customers in the bar, and the bartender and waiters were finishing up their night's business, when the cafe phone rang in the first-floor restaurant. Slightly incoherent from exhaustion, West walked downstairs and answered the phone. Grauman was on the line, relaying the message that Thelma was about to head home and would be back by 2:30 or so.

"Ask her if she remembers what I told her," West said as he hung up the phone. He was referring to the argument at the door, when he halfheartedly threatened to lock her out if she came home after two. The time was ten minutes of two.

West left the restaurant, walked to his apartment, grabbed White King's leash, and took him for a short walk around the cafe grounds. West returned to his apartment through the side door and bolted it, assuming Thelma would enter through the rear, outside door, which required two keys. West then shot one of the bolts on the door, locking Toddy out of the building. Later speculation was that West knew Todd would be home well past 2:30 and knew she did not have her keys. He either subconsciously locked her out, or deliberately locked her out with the intention of making her stand outside as "punishment" for some length of time before he would let her in.

West put White King in his apartment for the night and put a light cover on the dog and went to bed. It was 2:15.

In spite of her good intentions, Toddy could not walk away from fun. It was well past 2:45 when Harvey Priester called it a night, and Toddy was still going strong, laughing the night away with Grauman, Arthur Prince (who taught Toddy several new dance steps), and the Lupinos. The group dwindled down to a few, but they were still very much in a party mood. Prince and Toddy were dancing the tango, sipping champagne on the dance floor, when a Trocadero waiter interrupted.

"Excuse me, Miss Todd."

Thelma stopped dancing and turned to the young man.

"Would you follow me, please?"

Thelma kissed Prince on the cheek and excused herself, still smiling and full of fun.

The fun stopped when she saw a dark-haired man standing in the back of the downstairs cocktail lounge. The waiter left immediately when Todd saw the man. The room was empty and the lights were dim.

The man said very little, but what he said told Thelma everything she needed to know and something she desperately did not want to hear.

"Lucky is waiting at the beach."

The man quickly disappeared into the shadows. The color drained from Thelma's face. She had been waiting for Luciano to make some sort of move. She had dealt the cards two weeks ago when she had put up the sign on the front door; Luciano was now going to play his hand. Her shock quickly escalated into terror as the reality of the situation hit her. She ran back upstairs into the dining area to retrieve her purse, and took a deep breath to calm down. By the time she reached the table, she was somber and silent.

"Ernie's here. I have to go."

The Lupinos kissed her good-bye. Prince made a joking gesture to usher her out the door with a tango. Thelma played along, but she clearly was not in the mood. She took her mink coat from the checker, and left the Troc. Peters had the car door open, waiting.

In an unusual gesture, Thelma stopped and turned toward the Trocadero. She saluted the building and said good-bye. Then she smiled and climbed into the back of the car. By the time Peters started the car, Thelma was once again in a state of panic. The time was approximately 3:00 A.M.

"Faster, Ernie! Faster!"

The car was already racing down Sunset Boulevard at sixty miles an hour. Peters kept one eye on the road, one in the rearview mirror, watching for the LAPD traffic cops.

"Can't you go faster?"

"I'm doing the best I can. When we hit Roosevelt Highway I can push it, Miss Todd."

Toddy was terrified and was running as if the devil himself were on her tail. She kept checking her watch, leaning forward across the back of the driver's seat, holding Peters's shoulder.

When Peters made the right turn from Sunset Boulevard onto Roosevelt Highway, he accelerated past 70 mph.

"For God sakes, Ernie, step on it!"

They finally arrived at the Sidewalk Cafe. Peters was

about to get out of the car to escort Thelma to the door as he always did when Toddy stopped him.

"No, Ernie. You don't have to walk me to the door. Stay in the car. I'll be all right."

Thelma opened her car door and stepped out. She turned and leaned back into the open door.

"I owe you some money. I'll settle up with you next time I see you. Don't worry about it." She paused as if asking for forgiveness and approval. "Okay?"

"I'm not worried, Miss Todd. Will you be okay?"

"Yes, Ernie. Good night."

"Good night, Miss Todd."

Thelma slammed the car door and Peters drove away. Thelma stood outside the cafe for a few moments and looked around. She saw no one.

Then, as she was about to walk up the steps toward the main door of the cafe, a chocolate-brown convertible emerged from out of the fog, slowly making its way toward her, down the hill to the west of the cafe. The headlights were off, the top was up, and the car steadily approached as if it were stalking Thelma in the night. The fog was so thick it distorted both the oncoming movement of the car and the low, muffled hum of the engine, adding to the eerie scene.

Her first instinct was to run, but she was smart enough to know there was no place to run to. Thelma would have to confront the demon, and the drama was already set in motion.

White King bolted out of his dog bed and looked around West's room, waking West, who sat up in bed and looked at his clock. It was 3:30 in the morning.

"White King! What's wrong, boy?"

West thought he heard water running in Thelma's apartment; it was a low, muffled, "gurgling sound." He assumed it was Thelma and lay back down. The sound may have been the soft hum of the car outside.

White King sniffed at the apartment door, stood motionless for some time, then sat on the floor by the door, still preoccupied with the noise he heard outside the apartment door.

"Quiet! Go back to sleep, boy."

White King lay back down.

When the car reached the front steps of the Sidewalk Cafe, it stopped, but the motor was still running. The passenger door opened. A voice inside whispered in a deep, soft tone, "Get in." It was a voice Thelma had heard many times before. Thelma did as she was told.

Chapter Nineteen

" "It's been several weeks. I hope you don't mind this late-night appointment. I just arrived in town."

Luciano, of course, was lying. He had been in town for several days, spinning this latest, deadly web. Thelma was very nervous and frightened. She was not quite sure what Luciano was up to.

"I thought we'd go for a drive up the coast. Santa Barbara. I assume you have no plans."

Luciano later related fragments of his drive and conversation with Thelma to several close associates; the story has been carefully passed down over the years.

"But I do." Thelma was hoping to find a way to get out of the treacherous situation. "I have to get up early tomorrow to take care of the cafe. Roland has to go somewhere and I'm grounded for the day."

"It will be taken care of. The cafe can manage without you for a few hours. There are some things we need to discuss."

Luciano and Todd drove up to Santa Barbara, a drive of a little more than two hours. They parked along the beach, but Thelma remained in the car. Luciano took several bottles of champagne from the trunk, opened them, and sipped while he encouraged Toddy to drink heartily. Still frightened, Thelma downed at least two glasses to steady her nerves. Luciano knew the alcohol would make Toddy more likely to let down her guard and respond to his questions. The time for the interrogation was approaching, but it was not yet upon them.

Toddy and Luciano chatted for two hours in the car near the Santa Barbara coast. Thelma's defenses were beginning to drop and she was slowly feeling more at ease with Luciano, who insisted his late-night rendezvous was nothing more than a social call.

Thelma asked Luciano to drive her back to the cafe; he agreed and headed the car back down coastal route 101, south toward Los Angeles. Thelma's sense of security shattered when Luciano whizzed past the Sidewalk Cafe and headed toward downtown Los Angeles.

"Lucky! Stop the car! I want to go home. Now!"

"You'll get home. I still want to talk with you. I probably will not be back in Los Angeles for a long time, and I would like to spend this time with you. It may be our last time together. The farewell could be permanent."

Luciano spoke in vague references to Nitti and business in Los Angeles. What puzzled Thelma the most, though, were his repeated statements about his "final" farewell. His words made Thelma wonder if it was really Luciano who was going to go somewhere, or if she was the one "taking a trip."

When they reached downtown Los Angeles around 9:00 A.M., Thelma grew increasingly edgy and ordered Luciano to stop the car, saying she wanted to take a taxi home. Her alcohol-fueled demands infuriated Luciano, who shouted at Thelma to quiet down.

"You will go when I tell you to go."

The inebriated Thelma yelled at Luciano, who slapped her hard across the face. She sobered slightly.

They were in the vicinity of Eighth and Figueroa streets when Todd again insisted he stop the car. When Luciano pulled up alongside the curb, Todd ran out of the car and into a cigar store owned by W. F. Persson. Persson was an avid movie fan and immediately recognized the frantic woman as Thelma Todd. Toddy was trembling, disheveled, crying, and near-hysterical when she leaned over the counter.

"I need you to dial a number for me. Hurry!"

Persson asked Thelma to follow him to the middle of the store, to a pay phone, where he dialed the numbers as Thelma called them out. As he dialed the last number, he saw Thelma turn and look out the door. She vanished. There was no answer on the line.

In court Persson could remember only the last four of the numbers Thelma asked him to dial; they were "7771." He could not remember the prefix, nor did police ever try to track the exchange down. Neither West nor Alice knew of any such number. Persson thought he saw a car waiting by the curb, but he was not positive.

But another man, Robert E. Fisher, was positive. He was an older man with a eye for the ladies. A knock-out blonde was hard to miss, especially wandering around Los Angeles on a Sunday morning, still dressed for a night on the town.

Fisher, a customer in the store, testified that he saw the woman, believed to be Thelma Todd, run out of the cigar store and meet a dark man who was holding a woman's fur coat on his arm. Thelma and the dark man walked across the street to the First Methodist Church at Eighth and Hope streets, where they sat for a few moments on the church steps. Todd appeared to calm down, and the couple returned to the car and sped away. Fisher looked at a clock in the cigar store. It read 9:10 A.M. He and Persson became the first two eyewitnesses to see Thelma Todd alive hours after 2:00 A.M., the time at which L.A. County Medical Examiner A. F. Wagner claimed she had died.

"I thought we would spend a nice quiet Sunday together. You have been invited to dinner with some friends of mine. I accepted on your behalf and I know you would not want to disappoint them or me. You and I parted on a bad note. I would like to leave you on better terms."

It was clear that this day would be all Luciano's and that Thelma was a hostage who had no choice but to go along for the ride.

Roland West woke from a restful sleep just before 10:00 Sunday morning. The apartments were quiet; he did not hear Thelma and assumed she was either downstairs in the cafe or had gone out. He showered and shaved, dressed and rang for his breakfast. When there was no sign of Thelma, West assumed she had been locked out for the night and checked the ladies' lounge.

"She slept on the couch in there when she had been locked out before. I thought maybe she had slept there again. I saw an indentation in the couch and assumed Thelma had been there."

Because of that indentation, West believed Thelma had gone out for the day. It was just before 11:00 A.M. when he went back into the cafe to take care of business. The cafe was empty except for a few guests, a bartender, and the kitchen staff who had just arrived. West was extremely irritated that Thelma had "gone back on her word" and had gone out after promising to give him the day off. West telephoned car salesman H. H. Cooper and asked him to come down to the cafe to discuss a car sale, saying, "Something came up and I can't get away."

West asked cafe bartender Robert John Anderson, who usually repaired West's, Carmen's, and Toddy's cars, which car Thelma had taken that morning. Anderson, whom West called "Bob," said he had been busy and did not have time to hike up to the main house to see, but when he had a moment, he would take care of it.

Cooper arrived at the cafe shortly after noon and West invited him to have lunch while they talked about the possible purchase of a car for Jewel Carmen.

"Mr. West was very nervous, almost distracted when we talked, as if he was expecting someone or as if something was wrong."

West told Cooper to go upstairs to the Posetano Road house and get a check from cafe treasurer Charles Smith to purchase the car. Cooper left, and West assumed he had received the check because he never heard anything more from Cooper that day. At 1:00, West returned to his duties at the cafe.

At 2:15 Bob Anderson left the bar area and walked up the three streets to the main house to check on Thelma's car. When he opened the wooden double doors, he saw her chocolate-brown Phaeton convertible parked inside. He told Deputy D.A. Johnson that the car was backed into the garage, not driven in front end first as it was found on Monday morning. He also said Thelma was definitely not in the car at that time.

Anderson hiked back down the hill and reported to West that Thelma's car was still in the garage.

He held firm to his testimony that the Phaeton was empty more than twelve hours after Wagner's finding. Anderson was the third witness to testify that Thelma Todd could not have been dead in her car at 2:00 A.M. Sunday morning.

"If Miss Todd did go out, she did not drive that car."

"What did Mr. West say to you after you told him Miss Todd's car was still in the garage?"

"Nothing. He nodded and walked back downstairs to the restaurant. I went back to my duties behind the bar. The cafe was getting busy with the Sunday afternoon brunch and dinner crowds, so there was not much time to talk."

Roland West's mother stopped by the cafe several minutes before 4:00. Her visit was initially meant as nothing more than a brief visit with her son, but the conversation immediately took on a serious and somber tone.

"I'm very worried about Thelma. I haven't seen her all day. I believe she came home late last night. Her car is still up in the garage."

"She's taken off like that before."

"This time she had given me her word she would be here today. I had a lot of things to do, and now I won't be able to get them done."

"Did you take care of the car for Jewel?"

"I had Cooper come here."

"I'd give her hell if I was you. She has one hell of a lot of nerve pulling this again."

"I probably should have waited up for her, like I did the other times, but I was just too tired."

"Straighten it out with her the second she comes back. With the upstairs opening soon, you can only take on so much. If you let it slide now, you'll be stuck handling the entire building yourself."

Mrs. West left at 5:00.

The whereabouts of Thelma and Luciano between the hours of 9:30 Sunday morning and 4:00 Sunday afternoon are uncertain. But Thelma resurfaced at 4:00, at a drugstore in Beverly Hills, a town approximately thirty minutes south of downtown Los Angeles. She was identified by two people—

one an eyewitness and one who spoke over the phone with a woman she believed was Thelma Todd.

Sara Kane Carter lived on Utica Drive, a wealthy, winding canyon area on the northwest edge of Beverly hills. Carter claimed she saw a blond woman in an evening dress and fur telephoning from a drugstore on the corner of Sunset Boulevard and Laurel Canyon (the Canyon road is also called Crescent Heights Boulevard at the intersection). Carter pinpointed the exact time as 4:04, claiming she was in the drugstore to buy sundries and noticed a woman who seemed inappropriately dressed for a Sunday afternoon. Now four witnesses had sworn under oath that they saw Thelma Todd alive on Sunday.

The story was verified by a fifth witness, Martha (Mrs. Wallace) Ford, who maintained she received a phone call, at her home, from a woman who identified herself at Thelma. The call was received sometime between 4:00 and 4:15, approximately the same time as Carter's sighting. Ford said she could not be more specific about the time since she was in the middle of preparing for a party, a party to which Thelma had been invited.

"Mrs. Ford, are you acquainted with Thelma Todd, the deceased?"

"Very well."

"When did you last see her alive?"

"About three or four weeks ago, downtown, I think it was near the Broadway Hotel."

"Have you talked with her since that time?"

"I haven't seen her since that time; I talked to her on Sunday."

"This last Sunday?"

"This last Sunday."

"About what time did you talk to her?"

"I should judge it was about four-thirty. I have been told it was ten minutes after four."

"Will you state the circumstances?"

"Yes, I had told Miss Todd's maid—it might be her mother or her maid, she didn't say when she talked—about a party, and gave her the address and the time and the phone number, so they would be all set."

"You had invited her to a party at your home?"

"I had invited her to be at a party at my home that was to be at seven on Sunday night."

Thelma assumed the party was at four o'clock, hence the call saying she would be over. Thelma was not one to show up at parties three hours before their start.

"What did she say in this conversation?"

"Well, the first thing she said was, 'Hello, this is Thelma,' and I said, 'When are you kids coming out?,' and I thought it was Velma, another girlfriend, and she said, 'Who do you think this is?,' and I said, 'Velma,' and she said, 'No, it is Hot Toddy.'"

"Was that a nickname?"

"That was a joke between us."

"All right, go ahead."

"I don't know the exact sequence, but the substance of the conversation was she said, 'What are you wearing at the party?,' and I said, 'I am wearing hostess pajamas,' and she said she had on an evening gown and I said, 'Whatever you are wearing will be all right,' and she said she was bringing someone with her and I asked if it was a girlfriend and she said, 'No,' and I asked who it was and she wouldn't tell me. She said, 'I want to have the fun of seeing your face when I come in the door. You'll drop dead when you see who it is.' And she mentioned something about going through a short-cut or something like that and I said I didn't know much about that part of the country and I said, 'If you know about it, all right there is such a place [meaning the shortcut],' and she spoke of the address being wrong, and said, 'I will be there in half an hour,' and I said, 'All the lights will be on and you can't miss the house because there will be plenty of cars there,' and she said, 'Okay.'"

This was another irregularity in Ford's testimony. Ford stated the party was not to start until 7:00; would there have been "plenty of cars" already at the house at 4:30? The driving distance from Sunset Boulevard and Laurel Canyon to Studio City where Ford lived was approximately half an hour, verifying the location of Thelma in the area. The shortcut was presumed to be over Laurel Canyon, which extended from Beverly Hills through the mountains, finishing in Studio City, a winding and dangerous drive in 1935.

"She didn't arrive?"

"No."

When Thelma was found Monday morning, she was wearing a faded camellia flower arrangement on her gown; the flowers were identical to those she had worn to the Trocadero on Saturday night. The flowers were faded, but not dried out as they should have been if they were the same arrangement she was wearing at the Troc.

Prosecutor Johnson pressed on. "Did you suppose if she had purchased a camellia on Saturday evening on her way to the Trocadero she would have that same faded camellia on her dress on Sunday afternoon at four o'clock?"

"I should think not. I should think it would be mussed up. Thelma was more particular than that."

"And you think if she was found dead in the same gown with that camellia, you still feel she talked to you Sunday afternoon?"

Thelma was obviously not thinking of fresh flowers Sunday afternoon.

"I know she talked to me Sunday afternoon."

"Do you think you could be mistaken?"

"Oh, no. I could not be."

"Well, you believe you could not be?"

"Well, as sure as any human being could be."

Thelma still had not arrived at the party by 4:45. She and Luciano remained in Beverly Hills well after the call. They were seen driving on Wilshire Boulevard by J. A. Clough, who was an official with the city of Santa Monica and considered a very credible witness. Clough, his wife, and his son were driving down the boulevard when he saw a chocolate-brown Phaeton pass them. He initially claimed he saw two women in the car and identified the driver as Thelma wearing a mink coat. He testified there was a woman in the passenger's seat, a "lightly built, rather short, beautiful blonde girl."

When he was pressed, his memory failed to a large degree. He said Thelma was not the driver but the passenger he had previously described. He claimed he could not remember who was driving the car. Later he told Johnson he assumed the driver was Thelma after he read press clippings about her death. It was there he learned she drove a chocolate-brown

Phaeton and his memory was muddled. His wife and son did not remember the incident at all.

His testimony as the sixth witness was not as solid as the others', but it was considered further documentation of Todd's whereabouts.

What Clough had seen was Toddy and Luciano. What he did not know was that the pair was headed to an expensive home in Beverly Hills, the home of a friend of Luciano's, where Thelma was to dine for the last time in her life.

According to accounts related by former associates of Luciano's, the home was owned by an underworld businessman who had dealings with the crime boss; his identity must remain confidential. Whether the friend knew of the diabolical plot Lucky was hatching will never be known, but in any event, the associate played an important part in the final act of the macabre play.

Meanwhile, Roland West was struggling between two emotions—all-out hostility at Thelma for her failure to show at the cafe all day, and very real concern that something might have happened to her. No one had seen Thelma, nor had anyone on the staff heard from her. West phoned Alice to find out if Thelma had been with her. Alice said she had not seen her daughter since Saturday night and also became worried. They discussed the possibility of calling the police but never did.

Around 6:00, West received a call from one of the Skouras brothers, confirming the dinner reservation for eleven people for around 7:15. When he asked to speak with Toddy, West explained that she had just stepped out but would be back by the time they arrived for dinner, and everything had been arranged for them. Skouras joked again about the $100 bet, telling West to remind Toddy that he was going to collect. West said he would pass along the message when Thelma returned.

At 7:15, on schedule, the Skouras party of eleven arrived for dinner. West made apologies for Thelma, saying she was delayed and would return "any moment now." West was increasingly nervous and jumpy. He began to sweat and was clearly distracted as he moved among his guests.

Fifteen minutes later, George Baker, assistant director at the Roach Studios, called and asked to speak with Thelma. West gave the same excuse, that she stepped out, but he would gladly take a message. Baker related the details of the previous 4:15 phone exchange between Toddy and Martha Ford, and said Ford was very upset that Thelma had failed to show.

"You actually spoke with her?"

"Yes, Martha did. But that was more than three hours ago. She never showed and we haven't heard from her. Where is she?"

West was vague and distant. "Where was she when she called?"

"I don't know. Sounded like a pay phone." Baker was abrupt. "Look, when she comes in have her call Martha, okay?"

At 8:45 Thelma, Luciano, his associate, and his associate's wife reportedly dined on roast beef, potatoes, peas, and carrots, washed down with champagne. Shortly after dinner, the wife left, leaving Toddy alone with the two men. Luciano and his pal kept the drinks flowing. Again, Luciano plied Thelma with alcohol hoping to get her to lower her guard, to force her to open up. Only this time it was not for fun and games and general "friendly" chatter. Luciano wanted to find out how much Toddy knew about his dealings in Los Angeles—his drug, prostitution, and gambling rackets, his infiltration of restaurants and unions, and the Million Dollar Movie Shakedown. He wanted the interrogation done in a place large enough to prevent anyone from eavesdropping, a place in which he felt comfortable about taking his time to get what he needed, and where there was someone who would stop at nothing to help him get the truth.

During the course of the conversation in the living room, Luciano's eyes narrowed; they found their mark and zeroed in. Luciano wasted no time in making his point.

"Why did you call the D.A.?"

"I didn't call the D.A."

"Let's get one thing straight. I know what you did. Do not lie. I have people in the office who tell me everything. They are there for a reason. Do not lie!"

With that, Lucky slapped Toddy, reducing her to tears. Luciano's associate watched in silence.

"I ask you again. Why did you make the call?"

Thelma struggled to talk through the tears and the effects

of the champagne. She found enough courage to try to cover her tracks, hoping Lucky was only guessing and knew nothing of the real purpose of her call. "I had some questions about the restaurant, some legal stuff, about the books. You know. I thought Smith was cheating. That's all. Why should it concern you?"

Luciano did not believe Thelma and Thelma knew it by the look in his eyes. She was terrified and she had no one to help her. Charley Lucifer was silent, stalking his victim, plotting his next move. He poured another glass of champagne and forced Thelma to drink. Lucky later bragged that Thelma did as she was told.

"I could beat it out of you. I could also kill you. But you are a smart girl. If you tell me what I want to know I will be satisfied. I will have no reason to hit you. I will not lay a hand on you. I care about you, I always have. I just want to know if you have caused any trouble for me yet, and if you have I must know because I must repair the damage."

"Care about me? You got me hooked on hard drugs. You tried to steal the cafe from me. You busted up my marriage to Pat. Go ahead and kill me. There's just about nothing else you can do to me."

"Just answer one question. What were you going to tell Buron Fitts? That is all I want to know. I will make a deal with you."

"Such as?"

"If you tell me what I want to know, I will give you what you want. You and I will never cross paths again after this night. I will stay away from the Sidewalk Cafe, my men will no longer follow you. You will never see me again after tonight."

"What good is your word?"

"I may be many things, but I do not lie. I will keep this promise to you."

"I don't have anything to tell you."

Luciano was angry at Thelma's brave refusal to cave in to his demand for information. He and his friend crowded Toddy, one on either side of the blonde as a show of force and intimidation.

"You would then prefer to die? You know I find no sorrow in death and you know you would not be the first to die. What I want is by the far better choice."

Luciano was a man of his word, at least when it came to killing. Thelma knew he was capable of murder and had no remorse. Toddy had heard stories that Luciano would sometimes stay in the same room with one of his bloodied victims, talking, drinking, laughing, climbing over the body as if it were not there.

Thelma quieted down. She stopped crying, took a deep breath, and stared down at the floor. What went through her mind at that time will never be known; one can only speculate. But she must have realized that with Luciano there was no walking away. She must have known she was a dead woman no matter what she did or did not tell Lucky.

Knowing Toddy's background with gangsters, from infancy on, it can be assumed she knew what fate awaited her, and from that knowledge, she drew the courage to win one final victory against Luciano. She told him what he wanted to know, and then some.

"Okay. I was going to tell Mr. Fitts about the way you've been squeezing Roland and me at the cafe, forcing us to order from your men at inflated prices. I know you've been doing the same thing to other people because we've talked. I have a list of names, dates, and amounts. I also have photographs of your men who have been hanging around my cafe and selling the food and alcohol to Roland. It's all tucked away where you'll never get your hands on it, but enough people know about it and are ready to use it against you. You're through in Los Angeles, Lucky."

Thelma had no list, had talked with no other people and had taken no pictures. She only hoped her bluff would be enough to make Luciano think twice, perhaps even to undermine his operation. She hoped it would keep Luciano on his guard in Los Angeles, never knowing who had the information or where it might turn up. He "owned" a lot of officials, but he did not "own" everybody.

Luciano exploded into a vile rage, shouting, swearing in Italian, waving his arms, ready to attack the beautiful blonde. His friend held him back, telling him quietly, "It's not time

. . . calm down." If what Toddy said was true, Luciano knew he'd been had.

Thelma was not through talking; she had one more blow to strike. "I also know about the connection between you, Nitti, Bioff, Browne, and the movie unions. I have documentation and details. And with that, I've already gone higher than Fitts. I've turned the information over to the FBI here in Los Angeles, the same people who were my bodyguards. I got to know them pretty well and I gave them an earful. I'm going to turn state's evidence and it's all going to blow up in your face."

Toddy again was bluffing. What she knew probably only skimmed the surface; she had linked names together only through the previous rantings and ravings of Luciano when he was threatening to kill the B&B kids. When she finished her story, she sat up straight and smiled. Thelma knew her statements would rattle Luciano and he would never know when someone else might rise up with information to destroy him. Thelma had won the final battle.

"To use your words, I have no fear of death either, Luciano. Your luck just ran out. Do what you wish, but it won't stop with me. You, too, are a dead man. It's all blowing up and there's not a damn thing you can do."

Luciano stormed out, still swearing in Italian. His associate stayed behind in the room with Toddy and said nothing.

Those who remember the story claim Luciano made a call from another room. He dialed a room in a small, rundown apartment house in downtown Los Angeles. He said only one word into the phone: *"Cominciare,"* which means "begin." The man on the other end of the wire said nothing and hung up the phone. It was 10:30 Sunday night. Luciano and Todd left the Beverly Hills home.

Thelma had found peace and was almost in a happy mood. Perhaps it ran through her mind that she might not die after all, that Luciano would see no point in killing her because information had already been spread too far and her death would be pointless. Or perhaps she felt it no longer mattered.

West was nervous on the stand when Johnson asked him to repeat his testimony about his last movements Sunday night.

"I stayed in the bar area for about an hour; then I went back downstairs to the cafe. The Skouras party was still there. It was after ten, and they kept asking for Thelma. Finally Mr. Skouras said they could not stay at the cafe any longer and left."

"What time was that?"

"It was about eleven o'clock. The crowd in the cafe had dwindled down by that time; it was pretty empty. I stayed there for about another hour or so then I went to my apartment."

"Had you ever heard from anyone who had seen Miss Todd all day Sunday, or did you know anything of her whereabouts on Sunday?"

"No, sir, I did not. If anyone had seen Thelma they did not mention it to me. The only information I received on Thelma all day was the call from Mr. Baker saying Mrs. Ford spoke with Thelma. Because of that call, I had no reason to suspect she was not alive. I assumed she was out somewhere and either lost track of time or had been delayed. I always assumed she would return to the cafe."

"Did you make any other inquiry anywhere regarding the whereabouts of Miss Todd?"

"No, I never did that."

"Did you leave the cafe—I mean the building there itself that day at all, Sunday?"

"No."

"Then you remained there at the cafe Sunday evening, too?"

"Sunday evening, I stayed there until twelve o'clock Sunday night, and then went to bed, took the dog for a walk and was in bed by twelve o'clock."

West was rambling.

"And you had heard nothing from Miss Todd, of course."

"Not a word."

"Then you slept as usual there Sunday evening after you went to bed, about midnight?"

"No, I did not sleep."

"What did you do?"

"Just lay awake until about five o'clock."

"You mean you could not sleep?"

"Could not sleep. I think I fell asleep around five or six

o'clock, and I was awakened by the house phone, buzzing very heavily."

While West was wrapping up turbulent Sunday evening, Toddy and Lucky were on their way back to the Palisades, to the cafe. After placing the phone call from the Beverly Hills home, Luciano told Thelma he would take her back to her apartment, which relieved Thelma to a great extent, bolstering her belief that Lucky would not kill her and she would come out of the situation alive.

They traveled the route from Beverly Hills to Hollywood to Santa Monica down Wilshire Boulevard. Once in Santa Monica, they picked up Sunset Boulevard through the Palisades and continued down to the Roosevelt Highway, to Posetano Road above the cafe.

They were spotted in Hollywood by Jewel Carmen, whom Thelma pointed out to Luciano. Luciano made every possible effort to avoid close contact and positive identification by Carmen.

"I'm positive it was Miss Todd. I recognized the chocolate-brown car; they were heading toward the beach."

"What was their exact location?"

"It was on Sunset and Vine in Hollywood."

"How did you happen to be in the area at the time?"

"I was driving from the San Fernando Valley when I saw Thelma driving east on Hollywood Boulevard. I stepped on the gas to get as close as possible to the car."

"The car you believe was Miss Todd's?"

"Yes."

"Continue."

"I saw Thelma sitting next to a dark, foreign-looking man wearing a salt-and-pepper hat and overcoat to match. He had a dark complexion."

"Did you recognize this man?"

"No. He did not at all look familiar to me."

"Then what did you do?"

"When I accelerated to get a closer look at the car, the car turned south on Vine Street. I followed the car as far as Santa Monica Boulevard. At that point, the car turned west and sped away."

"You have no idea as to the identity of the man behind the wheel of the car?"

"No, I had never seen him before. He just appeared to be dark and foreign-looking. In his forties."

If it was Pat DiCicco driving the car, as some assumed, Carmen would have recognized him. She did not know Luciano, who could readily be described as "dark" and "foreign-looking." Luciano was forty-two years old. Jewel Carmen was the seventh person to positively identify Thelma Todd on Sunday.

As Carmen concluded her testimony, grand-jury foreman George Rochester stood up and very confidently made a startling announcement. "I have obtained independent information that could indicate foul play in Miss Todd's death!"

The timing of the statement seemed to indicate a connection between the "dark, foreign-looking man" and this new information. Johnson called for a recess to speak to Rochester. The hearing was adjourned until the following day.

The first witness called in the morning was Rochester, who was asked by Johnson to explain his statement regarding "independent information." Rochester's demeanor changed entirely on the stand; he was nervous and cautious and uttered only one sentence: "I believe I was mistaken."

Johnson did not press the point and Rochester returned to the jury box.

Rochester's announcement once again stirred hints of mob involvement. Had someone gotten to Rochester to silence him? Johnson believed there could have been a tie between Rochester's announcement about "foul play" and the encounter between Thelma and the "mystery man" in the Café Trocadero. Johnson backtracked to the party at the Troc.

Choreographer Arthur Price told authorities about the "last tango," as he put it, and the interruption by a Troc waiter. He was unable to identify the waiter, involved as he was with the dance and unaware of the significance the incident would later assume.

"I ushered the dear soul out with a dance," Prince said. "I always expected her to come back and pick up right where we left off."

Johnson interrogated each of the waiters and bartenders who might have seen the fateful encounter. Joe Bart, Eddie

Ybares, Pat Purcell, Pat Rynelli, John Barrajas, John Linden, and Peter Imfeld each told what little he had seen, or thought he had seen.

"Miss Todd had one glass of champagne, maybe two at the most" was the consensus. "She was not drunk by any means." Johnson then realized Thelma must have gone somewhere else after leaving the Troc in order to account for the intoxication level of .13 found in her blood by the coroner.

Two waiters also backed statements made by Ida and Stanley Lupino, Sid Grauman, Harvey Priester, and Arthur Prince. "She didn't eat very much, and there were no peas and carrots served at the Lupino party."

Johnson believed that wherever Todd had stopped for a drink, she had also had a bite to eat, accounting for the vegetables found in her stomach. He called Troc headwaiter Alex Hounie to the stand.

"Do you have any knowledge of Miss Todd leaving the Stanley Lupino party during the course of the evening?"

"She might have . . . yes."

"Do you have any knowledge that Miss Todd was escorted downstairs to the cocktail area at approximately two-forty-five A.M.?"

Hounie was nervous and distracted. "Yes."

"Mr. Hounie, are you the man who interrupted the dance with Arthur Prince and escorted Miss Todd downstairs?"

The courtroom was silent. A significant clue was about to be revealed. Hounie looked around the room, waited several moments, then pulled a postcard from his pocket. He handed it to Johnson as he spoke.

"I can't speak out of fear I'll be kidnapped and killed."

A loud gasp erupted from the spectators, then a wave of mumbling. The judge pounded his gavel. Johnson took the postcard and read it before handing it to the judge.

The card was postmarked December 19, 1935. Hounie had received it in the mail, at the Cafe Trocadero, that morning. His name was clipped out and pasted on, as was the note on the reverse side.

MR. ALEX . . . CAFE EMPLOYEE . . . TROCADERO CAFE.

Though the grammar on the reverse side was poor, it made its point.

WITHHELD TESTIMONY OR KIDNAP TRIP.

The words were clipped from the *Los Angeles Times*, the exact issue to be determined when and if the LAPD, and possibly the FBI, investigated.

"When did you receive this?"

"This morning, sir. I went to the Trocadero to finish up some business before coming here. It was waiting for me in the office. I wasn't sure what to do."

Johnson called for a recess to examine these startling developments.

Newspaper and wire-service reporters crowded Buron Fitts's office for his reaction to these threats. They asked point-blank if the mob was involved. Fitts rocked back in his office chair and smugly made one statement. "Witnesses before the grand jury are not being as helpful as they might be. Why? Are they afraid?"

On their way back to the Palisades, Luciano and Thelma had stopped at a Christmas-tree lot in Santa Monica. The stop seemed unusual on the surface, but Luciano agreed for several reasons—it reassured Thelma that things were settled between them, preventing any further arguments in the car during the forty-five-minute drive back to the cafe; it also bought Luciano time to make sure everything would be in place, as planned, upon his arrival there.

Lot proprietor S. J. Cummings, his wife and daughter, all described seeing Thelma Todd laughing and joking. She told Cummings privately that she had just "put one over on someone." He said he assumed it was an inside joke or had something to do with a Christmas tree. He said it appeared as if Miss Todd had been drinking in that she was slightly off balance in her walk. He described her companion as a man with black hair, black eyebrows, and dark eyes, who was extremely well dressed in a black overcoat and navy-blue suit. Cummings, though, claimed the man was only "about twenty-five or so." Thelma asked him to "silver" the tree they chose and said she would return for it. He testified the two drove off, heading west on Wilshire toward the beach, at about 11:45.

Though his statement contradicted Carmen's on several key items, it did establish one major point—Thelma was alive Sunday night shortly before midnight. Cummings's wife and daughter verified his testimony, making them the eighth, ninth, and tenth witnesses to see Thelma Todd alive.

Roland West returned to his apartment just after midnight, after taking White King for his walk. If he had delayed that walk by just ten minutes, he might have stopped the desperate scene that was unfolding in front of the garage on Posetano Road, out of view of cafe guests, deep in the shadows and brush surrounding the twin garages.

Thelma Todd was about to keep her appointment with death.

Chapter Twenty

The chocolate-brown Phaeton crept up the three winding roads, reaching its destination near the end of the street by the brush of the Posetano Road garage. Luciano dimmed the lights, and kissed Thelma good-bye.

"I am a man of my word. Our paths will never cross again."

He reached across Toddy and opened her door from the inside.

"There are battles and there is the war, Lucky. May you burn in hell."

Thelma slowly climbed out of the car and slammed the door. The noise did not awaken anyone in the house. Luciano continued down the road, making a right turn at Stretto Way, and winding down the roads leading to Roosevelt Highway. Thelma watched as the car faded into the cold night fog.

She turned and walked toward the garage, pulling her fur coat around her shoulders and neck to ward off the chill. Suddenly, from out of the shadows, a strong, thin-fingered hand grabbed her throat from behind, pulling the fur coat from around her body. Thelma tried to scream as the other hand closed tightly around her neck, choking off the last bit of air. She grabbed the hands but was unable to pry them loose.

As she twisted in the struggle, one of the hands released its deadly grip. Toddy tried to break away. The hand returned as a fist and pounded Thelma on the left side of her face, breaking her nose. Blood drained over her mouth in a steady stream. Dizzy and weak from the terror of the evening, the intake of champagne, and the blow to her face, Thelma collapsed onto the pavement, barely conscious.

The stranger behind the fist was tall and thin and deadly silent. He carried out his duties as an emotional robot, mechanically and without feelings. To him, Thelma Todd was just another in the long line of bodies that were to be systematically dealt with as pieces of excess baggage. Luciano liked it that way. He bent down and scooped the bloodied body in his arms and carried his victim to the garage.

The stranger opened the driver's door of Thelma's car and brutally shoved the body onto the seat. He miscalculated the distance between the seat and the steering wheel and jammed Thelma's limp body hard against the wheel, fracturing two ribs on her right side.

When he finally had the body in the car, he propped it against the back of the seat. It was approximately one foot to the right of the steering wheel and not directly behind the wheel, where a person would have to sit when driving or starting the car. He slowly reached into the car and found the keys still in the ignition, where Thelma so often left them so that Mae Whitehead could bring the car to the cafe apartment in the morning. He started the ignition, left the car door ajar, and walked out of the garage, closing the right wooden garage door but not locking it.

The small dank garage rapidly filled with deadly carbon monoxide. Thelma's breathing was shallow, but enough to fill her lungs with the poisonous gas. She coughed, bringing herself to a state of semiconsciousness. The cough jerked her body forward and to the left, throwing her head against the steering wheel. As she struggled to lift her head off the wheel, she coughed again, this time bringing up more blood that slowly trickled out of the corner of her mouth. It was a warm sensation against her cold skin, which was growing numb from the effects of the beating and suffocation from carbon monoxide.

Still drowsy, still teetering on the brink of death, Thelma

clumsily reached for the keys, dangling in the ignition near the steering column. She could not muster the strength to turn off the engine. She clenched her fists in agony.

Taking one last breath, she tried to push the thick leather-lined car door but fell sideways, wedged between the steering wheel and the car seat. Her life slipped away, her once beautiful body now brutally disfigured from a beating, her once creamy-white skin a contorted crimson-red, her blond curls scattered across her face—the face that had catapulted a naïve little girl from Lawrence, Massachusetts, to Hollywood, California.

With her body wedged partially upright against the car seat, the last bit of life flowed from her mouth across her cheek and onto her fur coat. She died alone in a garage three roads above the restaurant that had promised hope but had eventually led to death.

Thelma Todd died shortly after midnight, Monday, December 16, 1935. Several hours later, the right garage door crept open six inches. The doors never did close properly unless they were shut tight and locked.

Mae Whitehead went to the garage as she usually did, arriving shortly after 10:00 A.M.

"I went to the garage Monday morning to get the Phaeton and drive it down to the cafe, as I always did."

"This was part of your duties as maid?" Johnson asked.

"Yes. I opened the door, which was closed but not locked. When I saw Miss Todd, her head was just beneath the steering wheel and her body sort of crumpled; I thought at first she was asleep. But I realized almost at once that she was dead. I ran to the cafe and told them to call Mr. West."

West continued the story from there.

"I had been asleep, and was awakened by the house phone, buzzing very heavily."

"What was that?"

"That was from Smith; he told me the maid had come from the garage and told him there was something terribly wrong with Miss Todd and she said she thinks she is dead."

"And did you go to the garage then?"

"I put on a pair of trousers and shirt and coat and climbed the steps that took me up to the garage. I came to the garage and rushed in the door and there was Miss Todd lying over there. I put my hands onto her face and there was blood and I wiped it off on my handkerchief and I then sent Mae to go up into the house. She could not go through the garage into the house because the garage door leading to the house was locked. I said, 'Go get Schaefer and his wife as quick as you can.' And she sent them down and they came down and opened the garage door from the inside. I told Schaefer, 'Better go get the police and get a doctor.' And he jumped in the car [West's car] and I said, 'Mae, you go down and get the mother.' The ignition was on, but the gas tank was empty. Thelma rarely filled the tank, it was always almost empty. . . . From the way Miss Todd was, it looked as if she was trying to get out of the car."

"What position was the body when you found it?"

"The door was wide open and the body was upright."

Rudy Schaefer offered the same story.

"I went into the garage and felt Miss Todd's neck and it was cold. It was my impression she was sitting up, nearly upright but slumped forward toward the door."

Their statements contradicted that of Whitehead, who remembered the body as being slumped over almost on its side. When police found the body, it had fallen completely over to the left, indicating rigor mortis had not yet set in by 11:25 A.M.

Medical Examiner Wagner changed the time of death twice after his initial statement that Todd was killed at 2:00 A.M. Sunday morning. He moved the time up to noon Sunday, then finally decided 6:00 P.M. seemed an appropriate time. L.A. County Coroner Frank Nance placed the time no earlier than 5:00 P.M. Sunday. They both agreed the cold, damp, foggy night air preserved the body, staving off rigor mortis, making it difficult to pinpoint the actual time of death.

Luciano headed out on a flight to New York at 7:45 A.M. Monday, never to set foot in Los Angeles again. Pat DiCicco flew out of Los Angeles for Long Island at 9:00 A.M. the same day to spend the Christmas holidays with his mother. He offered to return on Friday to testify if needed. He was never called.

Several weeks after the murder, the Los Angeles Police Department Homicide Division received a telegram from Rial Moore, Ogden, Utah, police chief. Moore stated he was in direct contact with a woman who claimed she knew the identity of the man who had killed Thelma Todd, and that man was staying in an Ogden hotel. Moore awaited a reply from the LAPD. He never received an answer.

The murder investigation skidded off course, and with a jumble of contradicting testimonies, altered and destroyed evidence, threats to witnesses, cover-ups and chaos, it proved a complete fiasco. It remained one of the darkest stains on Buron Fitts's career, a career riddled with scandal.

The case was closed in time for the Christmas holidays. The inquest's final ruling—Thelma Todd died an accidental death.

Thelma did win her final victory against Luciano. Not only did she undermine his operations in Los Angeles to the point where he steered clear of the town, the cafe itself provided the last laugh on the mobster. Thelma Todd's Sidewalk Cafe had its own business address, independent of Roosevelt Highway: the "Castellammare Business Center." It was named after an old village in Italy, Castellammare di Stabia, called the jewel of the Gulf of Naples—the birthplace of Al Capone, the man Luciano despised more than anyone else in the world.

Conclusion

Roland West and Rudy Schaefer accompanied Alice Todd to the Pierce Brothers Mortuary to help her make the final arrangements for Toddy's burial. Thelma's body was placed in an open gold casket lined with orchid satin, her hair fixed as she liked to wear it: big blond curls piled up on her head. Her body remained on view from 8:00 A.M. to 1:00 P.M., Thursday, December 19, at the Pierce Brothers chapel. Thousands of movie fans, friends and curiosity seekers jammed the chapel to get one last look at their beloved Hot Toddy. Police were called in for security, but the mourners conducted themselves in an orderly manner.

Funeral services for Thelma Todd were conducted later that afternoon, at one o'clock at the Wee Kirk o' the Heather Chapel at the Forest Lawn Cemetery in Glendale. The Reverend Harold Proppe of the Hollywood Baptist Church officiated. The service was private, attended only by Alice, West, Priester, ZaSu Pitts, Patsy Kelly, Hal Roach, a few of Thelma's friends from the Roach Studios, and other close friends and associates. Her body was cremated later that afternoon.

During the service Pitts whispered to a friend, "Why, Thelma looks as if she was going to sit up and talk."

Thelma was through talking. But in a sense, she did have

the last word. Toddy got her revenge, almost as if she had reached out from the grave. No one who contributed to those bitter last days of her life, or played a hand in her ultimate demise, seemed to find much happiness after her death; most lived out their remaining years in bitterness and sorrow.

Roland West, always considered a prime suspect in the murder, never made another picture after *Corsair*; he never returned to motion pictures in any capacity. Shortly after Thelma's death, he and Jewel Carmen were divorced; she moved to a home on 317 S. Ardmore in Los Angeles; he eventually sold the cafe and went into seclusion. His health began falling in 1950, and he suffered a stroke and a nervous breakdown.

On his deathbed, delirious, he "confessed" to murdering Thelma Todd, saying he had locked her out to "teach her a lesson." He even went on to say he followed her up to the garage after he heard her trying to get in through the outside door (which he had double-locked). West claimed he and Thelma argued in the garage, and she climbed in her car and turned on the ignition after she got cold, drowning out West's half of their quarrel. West said he walked out and locked the garage door in anger, locking Thelma in the garage with the car motor running. When he went back to the garage a few minutes later, he maintained, Thelma was dead. He said he ran back to his apartment in a panic. He had played the scenario so many times in his mind, and was believed by so many people to be Thelma's killer, that he eventually convinced himself and others of this death scene.

But West had also convinced himself of another story that, if true, contradicted his own murder tale because it indicated a suspicion that Thelma was killed by gangsters. West told friends he had played a significant part in Thelma's death because he caved in to pressure from Luciano's men who had infiltrated the restaurant, putting Thelma on a collision course with Luciano. It seems that even Roland West was never certain if he had actually killed his beloved blonde or if she died at the hands of the underworld.

West could not have killed Thelma; he was in the wrong place at the wrong time. Also, the cover-up was so elaborate and well orchestrated that it was obvious that someone with a tremendous amount of power was calling the shots. By 1935,

West had no power in Hollywood, and few would have cared if he took the fall for the murder.

There were reports that Fox Film executive Joe Schenck (who was later nailed for income-tax fraud) paid to cover up the crime for West, who was a business partner and friend. Even someone as powerful as Schenck did not carry enough clout outside the movie industry to order evidence altered and destroyed, to silence authorities and pass along death threats. West was too faint a spark to ignite all those fires.

In some ways, though, West did kill Thelma; he drained her spirit, consumed her energy with the restaurant, and stood by as she drowned herself in drugs and alcohol. When she really needed a friend, West was never there for her. He dearly loved her and what he did, he believed he did out of love and friendship. His deathbed "confession" was his release, a catharsis to give his tormented soul some peace. It was also his last chance at immortal fame, again at Thelma's expense. West died alone and obscure in 1952.

Pasquale "Pat" DiCicco worked his way back in with the monied movie crowd, and was one of the "fast lane" boys, the gang of Errol Flynn and John Barrymore who drank and caroused with wealthy heiresses and rich actresses. He married seventeen-year-old Gloria Vanderbilt in 1939; she was to inherit $4 million when she reached "legal age." DiCicco's violent temper quickly strained the marriage and there were reports of beatings, thrashings, and continued verbal abuse of Gloria at the hands of her hot-tempered spouse. The marriage ended in divorce three years later. Gloria wired Pat from New York, where she had sought refuge with her family, saying she would not return to California. Her family allegedly paid DiCicco half a million dollars to get him out of the family's hair.

He married RKO contract actress Mary Joanne Tarola, age twenty-four, on December 12, 1952. He was forty-three, and at the time living in California, in Benedict Canyon. He worked his way up to become the vice-president of United Artists Theatres. He died of "natural causes" in New York in 1980.

DiCicco was also a prime suspect in Todd's death. He was thought by many to be the last person to see Todd alive. Some witnesses believed it was DiCicco in the car with Thelma on that fatal night, driving around town. Pat and Thelma had a few sharp words at the Trocadero, and it was apparent that DiCicco was trying to get back with, or back at, Thelma for some reason, most likely to take over the third floor of the cafe for personal financial gain. Todd left Pat one dollar in her will to make sure he could not contest the document or lay claim to any of her estate.

When Todd was found battered and bloody, DiCicco's name immediately came to mind; beating her up was just the thing he would do in a fit of anger. He had done it before. DiCicco's name was continually linked with New York, Los Angeles, and Las Vegas gangsters, including Lucky Luciano.

Charles Smith disappeared shortly after Todd's death. It is believed he either moved out of the area or went into seclusion with his wife. The Sidewalk Cafe books were handed over to a professional accountant, Erwin Luttermoser, who was to explain "certain and unusual entries" in the cafe books. There is no record of his testimony, however, nor is there any further report that he was even called to the stand. In the event, any irregularities in the books were brushed aside, and the thread leading to Smith's possible involvement was broken. Thelma carried her suspicion of Smith to her grave.

Scandal, rumors of corruption and ineptitude, plagued District Attorney Buron Fitts, who was linked to a series of other unsolved murders and questionable movie-colony suicides. Fitts was accused of railroading opponents into jail and ruining political enemies through the misuse of his office's power. The grand jury even investigated charges of fraud in a scam involving a Southern California citrus-grove swindle, but the jury was in Fitts's pocket and the case was surreptitiously dropped. (The grand jury was so much a puppet of the D.A. in the thirties that it even provided security for the Santa Anita racetrack!)

But the mess that was made of the Todd investigation haunted Fitts for the remainder of his career. He finally lost his bid for D.A. in 1940, on a three-to-one majority, to John Dockweiler. Considered the head of one of the most corrupt administrations in the history of the Los Angeles District Attorney's office, Fitts killed himself on March 29, 1973, with a

.38-caliber pistol, one shot to the temple. He was seventy-eight years old.

Maid Mae Whitehead raised a family and continued working for other households. She was still alive in 1980, but somewhat infirm. She was left one dollar in the will. Thelma liked Whitehead, but considered her nothing more than a maid. As with DiCicco, the dollar was a means of preventing Whitehead from claiming any portion of Todd's estate.

Alice Todd took her daughter's cremated remains back home with her to Lawrence, Massachusettes. Every night, Alice moved the urn from her fireplace mantel to her bedside. She was named sole inheritor of Thelma's estate, valued "in excess of $250,000" after Thelma's share of the cafe was divvied up. After the inquest, Alice never returned to California, living out her remaining years alone as a Lawrence society matron. She died at age ninety-two. Thelma's funeral urn was placed in Alice's coffin and buried with her mother. Even in death, Alice refused to release her grip on her daughter.

In private, Alice always insisted Roland West did not kill Thelma, and claimed she knew who had murdered her daughter. But when Mac and other friends back home pressed Alice to tell what she knew, Alice turned pale and locked herself inside her house. Whenever the name "Luciano" was mentioned, Alice trembled and avoided contact with anyone for days.

However, she left newspaper reporters with what she hoped would be the definitive public explanation of Thelma's death. "I am just as certain that it was accidental as I am that I am present here at this moment. If at any time there had been the least doubt in my mind that it was anything other than accidental, I would have been the first person in this world to want justice. I am absolutely satisfied and have been right along, though, that my daughter's death was purely accidental."

Alice refused to explain her initial reaction at the scene of the crime, when she insisted her daughter had been murdered.

Charles "Lucky" Luciano never returned to Los Angeles after the murder. He was eventually squeezed out of his West Coast holdings by Chicago mobsters, the takeover railroaded through with the backing of Nitti and his successors. Los Angeles proved the one place that was unlucky for him; it was the beginning of his fall from power.

After working with the government during World War II, Luciano was finally deported in 1946 to his hometown in Sicily as an undesirable alien for crimes ranging from extortion to racketeering to murder. He was never convicted, tried, nor called to testify about the murder of Thelma Todd, though his name was mentioned by everyone who knew Thelma or knew of his mob dealings on the West Coast. Luciano was above the law. He also cleared the way for DiCicco to escape questioning in the affair.

Luciano was the only man capable of pulling off such a murder and such an elaborate cover-up. If Luciano had not been the man pulling the strings, he, or at least DiCicco, would have been subpoenaed. Only Luciano could have ordered the fraudulent medical reports, the destruction of evidence, the disarray of witnesses. Only Luciano could have achieved the unbelievable ending to such a macabre murder. The murder and its aftermath were textbook Luciano, typical 1930s gangland.

Luciano died on January 26, 1962, at age sixty-nine of "natural causes." Those who associated with Luciano maintain to this day that he was the person responsible, the one who ordered the hit on Thelma Todd.

The Beverly Hills "associate" of Lucky Luciano emerged as one of Los Angeles's most powerful and prominent citizens with strong ties to the movie industry, the Syndicate, and Las Vegas gambling operations. A meeting with this man was arranged through a third party, and details of the meeting with Luciano and Toddy in his Beverly Hills home were given on condition that he remain anonymous because of his stature and influence. He was alive in 1987.

The hit man, ordered to Los Angeles by Luciano and contacted from his Beverly Hills home, was from Detroit and had alleged ties to the Purple Gang. He never rose to any prominence in the underworld and died of unknown causes in the early 1970s.

As for those involved in the Million Dollar Movie Shakedown, fate dealt them a harsher blow.

The shakedown began unraveling shortly after Thelma's death, when Hearst syndicated newspaper columnist Westbrook Pegler saw Bioff, with Joe Schenck, at a Hollywood party. He knew of Bioff's sleazy reputation in Chicago and did a little digging. He eventually uncovered the outstanding conviction—Bioff still owed the state of Illinois six months for slugging a whore.

In spite of a tremendous amount of publicity against Pegler, instigated by Bioff, Browne, Nitti, and the boys, his continual hammering at the union goons eventually brought justice. The Feds began a probe into the racket and eventually nailed Bioff and Browne on film-industry extortion. Both were found guilty on October 25, 1941. Indictments were returned against Nitti and the Capone gang on March 18, 1943. Nitti was chosen to take the fall for the mob.

Nitti was not one to take the rap for anyone. He threatened to turn state's evidence against the rest of the gang. He thought he was indestructible, but he was wrong. He was gunned down at point-blank range, with two bullets to the brain, on some railroad tracks in North Riverside, Illinois, on March 19. The hit was listed as a suicide.

George Browne worked out a scheme that, through a special union assessment, brought in an additional $6 million never recorded during the shakedown of the movie industry. He split the take with Willie Bioff, cheating Nitti and the Capone Syndicate out of a substantial fortune. He later turned state's evidence against the Syndicate, pocketed the money, and was a free man while the rest of the Syndicate served hard time behind bars. Browne said it was always his dream to be able to drink one hundred bottles of beer a day. He retired to a ranch in Woodstock, Illinois, where he reportedly fulfilled that dream. He died in the 1950s of "natural causes."

Willie Bioff also squealed on the mob, and took his $3 million to a little farm outside Phoenix, Arizona. He was not as fortunate as his chubby partner. He changed his name to Al Nelson, but finally met his fate on November 4, 1955. His pickup truck exploded into thousands of little pieces, Bioff along with it, when he turned on the ignition. It took a long time, but the mob got its revenge.

Al Capone went insane from the ravages of syphilis. He was released from Alcatraz on January 6, 1939, his mind completely gone. He returned to his home in Key Biscayne, Florida, mumbling to himself, seeing imaginary killers, "deep sea" fishing in the swimming pool. He was organizing take-overs and contract killings right up to the end. As Capone gang accountant, Jake "Greasy Thumb" Guzik put it, "Al's nuttier 'n a fruitcake." Al Capone died January 25, 1947.

Perhaps one of the most bizarre stories of all centers on a black and gold sardonyx ring, given to Toddy by Pat DiCicco shortly after their marriage. Inside the band was an inscription, TO LAMBIE, a pet name DiCicco called Thelma. She wore the ring after her divorce from DiCicco. It reportedly disappeared the night Thelma was killed.

While touring in Warren, Ohio, in 1979 with the musical *Irene*, Patsy Kelly claimed a mysterious man approached her backstage, opened his hand, and held out a sardonyx ring identical to Thelma's missing band. The man said he was from Florida and that he had been in California. Then he stated, "This was Miss Todd's," and left. Kelly repeated the story to several people before her death on September 24, 1981.

In eulogizing Thelma, Hal Roach said, "She was a favorite with everyone on the lot from the lowest employee to the highest. She was always joyous and happy and seemed thoroughly to enjoy her work. She was well-loved and we will miss her." More than fifty years later Roach still had fond memories of Thelma.

Upon returning home to Lawrence, Alice told reporters, "I am glad to be back home in Lawrence among relatives and friends. The people here were loyal and, I know, devoted to my Thelma. Just as she loved Lawrence, I know Lawrence loved her."

As for the Sidewalk Cafe, the building is now owned by Paulist Productions. The area Todd and West subdivided into two apartments is now one work area. The downstairs cafe is a storage room for tapes and archives. There are rumors that the third floor had eventually opened to gambling. Whether Luciano had a hand in the operation has never been clear. It is now an apartment. The main entrance still has the two wooden doors, each with a glass diamond-shaped panel etched with the word JOYAS, just as Thelma left it in 1935. The footbridge still stands, as does the secluded courtyard off Castellemmare. Some who work in the building insist they have seen Thelma's ghost passing through the hall at the top of the staircase near the outside doors to the courtyard. They say they have also seen her ghost moving through her old apartment.

The West/Carmen house on Robelo Drive still stands, appearing much as it did in 1935. Also virtually unchanged is the twin garage in which Thelma died. Posetano Road is no longer a through street, the garage accessible only from Stretto Way. The area is almost completely developed with houses, but the brushy area where Thelma's killer hid has yet to be paved over, serving as an eerie reminder of the horror on that cold December night in 1935.

After more than fifty years of turmoil surrounding her death, maybe Thelma Todd can now find peace. She died fighting, in a sense, for what she thought was right, trying to stop Lucky Luciano's operations in California. The mobster won the first round, but perhaps, Thelma has won the final battle.

Many of Thelma Todd's comedies, including the Todd/ Pitts and Todd/Kelly films, are finding new audiences today on cable television. Perhaps Thelma Todd will once more be appreciated for her beauty and wonderful comedic skills, rather than remembered for her tragic death.

The Films of Thelma Todd

(Films are listed by year. Information includes date of release, studio, director, and featured players when available.)

1926:

FASCINATING YOUTH (3/17/26). Paramount. Dir. Sam Wood. Co-stars: Buddy Rogers, Josephine Dunn, Richard Dix, Clara Bow, Adolphe Menjou.

GOD GAVE ME TWENTY CENTS (11/19/26). Paramount. Dir. Herbert Brenon. Co-stars: William Collier, Jr., Jack Mulhall, Lois Morgan.

1927:

RUBBER HEELS (6/11/27). Paramount. Dir. Victor Herman. Co-stars: Ed Wynn, Chester Conklin, Robert Andrews.

NEVADA (8/8/27). Paramount. Dir. John Waters. Co-stars: Gary Cooper, William Powell, Philip Strange.

THE POPULAR SIN (11/22/27). Paramount. Dir. Malcolm St. Clair. Co-stars: Clive Brook, Greta Nissen, Florence Vidor, André Beranger.

THE GAY DEFENDER (12/10/27). Paramount. Dir. Gregory La-Cava. Co-stars: Richard Dix, Fred Kohler.

SHIELD OF HONOR (12/10/27). Universal. Dir. Emory Johnson.

Co-stars: Neil Hamilton, Dorothy Gulliver, Ralph Lewis, Nigel Barrie.

1928:

THE NOOSE (1/29/28). First National. Dir. James Francis Dillon. Co-stars: Richard Barthelmess, Montague Love, Jay Eaton, Robert E. O'Connor.

VAMPING VENUS (3/22/28). First National. Dir. Eddie Cline. Co-stars: Charlie Murray, Louise Fazenda.

HEART TO HEART (7/22/28). First National. Dir. William Beaudine. Co-stars: Mary Astor, Lloyd Hughes, Louise Fazenda, Lucian Littlefield.

THE CRASH (10/7/28). First National. Dir. Eddie Cline. Co-stars: Milton Sills, Wade Boteler, William Demarest.

THE HAUNTED HOUSE (11/4/28). First National. Dir. Benjamin Christensen. Co-stars: Edmund Breese, Chester Conklin, Montague Love, Larry Kent.

1929:

NAUGHTY BABY (1/19/29). First National. Dir. Mervyn LeRoy. Co-stars: Alice White, Jack Mulhall, Jay Easton, Andy Devine.

SEVEN FOOTPRINTS TO SATAN (2/17/29). First National. Dir. Benjamin Christensen. Co-stars: Creighton Hale, Ivan Christie, Sheldon Lewis, Cissy Fitzgerald.

TRIAL MARRIAGE (3/10/29). Columbia. Dir. Erle Kenton. Co-stars: Jason Robards, Norman Kerry, Sally Eilers, Charles Clary.

THE HOUSE OF HORROR: (4/28/29). First National. Dir. Benjamin Christensen. Co-stars: Louise Fazenda, Chester Conklin, James Ford.

UNACCUSTOMED AS WE ARE (5/4/29). Hal Roach/MGM. Dir. Lewis Foster. (Laurel & Hardy Comedy.) Co-stars: Stan Laurel, Oliver Hardy, Mae Busch, Edgar Kennedy.

THE BACHELOR GIRL (5/20/29). Columbia. Dir. Richard Thorpe. Co-stars: William Collier, Jr., Jacqueline Logan, Edward Hearn.

CAREERS (6/2/29). First National. Dir. John Francis Dillon. Co-stars: Billie Dove, Antonio Moreno, Noah Beery.

SNAPPY SNEEZER (7/29/29). Hal Roach/MGM. Dir. Warren

Doane. (Chase Comedy). Co-stars: Charley Chase, Anders Randolf.

LOOK OUT BELOW (8/18/29). Educational. Dir. Jack White. (Jack White Talking Comedy). Co-stars: Edward Everett Horton.

HER PRIVATE LIFE (8/25/29). First National. Dir. Alexander Korda. Co-stars: Billie Dove, Roland Young, Montague Love, Walter Pidgeon, ZaSu Pitts.

HOTTER THAN HOT (8/26/29). Hal Roach/MGM. Dir. Lewis Foster. Co-stars: Harry Langdon, Edgar Kennedy, Frank Austin.

CRAZY FEET (9/7/29). Hal Roach/MGM. Dir. Warren Doane. (Chase Comedy). Co-stars: Charley Chase, Anita Garvin.

SKY BOY (9/23/29). Hal Roach/MGM. Dir. Charley Rogers. Co-stars: Harry Langdon, Eddie Dunn.

THE LONG, LONG TRAIL (10/14/29). Universal. Dir. Arthur Rossen. Co-stars: Hoot Gibson, James Mason, Sally Eilers.

STEPPING OUT (11/2/29). Hal Roach/MGM. Dir. Warren Doane. (Chase Comedy). Co-stars: Charley Chase, Anita Garvin.

THE HEAD GUY (12/26/29). Hal Roach/MGM. Dir. Fred Guiol. Co-stars: Harry Langdon, Edgar Kennedy, Eddie Dunn.

1930:

THE FIGHTING PARSON (1/6/30). Hal Roach/MGM. Dir. Charles Rogers. Co-stars: Harry Langdon, Eddie Dunn, Charlie Hall.

THE REAL MCCOY (2/1/30). Hal Roach/MGM. Dir. Warren Doane. (Chase Comedy). Co-stars: Charley Chase, Edgar Kennedy, Charlie Hall.

THE SHRIMP (3/3/30). Hal Roach/MGM. Dir. Charles Rogers. Co-stars: Harry Langdon, Max Davidson, James Mason.

ALL TEED UP (4/19/30). Hal Roach/MGM. Dir. Edgar Kennedy. (Chase Comedy). Co-stars: Charley Chase, Edgar Kennedy, Harry Bowen.

THE KING (4/21/30). Hal Roach/MGM. Dirs. James W. Horne & Charles Rogers. Co-stars: Harry Langdon, Dorothy Granger.

HER MAN (9/21/30). Pathé. Dir. Tay Garnett. Co-stars: Helen Twelvetrees, Ricardo Cortez, James Gleason, Phillips Holmes, Franklin Pangborn, Slim Summerville.

FOLLOW THRU (9/27/30). Paramount. Dirs. Lawrence Schwab & Lloyd Corrigan. Co-stars: Buddy Rogers, Nancy Carroll, Eugene Pallette, Frances Dee.

DOLLAR DIZZY (10/4/30). Hal Roach/MGM. Dir. James W. Horne. (Chase Comedy). Co-stars: Charley Chase, Edgar Kennedy, James Finlayson, Dorothy Granger.

LOOSER THAN LOOSE (11/15/30). Hal Roach/MGM. Dir. James W. Horne. (Chase Comedy). Co-stars: Charley Chase, Dorothy Granger, Edgar Kennedy.

ANOTHER FINE MESS (11/29/30). Hal Roach/MGM. Dir. James Parrott. (Laurel & Hardy Comedy). Co-stars: Stan Laurel, Oliver Hardy, James Finlayson, Harry Bernard.

HIGH C'S (12/27/30). Hal Roach/MGM. Dir. James Horne. (Chase Comedy). Co-stars: Charley Chase, Carlton Griffin, The Ranch Boys.

1931:

NO LIMIT (1/23/31). Paramount. Dir. Frank Tuttle. Co-stars: Clara Bow, Norman Foster, Stuart Erwin, Harry Green.

COMMAND PERFORMANCE (1/24/31). Tiffany Films. Dir. Walter Lange.

ALOHA (2/4/31). Tiffany Films. Dir. Albert Rogell.

CHICKENS COME HOME (2/21/31). Hal Roach/MGM. Dir. James W. Horne. (Laurel & Hardy Comedy). Co-stars: Stan Laurel, Oliver Hardy, James Finlayson, Baldwin Cooke.

SWANEE RIVER (2/23/31). Sono Art World Wide Films. Dir. Raymond Cannon.

THE PIP FROM PITTSBURGH (3/21/31). Hal Roach/MGM. Dir. James Parrott. (Chase Comedy). Co-stars: Charley Chase, Dorothy Granger, Carlton Griffin, Kay Deslys.

LOVE FEVER (4/11/31). Hal Roach/MGM. Dir. Robert McGowan. (Boy Friends Comedy). Co-stars: Mickey Daniels, Grady Sutton, Mary Kornman, Dorothy Granger, Edgar Kennedy.

BEYOND VICTORY (4/12/31). Pathé. Dir. John Robertson. Co-stars: Horace Jackson, James Gleason.

ROUGH SEAS (4/25/31). Hal Roach/MGM. Dir. James Parrott. (Chase Comedy). Co-stars: Charley Chase, Carlton Griffin, Harry Bernard, The Ranch Boys.

THE MALTESE FALCON (5/28/31). Warner Bros. Dir. Roy Del

Ruth. Co-stars: Ricardo Cortez, Bebe Daniels, Dudley Digges.

LET'S DO THINGS (6/6/31). Hal Roach/MGM. Dir. Hal Roach. (Todd/Pitts Comedy). Co-stars: Charlie Hall, Jerry Mandy, George Byron.

BROAD-MINDED (6/26/31). First National. Dir. Mervyn LeRoy. Co-stars: Joe E. Brown, William Collier, Bela Lugosi.

CATCH AS CATCH CAN (8/22/31). Hal Roach/MGM. Dir. Marshall Neilan. (Todd/Pitts Comedy). Co-stars: Guinn "Big Boy" Williams, Reed Howes, Billy Gilbert.

MONKEY BUSINESS (9/17/31). Paramount. Dir. Norman Z. McLeod. Co-stars: The Four Marx Brothers, Rockliffe Fellowes, Ruth Hall, Tom Kennedy.

THE PAJAMA PARTY (10/3/31). Hal Roach/MGM. Dir. Hal Roach. (Todd/Pitts Comedy). Co-stars: Elizabeth Forrester, Eddie Dunn, Billy Gilbert, Charlie Hall.

THE HOT HEIRESS (10/10/31). First National. Dir. Clarence Badger. Co-stars: Walter Pidgeon, Tom Dugan, Inez Courtney.

THE FIGHTING MARSHAL (10/25/31). Columbia. Dir. D. Ross Lederman.

CORSAIR (10/28/31). United Artists. Dir. Roland West. Co-stars: Chester Morris, Frank McHugh, William Austin, Gay Seabrook.

WAR MAMAS (11/14/31). Hal Roach/MGM. Dir. Marshall Neilan. (Todd/Pitts Comedy). Co-stars: Guinn "Big Boy" Williams, Charles Judels, Allan Lane.

ON THE LOOSE (12/26/31). Hal Roach/MGM. Dir. Hal Roach. (Todd/Pitts Comedy). Co-stars: John Loder, Billy Gilbert, Stan Laurel, Oliver Hardy.

1932:

ONE MAN LAW (1/11/32). Columbia. Dir. Lambert Hillyer.

SPEAK EASILY (1/12/32). MGM. Dir. Edward Sedgwick. Co-stars: Buster Keaton, Jimmy Durante, Ruth Selwyn, Hedda Hopper.

THE FIGHTING FOOL (1/23/32). Columbia. Dir. Lambert Hillyer.

SEAL SKINS (2/6/32). Hal Roach/MGM. Dir. Gil Pratt. (Todd/Pitts Comedy). Co-stars: Charlie Hall, Leo Willis, Billy Gilbert.

BIG TIMER (2/27/32). Columbia. Dir. Eddie Buzzell.

THE NICKEL NURSER (3/12/32). Hal Roach/MGM. Dir. Warren Doane. (Chase Comedy). Co-stars: Charley Chase, Billy Gilbert, Harry Bowen.

RED NOSES (3/19/32). Hal Roach/MGM. Dir. James Horne. (Todd/Pitts Comedy). Co-stars: Blanche Payson, Billy Gilbert, Wilfred Lucas.

STRICTLY UNRELIABLE (4/30/32). Hal Roach/MGM. Dir. George Marshall. (Todd/Pitts Comedy). Co-stars: Billy Gilbert, Charlie Hall, Bud Jamison.

NO GREATER LOVE (5/16/32). Columbia. Dir. Benjamin Stoloff.

THE OLD BULL (6/4/32). Hal Roach/MGM. Dir. George Marshall. (Todd/Pitts Comedy). Co-stars: Otto Fries, Robert Burns.

HORSE FEATHERS (8/18/32). Paramount. Dir. Norman Z. McLeod. Co-stars: The Four Marx Brothers, David Landau, Nat Pendleton, Florine McKinney, Reginald Barlow, Robert Greig.

SHOW BUSINESS (8/20/32). Hal Roach/MGM. Dir. Jules White. (Todd/Pitts Comedy). Co-stars: Anita Garvin, Monty Collins, Charlie Hall.

KLONDIKE (8/25/32). Monogram. Dir. Trem Carr.

THIS IS THE NIGHT (9/12/32). Paramount Studios. Dir. Frank Tuttle. Co-stars: Cary Grant, Lily Damita, Charles Ruggles, Roland Young.

ALUM AND EVE (9/24/32). Hal Roach/MGM. Dir. George Marshall (Todd/Pitts Comedy). Co-stars: James C. Morton, Almeda Fowler.

DECEPTION (11/1/32). Columbia. Dir. Lew Seiler.

CALL HER SAVAGE (11/14/32). Fox Films. Dir. John Francis Dillon.

SNEAK EASILY (12/10/32). Hal Roach/MGM. Dir. Gus Meins. (Todd/Pitts Comedy). Co-stars: Robert Burns, James C. Morton, Billy Gilbert, Rolfe Sedan, Harry Bernard, Charlie Hall.

1933:

AIR HOSTESS (1/4/33). Columbia. Dir. Albert Rogell.

ASLEEP AT THE FEET (1/21/33). Hal Roach/MGM. Dir. Gus Meins. (Todd/Pitts Comedy). Co-stars: Billy Gilbert, Anita Garvin, Eddie Dunn.

MAIDS À LA MODE (3/4/33). Hal Roach. Dir. Gus Meins. (Todd/Pitts Comedy). Co-stars: Billy Gilbert, Harry Bernard, Kay Deslys.

THE BARGAIN OF THE CENTURY (4/9/33). Hal Roach/MGM. Dir. Charley Chase. (Todd/Pitts Comedy). Co-stars: Billy Gilbert, James Burtis, Harry Bernard.

THE DEVIL'S BROTHER (FRA DIAVOLO) (5/4/33). Hal Roach/ MGM. Dirs. Hal Roach & Charles Rogers. (Laurel & Hardy Comedy). Co-stars: Stan Laurel, Oliver Hardy, Dennis King, James Finlayson.

ONE TRACK MINDS (5/20/33). Hal Roach/MGM. Dir. Gus Meins. (Todd/Pitts Comedy). Co-stars: Billy Gilbert, Lucien Prival, Sterling Holloway, Spanky McFarland, Charlie Hall.

MARY STEVENS, M.D. (6/12/33). Warner Bros. Dir. Lloyd Bacon. Co-star: Kay Francis.

CHEATING BLONDES (7/20/33). Equitable. Dir. Joseph Levering. Co-stars: (Todd in dual role), Rolfe Harold, Inez Courtney, Milton Wallis, Mae Busch.

BEAUTY AND THE BUS (9/16/33). Hal Roach/MGM. Dir. Gus Meins. (Todd/Kelly Comedy). Co-stars: Don Barclay, Charlie Hall, Tiny Sanford, Tommy Bond, Eddie Baker.

BACK TO NATURE (11/14/33). Hal Roach/MGM. Dir. Gus Meins. (Todd/Kelly Comedy). Co-stars: Don Barclay, Charlie Hall.

SITTING PRETTY (11/22/33). Paramount. Dir. Harry Joe Brown. Co-stars: Jack Oakie, Jack Haley, Ginger Rogers.

COUNSELLOR-AT-LAW (12/5/33). Universal. Dir. William Wyler. Co-star: John Barrymore.

SON OF A SAILOR (12/16/33). First National. Dir. Lloyd Bacon. Joe E. Brown, Sheila Terry, Johnny Mack Brown, Frank McHugh.

AIR FRIGHT (12/23/33). Hal Roach/MGM. Dir. Gus Meins. (Todd/Kelly Comedy). Co-stars: Don Barclay, Billy Bletcher, Charlie Hall.

1934:

HIPS, HIPS HORRAY (2/2/34). RKO. Dir. Mark Sandrich. Co-stars: Bert Wheeler, Robert Woolsey, Ruth Etting, Dorothy Lee, George Meeker.

BABES IN THE GOODS (2/10/34). Hal Roach/MGM. Dir. Gus

Meins. (Todd/Kelly Comedy). Co-stars: Jack Barty, Arthur Housman, Charlie Hall.

THE POOR RICH (2/15/34). Universal. Dir. Edward Sedgwick. Co-stars: Edward Everett Horton, Edna May Oliver, Andy Devine.

YOU MADE ME LOVE YOU (3/21/34). British Film/Universal. Starring Stanley Lupino.

BOTTOMS UP (3/13/34). Fox Films. Dir. David Butler.

SOUP AND FISH (3/31/34). Hal Roach/MGM. Dir. Gus Meins. (Todd/Kelly Comedy). Co-stars: Gladys Gale, Billy Gilbert, Don Barclay, Charlie Hall.

PALOOKA (5/8/34). United Artists. Dir. Benjamin Stoloff. Co-stars: Jimmy Durante, William Cagney, Stuart Erwin, Lupe Valez.

MAIN IN HOLLYWOOD (5/19/34). Hal Roach/MGM. Dir. Gus Meins. (Todd/Kelly Comedies). Co-stars: Eddie Foy, Jr., Don Barclay, Charlie Hall, James C. Morton.

I'LL BE SUING YOU (6/23/34). Hal Roach/MGM. Dir. Gus Meins. (Todd/Kelly Comedy). Co-stars: Eddie Foy, Jr., Douglas Wakefield, Billy Nelson, Benny Baker.

COCKEYED CAVALIERS (6/29/34). RKO. Dir. Mark Sandrich. Co-stars: Bert Wheeler, Robert Woolsey, Noah Beery, Billy Gilbert, Harry "Snub" Pollard, Franklin Pangborn.

THREE CHUMPS AHEAD (7/14/34). Hal Roach/MGM. Dir. Gus Meins. (Todd/Kelly Comedy). Co-stars: Benny Baker, Frank Moran, Harry Bernard.

ONE HORSE FARMERS (9/1/34). Hal Roach/MGM. Dir. Gus Meins. (Todd/Kelly Comedy). Co-stars: James C. Morton, Charlie Hall, Billy Bletcher.

OPENED BY MISTAKE (10/6/34). Hal Roach/MGM. Dir. James Parrott. (Todd/Kelly Comedy). Co-stars: William Burress, Nora Cecil, Fanny Cossar, Charlie Hall.

DONE IN OIL (11/10/34). Hal Roach/MGM. Dir. Gus Meins. (Todd/Kelly Comedy). Co-stars: Arthur Housman, Eddy Conrad, Rolfe Sedan, Leo White.

BUM VOYAGE (12/15/34). Hal Roach/MGM. Dir. Nick Grinde. (Todd/Kelly Comedy). Co-stars: Adrian Rosley, Constance Franke, Noah Young, Albert Petit.

1935:

TREASURE BLUES (1/26/35). Hal Roach/MGM. Dir. James Parrott. (Todd/Kelly Comedy). Co-stars: Sam Adams, Arthur Housman, Tiny Sandford, Charlie Hall.

SING, SISTER, SING (3/2/35). Hal Roach/MGM. Dir. James Parrott. (Todd/Kelly Comedy). Co-stars: Arthur Housman, Harry Bowen, Charlie Hall.

THE TIN MAN (3/30/35). Hal Roach/MGM. Dir. James Parrott. (Todd/Kelly Comedy). Co-stars: Matthew Betz, Clarence Wilson.

THE MISSES STOOGE (4/20/35). Hal Roach/MGM. Dir. James Parrott. (Todd/Kelly Comedy). Co-stars: Herman Bing, Esther Howard, James C. Morton.

AFTER THE DANCE (7/30/35). Columbia. Dir. Leo Bulgakov.

TWO FOR TONIGHT (8/12/35). Paramount. Dir. Frank Tuttle. Co-star: Bing Crosby.

SLIGHTLY STATIC (9/7/35). Hal Roach/MGM. Dir. William Terhune. (Todd/Kelly Comedy). Co-stars: Harold Waldridge, Dell Henderson, Harry Bowen, Carlton Griffin, Eddie Craven.

TWIN TRIPLETS (10/12/35). Hal Roach/MGM. Dir. William Terhune. (Todd/Kelly Comedy). Co-stars: John Dilson, Greta Meyer, Bess Flowers, Billy Bletcher, Charlie Hall.

HOT MONEY (11/16/35). Hal Roach/MGM. Dir. James Horne. (Todd/Kelly Comedy). Co-stars: James Burke, Fred Kelsey, Charlie Hall, Brooke Benedict.

LIGHTNING STRIKES TWICE (12/7/35). RKO. Dir. Ben Holmes. Co-stars: Pert Kelton, "Skeets" Gallagher, Ben Lyon, Laura Hope, Chick Chandler.

TOP FLAT (12/21/35). Hal Roach/MGM. Dir. William Terhune. (Todd/Kelly Comedy). Co-stars: Grace Goodall, Fuzzy Knight, Gary Owen, Harry Bernard.

MOVIES RELEASED AFTER TODD'S DEATH:

ALL-AMERICAN TOOTHACHE (1/25/36). Hal Roach/MGM. Dir. Gus Meins. (Todd/Kelly Comedy). Co-stars: Mickey Daniels, Johnny Arthur, Charlie Hall, Bud Jamison, Billy Bletcher.

BOHEMIAN GIRL (2/14/36). Hal Roach/MGM. Dirs. James Horne & Charles Rogers. (Laurel & Hardy Comedy). Todd was found dead five days after film preview. Her scenes were reedited with Mae Busch and Zeffie Tilbury.

The Films of Roland West

SILENTS:

A WOMAN'S HONOR (6/11/16). Fox Films. Producer and Director.

LOST SOULS (8/12/16). Fox Films. Director only.

THE SIREN (6/24/17). Fox Films. Director only.

DELUXE ANNIE (5/13/18). Norma Talmadge Films. Director and Writer.

THE SILVER LINING (12/29/20). Iroquois Films/Metro. Producer/Director/Writer.

NOBODY (6/23/21). Roland West Films. Producer/Director/Writer.

THE UNKNOWN PURPLE (5/8/23). Truart Films. (Adapted from West's stageplay.) Director and Writer.

THE MONSTER (3/9/25). Metro-Goldwyn Pictures. Producer and Director.

THE BAT (3/23/26). Feature Productions. Producer/Director/Writer.

THE DOVE (6/9/27). Roland West Films. Producer and Director.

TALKIES:

ALIBI (5/1/29). Feature Productions (10 reels). Producer/Director/Writer.

THE BAT WHISPERS (11/24/30). Art Cinema Corp./Joseph Schenck. Director and Writer.

CORSAIR (10/28/31). United Artists. Producer and Director.

INDEX

DATE DUE
